European Business
Four Centuries of
Foreign Expansion

This is a volume in the Arno Press collection

European Business
Four Centuries of Foreign Expansion

Advisory Editor
Mira Wilkins

Editorial Board
Rondo Cameron
Charles Wilson

See last pages of this volume for a complete list of titles.

BRITISH INVESTMENTS IN LATIN AMERICA, 1822–1949

J. Fred Rippy

ARNO PRESS

A New York Times Company

New York / 1977

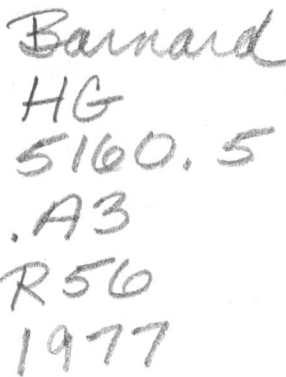

Editorial Supervision: ANDREA HICKS

Reprint Edition 1977 by Arno Press Inc.

Copyright © 1959, by the
University of Minnesota. All rights reserved.
Reprinted by permission of
The University of Minnesota Press

EUROPEAN BUSINESS:
Four Centuries of Foreign Expansion
ISBN for complete set: 0-405-09715-8
See last pages of this volume for titles.

Manufactured in the United States of America

Library of Congress Cataloging in Publication Data

Rippy, James Fred, 1892-
British investments in Latin America, 1822-1949.

(European business)
Reprint of the ed. published by University of
Minnesota Press, Minneapolis.
Includes bibliographical references.
1. Investments, British--Latin America.
I. Title. II. Series.
[HG5160.5.A3R56 1977]   332.6'7341'08   76-29755
ISBN 0-405-09771-9

British Investments in Latin America
1822–1949

⇋ J. Fred Rippy ⇌

BRITISH INVESTMENTS IN
LATIN AMERICA, 1822–1949

*A Case Study in the Operations of Private
Enterprise in Retarded Regions*

UNIVERSITY OF MINNESOTA PRESS, Minneapolis

© Copyright 1959 by the University of Minnesota. All rights reserved

PRINTED IN THE UNITED STATES OF AMERICA AT THE LUND PRESS, INC., MINNEAPOLIS

Library of Congress Catalog Card Number: 59-7950

The map on page 2 is from *Culture Worlds,* by Richard Joel Russell and Fred Bowerman Kniffen, copyright 1951, and is used by permission of the publishers, The Macmillan Company.

PUBLISHED IN GREAT BRITAIN, INDIA, AND PAKISTAN BY THE OXFORD UNIVERSITY PRESS, LONDON, BOMBAY, AND KARACHI AND IN CANADA BY THOMAS ALLEN, LTD., TORONTO

*To the memory of three persistent workers
in the vineyard*
CHARLES E. CHAPMAN
PERCY ALVIN MARTIN
HERBERT I. PRIESTLEY

PREFACE

I have published during the last fifteen years numerous articles on British overseas investments in various periodicals, including *Inter-American Economic Affairs*, *Hispanic American Historical Review*, *Pacific Historical Review*, *Journal of Business*, and others, to the editors of which I am indebted for permission to reproduce at this time, in modified form, a good part of the materials they have printed for me. I am also indebted to the University of Chicago for financial assistance, and to the library staff and graduate students of that university for other types of aid, in the preparation of this volume. I wish to thank them, each and all, for their help and at the same time to absolve them from any blame for such defects as this work may reveal. Lack of satisfactory information has made it impossible for me to extend the narrative of British investments beyond 1949.

In a short introductory chapter I have tried to describe the setting and explain the objectives and the prescribed limits of a work so vast in scope and so exacting in detail. Here I shall merely express the hope that readers will not be overwhelmed by the mass of statistics which I have felt it necessary to include, that the volume may prove useful to scholars and makers of policy, that nobody will be offended by what I have written so frankly, without malice or concealed purpose, and that those who take the trouble to examine the volume carefully may be led to ask themselves whether they should modify their views with reference to the role of British capital in Latin America.

In estimating the amount of British capital invested overseas and in calculating rates of return, I have used par values for two reasons: (1) they are more convenient in making comparisons and (2) I consider this method approximately as accurate as any other. Calculation of rates of return on any other basis, particularly on the basis of market values, seems unrewarding in view of the tremendous mathematical effort that it would involve: almost as futile as aimless perpetual motion. When not influenced by propaganda and market manipulation, the market value of securities rises and falls with the rise and fall of yields. I am fully aware that rates of return would be lower on very prosperous enterprises and higher on less prosperous ones if market values instead of par values were employed in calculating these rates; but I do not accept the view that rates of return arrived at in this manner, or even on the basis of book values largely determined by the investor, are an exact measure of profits. Who knows the precise value of assets, tangible and intangible? Who knows when each security holder bought his securities or what he paid for them? Who knows when he sold them or what he received for them? Who knows the precise value of securities in the possession of promoters and organizers? Such things are never a matter of general information. Are earnings withheld from shareholders and ploughed back into corporate capitalization real investment? Is not the sale of securities at a premium (namely, above par) the result of successful propaganda, or windfalls, or the restraint of management in the distribution of earnings?

Whatever the reader's view regarding methods of figuring rates of return, I shall not lead him astray, for I shall remind him again and again of the basis of my calculations of capitalization and yields. In fact, I shall no doubt tire him by constant repetition of the words "par" and "nominal." Moreover, I shall counterbalance any exaggeration of rates of return from very profitable enterprises by ignoring paper bonuses in calculating those rates.

Assuming that most readers will be interested in certain Latin-American republics and that some readers will be interested in all of them, I have added detailed regional and national surveys to the general summary presented in the initial chapters of this volume. I have loaded it rather heavily with statistics because I believe that such data are essential in useful economic history. Even with all these details, I have by no means exhausted the subject. I hope, however, that I have provided a suggestive introduction to this immense and important theme: the overseas ventures of investors residing in the British Isles, whose inhabitants have had, so far, more widespread economic interests than any group of people of equal numbers in the entire history of the world. Whatever their future in this respect, their past

Preface

cannot fail to attract the attention of historians, economists, and statesmen for many years to come. Let this be my apology for the abundance of statistics I have presented and the numerous enterprises whose dividend records I have analyzed. I have written not merely for the present decade but for the next and the next. But I repeat that I have deliberately terminated my story of British investments in Latin America (and elsewhere) with the end of the year 1949.

It has been suggested that *A Warning to Prospective Investors* might serve as an appropriate subtitle; but while it is true that British investors in Latin America frequently suffered vexations and disappointments, I am not certain that their experience should be exhibited either as a warning or as a guide for the future, whether for capitalists of the British Isles or others elsewhere. Tomorrow is likely to be different from yesterday. Nor should one assume that the fate of investors from all countries will be the same in Latin America.

J. Fred Rippy

CONTENTS

INTRODUCTION. RECENT PROBLEMS IN PRIVATE INTERNATIONAL INVESTMENT

I. The Crisis and British Experience in Latin America   3

PART ONE. GENERAL SURVEY OF BRITISH INVESTMENTS IN LATIN AMERICA

II. Early Imprudence and Vexation, 1822–1880   17

III. Two Decades of Brisk Investment and an Intervening Depression   36

IV. An Analysis of Investments at the End of 1913   66

V. British Investments at Their Peak, 1928   75

VI. A Decade of Rapid Contraction   84

PART TWO. COUNTRY-BY-COUNTRY INSPECTION OF THE BRITISH INVESTMENT

VII. Mexico: A Story of Bonanzas and Heartbreaks   95

VIII. The Small Caribbean Countries: A Story of Meager Profits   105

IX. Rainbow-Chasing in Northern South America   113

X. Ventures, Mostly Imprudent, in Paraguay, Bolivia, and Peru   124

XI. The Chilean Experience   133

XII. Surprisingly Profitable Ventures in Uruguay   142

XIII. Brazil: Large Latin-American Recipient of British Capital   150

XIV. Argentina: Late Major Field of British Overseas Investment   159

PART THREE. THE CRUX OF THE MATTER IN GLOBAL SETTING

XV. A Comparative Sample of British Overseas Companies   171

XVI. A Recent Decade of Income from British Overseas Investment   185

XVII. Some British Views on Foreign Investments   197

XVIII. Views of the Latin-American Recipients   208

Notes   223

Appendixes   239

Index   246

INTRODUCTION

*Recent Problems in
Private International Investment*

⇋ I ⇌

THE CRISIS AND BRITISH EXPERIENCE IN LATIN AMERICA

The Crisis

War and economic depression seem to be the major perils of the twentieth century, and many public officials and publicists appear to be convinced that international trade and international capital investment are among the major devices that must be employed to abolish these terrific evils. They must be abolished, it is said, in order to prevent the destruction of "free enterprise" and other freedoms, and even the destruction of civilization itself. If the closely related devices of international trade and investment are indeed among the most effective remedies for the diseases of war and depression, then scholars should be diligent in the investigation of these remedies.

But scholars are puzzled at the outset by two stubborn facts: first, the fact that international trade and investment began on a fairly large scale more than four hundred years ago with the discovery by the Europeans of land masses and peoples in Asia, the Pacific area, Africa, and the Americas; second, the fact that war and economic depression not only continued after these discoveries were made but continued to grow worse except for a brief century of relative peace following the Napoleonic Wars. Were the remedies ineffective because of intrinsic impotence, or did they fail to cure because they were not applied in sufficient doses? During the decades since World War I public officials, prominent writers, and many others have answered the second question in the affirmative. They have concerned themselves with the problem of increasing the size of the prescription and consequently with the problem of getting rid of the barriers to foreign trade and investment, barriers that have tended to become more rather than less formidable. They have tried, perhaps with too little persistence, to remove the multitude of restrictions that have hampered the movement of both capital and goods across national boundaries; but after the end of World War II their main concern seems to have been centered on the export of capital rather than the export of commodities — probably for the reason that they considered the financial problem fundamental in the attainment of higher levels of foreign trade, which they expected to expand tremendously by increasing the productive efficiency and purchasing power of the retarded peoples of the world. No other presumed remedy for the twin perils of war and economic depression has been discussed with greater fervor since 1945.

Two major methods of pumping capital into the underdeveloped countries are theoretically available: the old method of private investment and the new method of government grants and cheap government loans. The new method not only tends to expand bureaucracies and project governments into national and world economies; it involves a heavy load for taxpayers of the highly developed nations with capital to export. It means that such governments are no longer distributing lands and other resources among their people almost free of charge as they did during the four centuries following the Age of Discovery, but have begun to reverse the flow of benefits, depriving their people of wealth in order to apply in full measure the presumed major remedy for the banishment of war and depression.

While the new method may be the one preferred by the underdeveloped countries themselves, it seems not to be the method favored by many prominent political and economic leaders of the wealthier nations, who prefer the old method of private and voluntary international investment. But doubts have arisen with respect to the feasibility and efficacy of this old method of moving capital into the regions that require prompt development. Private capital will not flow out from the centers of surplus to those of deficiency at the beck and nod of governments. It flows out only when the inducements are attractive, when the "climate" looks favorable. And by and large the climate has not appeared favorable for a good many decades. It has not looked favorable for several reasons, concerning most of which there appears to be a consensus among promoters of private foreign investment — at least in recent years — as may be illustrated by statements made in 1950 by leaders in the United States interested in such investments.

The Crisis and British Experience

Alan Valentine, president of the University of Rochester, a man with business experience, said:

All that [foreign capital] asks is not to be discriminated against. But at present it encounters in many areas some or all of the following important difficulties: special labor and wage laws; discriminatory taxes; local monopolies protected by law; local participation in every industry required by law; . . . dread of expropriation; . . . competition on unequal terms from foreign government enterprise; the balance-of-payment squeeze; nonconvertibility regulations; multiple exchange rates; political insecurity — all these in addition to the normal hazards of business.[1]

Michael Heilperin, International Chamber of Commerce, asked:

What is it that makes private capital move not only into foreign countries but even into domestic investment? Clearly, it is the existence of an appropriate relationship between anticipated risks and prospective rewards. . . . In the past, private capital was far more venturesome in the foreign investment field than at present. This was due to two sets of reasons, one positive and one negative. The positive reason included prospects of rewards which were the higher, the greater the risks involved in the venture. . . . The negative reasons (which, of course, become particularly apparent now that they have ceased to exist) included the absence of legislative and administrative measures in the capital-receiving countries which place in jeopardy the rights of the foreign investor in terms of the disposal of his capital, the management of his enterprises, and the use of profits derived from his business activities.[2]

Henry W. Balgooyen, American and Foreign Power Company, reported:

In the spring of 1949, I attended a meeting of the Economic Commission for Latin America at Havana, Cuba. . . . I requested an opportunity to address the meeting. I am going to tell you some of the things I said. . . . I emphasized that, with economic freedom, private capital will flow toward those countries where the greatest opportunities exist for its safe and profitable employment. . . . One of the most important barriers, I said, . . . is the investor's lack of confidence in the political situation. . . . I mentioned as a second major reason . . . lack of confidence in the foreign exchange situation. . . . I mentioned as a third . . . the trend toward extreme nationalism which, in some countries, has resulted in expropriation of foreign-owned property without proper compensation, and in restrictive legislation directed against foreign enterprise and foreign personnel.[3]

Recent Problems

Why have the economically retarded countries erected such barricades? (They are not alone in this respect, but they are the main objects of concern here.) The word nationalism is used more often than any other to describe their motivation. Many of them have won their political independence only recently and are said to be afraid that they might be resubjugated by the process of foreign investment. Others, though they have had political independence for many years, feel that they cannot be free from outside domination until they have full control of their economy, and this usually signifies a mixture of government control and control by national ("native") capital. This nationalism is therefore economic as well as political: bulwarked by both the profit motive and national sentiment; by eagerness for material benefits, by patriotism, by distrust of foreigners and their capital.

Alluding to this problem in 1950, Heilperin commented:

It may well be that the advantages enjoyed by venture capital in the backward areas (during the nineteenth century and before) have been excessive in terms of the economic interests and national susceptibilities of the foreign countries themselves; [these advantages] have certainly left in their wake deep resentments which even overshadow those very real benefits which have accrued to the countries that served as outlets to those past flows of venture capital.[4]

Describing the passionate views of articulate groups in the retarded regions, a journalist named Harold Isaacs remarked on the same occasion:

The entire social, political, and economic balance that was built up during the last three centuries . . . was based on the exploitation of the so-called backward areas of the world by Western Europe. These areas contributed in the first place to the primary accumulation of capital and fueled the beginnings of European industrialism. Through decades and centuries they . . . contributed heavily to the national incomes of these [European] countries. . . . The economic legacy of empire is poverty . . . lopsided economies under which profitable raw materials have been extracted and . . . the welfare of the people ignored. . . . The psychological legacy of empire is hostility.[5]

A Summary of the British Experience

A more accurate knowledge of what actually occurred might help to remove from some countries these barricades of suspicion, fear, and hostility or enable those concerned with the promotion of international investment to arrive at a more sympathetic view of the reasons

The Crisis and British Experience

for their existence; and the hope of casting a few rays of light upon this subject has been one of the motives for the writing of this book. It deals with two main themes: (1) the size, nature, and chronology of British investments in Latin America and (2) approximate rates of return therefrom. A third topic, rates of return from British investments in other underdeveloped regions, has been considered to some extent for purposes of comparison and contrast; and a fourth, attitudes toward foreign investment in the British Isles, the United States, and Latin America, has been discussed briefly in order to suggest its importance.

Surprised at the meagerness of their returns from most of Latin America most of the time, I was on the point of concluding that Britishers who sent their funds overseas might have been the dupes of investment houses, manufacturers, exporters, and shipping companies, when it occurred to me that I should extend my research into other areas before reaching a firm conclusion. My eventual discoveries were another surprise. In fact, I was not only surprised but almost astounded by the large income returned by scores of the most profitable enterprises owned by British investors in India, Ceylon, Malaya, and Africa south of the Sahara Desert.

In stressing rates of return I have assumed that the primary aim of British private overseas investors — or those of any other country — has been profits, or the hope of profits. To consider the past activities of private investors in distant lands in any other light than the search for higher income than they thought they could obtain from investment at home is, in my opinion, to indulge in folklore or misrepresentation. For I am convinced that whatever benefits these investments may have brought to the home country as a whole, or taken to recipient countries, were in the main by-products — incidental or accidental benefits.

British investors in lands overseas had no master blueprint, no benevolent plan for "uplifting the natives." They made almost no improvements in sanitation unless they were paid for them, except possibly in the localities where they carried on their economic activities and with the objective of increasing the output of their labor crews. They rarely concerned themselves with the teaching of technical skills to foreign workers or built any hospitals with their own funds that they did not teach or build for the purpose of increasing the efficiency of their workers. They seldom financed any schools or orphan asylums, except indirectly through the purchase of government securities or by means of taxes they were compelled to pay.

Nor, on the other hand, is it likely that they were primarily devoted to serving the general economic interests of the United Kingdom. To stimulate exports therefrom was not their purpose, unless they happened to be manufacturers, exporters, or shippers as well as foreign investors. To obtain cheaper foods and raw materials was not their fundamental objective, unless they happened to require these in connection with other economic activities in which they were engaged. Neither was their primary aim that of supplying the home market, or any other, with cheaper manufactured goods resulting from increased volume of production, although this as well as more abundant foods and raw materials at lower prices may have been one of the consequences of their operations when they could not control the prices of such commodities. Most of the theories regarding the contribution of international investments to the welfare of the investing countries and the welfare of recipients are probably the rationalizations of promoters and economists.

I am not contending, however, that international investments of a private character, whether British or any other, have not benefited both lenders and borrowers. In most instances it is likely that they have. But that they have been beneficial to both investing and recipient countries in all times and circumstances has never been proved — or disproved — by any exact balance sheets.

As for the recipients, it is certain that foreign investors sent to Latin America and other similar regions almost every device of modern technology shortly after its invention. They accelerated the construction of more rapid means of transport and communications, of dams and irrigation projects, of waterworks and sewers, of gas plants and electric utilities. They hastened the development of material resources and increased the revenues of governments. They widened employment for labor, freeing some workers from peonage but perhaps (in connivance with local authorities) forcing others to toil for them involuntarily, compelling or inducing not a few to enter disease-infested regions to grow, harvest, and export rubber, tea, or bananas, to build railroads, or to search for metals and minerals, probably paying as a rule somewhat more than the customary wage, and eventually —

mainly because they expected by this means to expand their profits or because the local laws required it — providing better working conditions than might have prevailed otherwise. In short, private foreign investments raised the levels of living in underdeveloped areas to some extent.[6]

It is likewise certain, however, that this foreign capital and technology tended to disturb the status quo by the creation of new centers of power in the recipient countries, at least temporarily serving the interests of some groups therein while discommoding and injuring others: the handicraft industries, for instance, compelled to compete with new mechanized industries, or owners of pack-animals or other primitive transport systems forced to compete with railways and truck lines, or the makers of candles forced to meet the competition of kerosene lamps or gas and electric lights. It is also certain that foreign speculators may retard urban growth and agricultural development, or make them more expensive, by holding vacant lands for a rise in values, and that foreign capital, like any other vested interest, may retard progress by opposing the introduction of new forms of technology, as, for example, when foreign-owned gas companies oppose the installation of electric lights, or when foreign-owned railroads try to prevent the construction of highways, or when foreign-controlled tramways oppose the initiation of urban bus lines. In other words, nearly every economic innovation hurts somebody and benefits somebody; rapid change results in painful injuries as well as quick benefits, depending upon the occupation of the groups involved; foreign investors may sometimes hamper as well as stimulate progress.

In insisting that foreign private investments hitherto have been made primarily in a search for larger profits in distant lands than investors supposed they could obtain from domestic ventures, I am not condemning the foreign investor. I think that his attitude and efforts have been quite natural and very human. I might scold the management of the most profitable British overseas enterprises for lack of generosity if I were convinced that generosity could be assumed to be an essential element in the business world's pattern of values. But I feel that generosity is not an attribute of the capitalist system as such. Has it not been based upon the assumption that its benefits are derived from competition and the "survival of the fittest" (and that competition should not be softened by agreements among producers and distributors at the expense of consumers)? It is true that many businessmen have been generous with their fortunes, especially within their home countries. But this generosity has been an individual and personal trait and not a practice of the business system itself. Business enterprises operating abroad are usually corporations managed by boards presumably in the interest of stockholders, and the managers of corporations have no disposition or authority to engage in charity as a part of their function as corporation heads. Perhaps generosity can never become an effective force in the capitalistic way of life *per se*. Perhaps, on the other hand, generosity must become a part of the system's pattern of values — describing its new role as self-preservation or enlightened selfishness — in order to save the system from collapse; and perhaps this may be made possible by the growing separation of ownership from control. I do not know. I feel sure, however, that it will not be easy to find an effective and satisfactory substitute for the much-lauded and much-abused profit motive that has provided such a mighty impulse in the development and exploitation of the resources with which this planet is endowed.

Even in the absence of this benevolent disposition, foreign private capital probably has brought more benefits than injuries to the recipient countries. That most of these countries are still very poor cannot be denied; but they probably are in better condition than they would have been without such investment. It would certainly be a mistake to attribute their poverty solely or largely to the operation of foreign business enterprise; their poverty seems rather to be the result mainly of scanty resource endowment, debilitating climate, disease, illiteracy, psychological attitudes, and hampering value systems. The peoples of the retarded regions have neither practiced birth control nor devoted themselves enthusiastically and energetically to material progress.

I have already asserted that British investments in Latin America were not sent there for benevolent purposes but for profits, and remarked that I was surprised by the meagerness of the profits. I shall now attempt a few more generalizations. The profits varied, of course, with time and circumstance. They must have been most satisfactory from the investor's angle during the years 1879–1889 and 1902–1929 and the most unsatisfactory during the half-century following 1825 and the two decades starting in 1930. British investors suffered during

The Crisis and British Experience

both of these unsatisfactory periods because of the political disorders and public policies of the recipient countries. Income from government securities was very skimpy and irregular because the Latin-American governments lacked the capacity, and sometimes even the will, to make interest and sinking-fund payments. Returns on investment in business enterprises were meager during both periods, but for different reasons. Political turbulence was mainly responsible in the earlier period; during later years it was not so much political disorders as administrative interference and control by Latin-American governments that reduced profits. It should be added, however, that Latin Americans were not entirely to blame for these unsatisfactory returns. The blame must be shared by British imprudence and general disturbances in the outside world. And it was for the same reasons in the main that the flow of capital was not constant. There were interruptions, even shrinkages in some sectors; and finally, general contraction resulting largely from two world wars and a global economic depression between them.

The capital flow was very irregular. The major part of this British capital moved to Latin America in the 1880's and during the decade following 1902. The rest was mainly water and capitalization of reserves, which tended to depress nominal rates of return, which may also have been reduced in some instances by insiders who organized subsidiaries (whose dividend records are inaccessible) and siphoned out the earnings of their larger affiliates. Rates of return, however, as already suggested, are not a complete index of the benefits that accrued to the British Isles — or certain groups within them — since the investment expanded exports, probably increased total employment, augmented the supply of foods and raw materials, and perhaps reduced the costs of both, while preventing the sagging of interest rates and prices for manufactured products.

It appears likely that too much of the capital was invested in public services — railways, communications, waterworks, sewer systems, gas plants, electric utilities, and the like — but this was probably unavoidable in view of prevalent primitive conditions and the scarcity of domestic capital. The large investment in government securities was certainly imprudent in many instances. Commercial banks and other financial organizations were the most dependable sources of income, but only a little more dependable than the livestock industry in the

Río de la Plata countries, or two extractive industries dealing in scarce commodities; namely, nitrate of soda and a tanning material called *quebracho*. The petroleum industry, though risky, usually provided good income. The greatest losses in proportion to the capital involved were undoubtedly suffered in the failure to grow rubber on plantations. Many mining ventures also resulted in comparatively heavy casualties, but these were counterbalanced for investors in mines as a group and perhaps for Great Britain as a whole, though rarely for individual investors, by the discovery of a number of bonanzas. Manufacturing seems to have been a sound type of investment; but manufacturing seldom went beyond the processing of products of farm, ranch, forest, and orchard.

Finally, it should be noted that a minority of the countries — Argentina, Brazil, Uruguay, Chile, Peru, and Mexico — received the major part of British capital. Investments in the rest of them, however significant they may have seemed to the countries themselves, were small; and most of the capital in these, as also in Peru, might almost be described as frozen capital — money employed in the tenacious operation of rather unprofitable enterprises which had been taken over in the hope of ameliorating losses from earlier investments in mortgages or government securities. This was one of the reasons why the investment in the island republics and in the countries bordering the Caribbean failed to yield satisfactory returns. The railway capital in Peru, Central America, Cuba, and Paraguay, and some of the British-owned real estate in Ecuador and Paraguay, illustrate this category of investment. Capital ventured in Mexican lands was highly speculative and turned out to be unprofitable. The investment in public utilities in Bolivia, northern South America, and Central America was likewise mostly unprofitable, as was the railway investment, with a few notable exceptions, in Colombia, Venezuela, and Brazil — unprofitable even before the economic crash of 1929.

In general, it seems reasonable to conclude that the worst handicaps that vexed British investors were Latin-American revolutions, corruption, administrative whims, and nationalism, global wars and depressions, and occasional imprudence and dishonesty on the part of British promoters and investors. Furthermore, the British experience was more or less typical of the experience of other foreign investors. Frenchmen probably suffered a little more severely from their Latin-

The Crisis and British Experience

American ventures than did Englishmen. German investors appear to have been less unfortunate than either the French or the British until most of their properties were confiscated as a result of defeat in the two World Wars. Capitalists of the United States, except those who took part in the bond-buying extravaganza of the 1920's and the effort to grow plantation rubber, were probably the most fortunate of all.[7] But even those who had enjoyed the best luck seemed to be afflicted during the years following 1930 with doubts and fears about the future of foreign free enterprise in Latin America and other similar regions; and their doubts and fears were caused by the attitudes and policies of ruling groups in the retarded countries as well as by grave apprehensions about the world in general. The future of private international investment seemed insecure at the moment when the export of capital was felt to be one of the best remedies for a world in crisis.

PART ONE

*General Survey of
British Investments in Latin America*

⇋ II ⇌

EARLY IMPRUDENCE AND VEXATION, 1822-1880

Boom and Collapse

The inhabitants of the British Isles indulged in a wild speculation spree in the early 1820's, investing large sums in the bonds of foreign governments and in the securities of hundreds of joint stock companies organized for operation at home and abroad. Clever salesmen, scheming attorneys, and gamblers of every description swarmed through the business streets, subsidized journalists, induced members of Parliament to grant company charters, and peddled engraved paper. Poor and rich alike were soon scrambling for bonds of young and unstable governments and the stocks of almost every conceivable economic enterprise. A nominal sum of £25,308,486 was invested during 1824 and 1825 in the issues of foreign governments; and although only 156 British stock companies organized before 1824 had survived until the beginning of that year, 624 were founded or projected in 1824-1825, with an authorized capital of £102,781,600! The period marked the real beginning of British private investments in independent and semi-independent foreign nations, and the new nations of Latin America were important centers of attraction.[1]

The face value of Latin-American government bonds purchased by Englishmen during this two-year period was over £17,000,000. The authorized capital of the forty-six or more stock companies organized in 1824-1825 for the purpose of operating mainly or entirely in Latin America was probably not less than £35,000,000, although only a fraction of it was paid in before the crash that promptly followed. Associations were formed to obtain precious metals from the Andean cordilleras, where there were few workers, no fuel for the fires, and no roads for the vehicles; technicians and machinery were hurried off in utmost ignorance of the almost impenetrable mountains and matted jungles that awaited them. There were companies to fish for pearls,

17

General Survey

to inaugurate steamboat lines, to cut through the American isthmus, to furnish steam engines for mints, to establish colonies of farmers and herdsmen. A churning company was formed to send out milkmaids to the pampas; furs and warming pans were shipped to the tropics! "Too many were eager for gain, making haste to be rich; and of these the sharpers of society made an easy prey." [2]

British losses from their Latin-American ventures, to say nothing of other investments, were heavy. Every Latin-American bond issue went into default by the end of 1827; [3] over half of the some twenty-six mining companies organized for operations in Latin America collapsed by 1833 and only seven survived until 1842; [4] some twenty other enterprises set up to develop or exploit the region collapsed even more speedily.[5] As too often happens, only stock-jobbers, merchant-bankers, advertisers, and managing staffs too shrewd to risk their own funds profited from the orgy. Latin-American governments largely wasted the proceeds of their bond sales and gravely injured their credit.* For several decades after the debacle it was difficult to attract new British capital into the Latin-American mining districts; as late as the year 1875 only sixteen British mining companies of much significance were operating in the region.[6]

Latin-American investments had an especial appeal for Englishmen during the 1820's because Englishmen were deeply interested in the Latin-American independence movement — a struggle initiated in 1810, not without some anticipation of British assistance, and on the point of successful termination fifteen years later. Although the official attitude in London was at first cool toward the revolting Hispanic colonies and although the British government never conceded more than a benevolent neutrality at any time, the insurgents received aid and encouragement from His Britannic Majesty's subjects from the outset, and even more assistance after the end of the Napoleonic Wars. British officers paid the expenses of their recruits, British merchants extended credits for ships and supplies, and numerous expeditions of volunteers sailed for South America to join the patriot armies.[7] Thus, by the time their independence was won, and in some cases even be-

---

* There is no way to measure the extent to which their credit was injured, because it was affected by other factors besides the defaults — numerous civil wars and several little international conflicts, for instance — but the fact is that most of the borrowing governments had to wait for thirty or forty years before they could float new issues in the British Isles. (See the manuals cited in note 3.)

Early Imprudence and Vexation, 1822–1880

fore it was won, the new nations of Latin America were considerably indebted to British merchants, shipowners, soldiers, and army and navy officers; and since Great Britain was the only country in the world with a large surplus of capital, it was natural that the governments of the new Latin nations should float their first bond issues in the British market.

Four issues, with an aggregate face value of £3,650,000, were sold to British investors in 1822, and ten issues, with an aggregate face value of £17,479,000, in 1824–1825, making a grand total of £21,129,000. Mexico, the largest borrower, floated an aggregate of £7,000,000, including £600,000 for the Municipality of Guadalajara; but *La Gran Colombia*, then embracing what later became the three nations of Colombia, Venezuela, and Ecuador, was a close second, with £6,750,000. Brazil borrowed £3,200,000, Peru £1,816,000, and Chile £1,000,000. The Province of Buenos Aires (the national government of Argentina had hardly come into existence) borrowed £1,000,000, the ridiculous and largely mythical Kingdom of Poyais (on the east coast of Central America) floated a loan of £200,000, and the United Provinces of Central America (which were never really united and soon broke up into the republics of Costa Rica, El Salvador, Guatemala, Honduras, and Nicaragua) borrowed £163,000.

Putting aside the Poyais and the Central American issues, "the greater the risk the bigger the loan" would be an accurate description of the rest. The Poyais loan was comparatively small and Poyais bonds were completely worthless; the issue floated by the United Provinces of Central America was only a fraction of the £1,428,750 which the stock-jobbers and the government of that new state planned to sell.

These Latin-American bonds, which included issues by all the independent nations then in existence except three (Bolivia, Paraguay, and Haiti), were offered to the British public at prices ranging from 58 to 89.75, Mexican bonds being offered for the lowest as well as the highest price. The nominal interest rate was usually 6 per cent, but in three instances, two Brazilian loans and one Mexican, it was 5. For investors who bought the bonds for no more — and no less — than the price at which they were originally offered to the public the yield was — or might have been — from 5.9 to 10 per cent. Fuller details regarding these early issues are shown in Table 1.[8]

If British investors had bought the bonds at the price of issue an-

General Survey

Table 1. Latin-American Government Issues Floated in England, 1822, 1824, 1825

Date and Borrower	Face Value	Price to Public	Interest Nominal	Interest "Real"	Sums Realized
1822					
Colombia	£2,000,000	84	6%	7.1%	£1,680,000
Chile	1,000,000	70	6	8.6	700,000
Poyais	200,000	80	6	7.5	160,000
Peru	450,000	88	6	6.8	396,000
1824					
Peru	750,000	82	6	7.3	615,000
Buenos Aires	1,000,000	85	6	7.0	850,000
Colombia	4,750,000	88.5	6	6.8	4,203,750
Brazil	1,200,000	75	5	6.7	900,000
Mexico	3,200,000	58	5	8.6	1,856,000
1825					
Brazil	2,000,000	85	5	5.9	1,700,000
Mexico	3,200,000	89.75	6	6.7	2,872,000
Peru	616,000	78	6	7.7	480,480
Guadalajara	600,000	60	6	10.0	360,000
Central America	163,000	73	6	8.2	118,990
	£21,129,000				£16,892,220

nounced, their total actual investment would have been £16,892,220, as set forth in Table 1. But the market was rigged against them and they invested considerably more, possibly £19 million or £20 million altogether. The flotation process followed a uniform pattern. Representatives of the borrowing government came to London and negotiated contracts with issuing firms; space was bought in newspapers to extol the countries whose securities were to be marketed; pamphlets with glowing descriptions of their resources were circulated; prospectuses blazing with optimism were prepared and sent to agents and clients. After enthusiasm had been aroused to a high pitch, a selected group of insiders — participating merchant-bankers and swindlers — received large blocks of bonds and it was promptly announced that the issues had been completely sold out; but it was at the same time hinted and suggested that a few bonds could still be bought from original purchasers who might not recognize a gilt-edged security when they saw it. This caused further excitement and a feverish scramble by eager applicants. The contracting firms and their associates then unloaded all they had at a profit and the bonds declined forthwith to a fraction of their nominal value.[9]

The soar and swoop of quotations was something marvelous between

Early Imprudence and Vexation, 1822–1880

1822–1825 and 1827. The Colombian bonds of 1822, issued at 84, rose to 96.5 and dropped to 38.5. The Chilean bonds of the same year, issued at 70, rocketed to 93 and fell to 30. The Poyais loan of 1822, the bonanza investment offered by "King" Gregor McGregor, rose only a point above the issue price of 80, but soon descended to the appropriate level of 0. The Peruvian issue of 1824, offered at 82, soared to 89 and dived to 23.5. The Colombian loan of 1824, issued at 88.5, rose to 96.5 and plunged to 52.5, and the Province of Buenos Aires issue of the same year, originally offered at 85, kited to 97 and nosed down to 69.[10]

The great majority of the British investors — namely all, or nearly all, who were not admitted into the inner sanctum of the favored group — probably purchased their bonds somewhere near the peak. If they sold them in panic somewhere near the bottom, they lost most of their capital. If they continued to hold them, their losses were still large; but their heirs and assignees and the heirs of their heirs and assignees finally received interest at a reduced rate and recovered a good part of the principal — except in the case of the worthless paper of Poyais.*

The new Latin-American nations derived no benefit from the high prices paid by imprudent British investors. The loan contracts contained no provisions that entitled them to a share of the proceeds in excess of the original price at which the bonds were sold to the bankers. They received only the sums realized from flotations at that price, after the costs of distribution had been subtracted, and these costs were not moderate.

The profits of the financial agents were known only to the governments concerned and to the agents themselves. They were not revealed to the public at the time the bonds were sold,† and apparently they have not been fully revealed since. Enough has been disclosed, however, to indicate that their gross profits were enormous — probably between £4 million and £5 million. The commission on the two Colombian loans totaled £493,750 — 4.5 per cent of the face value of the first and 8.5 per cent of the second.[11] The commission exacted for floating

---

* In no instance save Brazil was interest paid at the full rate stipulated in the original contracts when service was finally resumed on these bonds, and only in a few cases was the principal fully redeemed.

† Embittered investors demanded and obtained a parliamentary investigation but no remedial legislation was enacted.

General Survey

the two issues of the Mexican national government was £356,000 — 8 per cent on the first and 3.75 per cent on the second.[12] The commission on the two Brazilian loans was £128,000, or 4 per cent on each.[13] The commission obtained from the Buenos Aires loan was £150,000 — 15 per cent of the face value of the issue![14] Similar commissions were probably charged against the issues of other countries. Nor were these by any means the only golden streams that flowed into the coffers of the financiers. Market manipulations probably brought in another million or more. Profits were obtained from interest and sinking-fund payments made in advance and left on deposit; interest and amortization for the first year and a half seem to have been subtracted from the proceeds in most instances and retained to help peg the market. Bills of earlier creditors were bought up at a discount and exchanged for bonds; agency fees were collected for remitting dividends; and the financiers, using the cash received from bond sales, often served as purchasing agents for the Latin-American governments.[15]

After all the commissions, fees, discounts, and printing costs had been deducted and service funds for the first eighteen months withheld, the Latin-Americans found themselves close to the short end of the deal, with cash in hand equivalent to about 60 per cent of the contracted debt. For a net of some £12 million they had obligated themselves to the extent of more than £21 million. The Mexican national government seems to have been shorn more thoroughly than any of the rest; for two issues of bonds with a par value of £6,400,000 it is said to have received a net of £2,358,578 in cash and supplies.[16] But British money would be expensive and the debt burden heavy only if the Latin-American governments faithfully lived up to their obligations, and most of them failed to take such obligations very seriously.

Such, in brief, is the story of the early issues of Latin-American government bonds. The history of the economic enterprises organized to take over the heritage of the Spaniards and the Portuguese was essentially the same. If the total losses were less, so was the aggregate of the venture capital. In relation to the actual investment the losses were even heavier. Little or no profit was derived from precious metals or pearls. No tolls were collected from the canal; it was not constructed. The projected steamship lines brought no returns; they were not inaugurated until fifteen years later. The colonization companies went down in the strange environment and amid the disorders of the time. There was no demand for pampas butter; the customary olive oil was preferred. There was no urgent need for furs and skates; the merchants could not change the climate.[17]

Of two things British promoters were most confident. They were certain that there were gold, silver, and copper in Latin America and that the Spaniards and Portuguese had found the metals even though their activities had been carried on behind a sort of "iron curtain." In fact, the long years of colonial secrecy served to stimulate imaginations and whet appetites; and the optimistic statements of Alexander von Humboldt and a few other European scientists whom the Hispanic monarchs had permitted to view the Land of Sharon made excellent quotations for prospectuses.[18] Englishmen did not know exactly where the treasures were, but they felt sure they could find them. They organized their mining associations at once, naming them for the countries in which they hoped to operate or for such mining districts as they could recall, and sent out searching parties and agents to negotiate contracts later.[19]

None of the new nations that had emerged from the wreckage of the American empires of Spain and Portugal by the middle 1820's was overlooked, with the exception of hermit-like Paraguay, which may not have been too secluded for the all-embracing grasp of the General South American Mining Association, formed primarily, however, for operation in Brazil. Seven associations were organized for Mexico; four for Brazil; three for Peru and three for Chile, not counting the Chilian and Peruvian Association obviously designed for both; three for La Gran Colombia; two for Argentina; and one each for Bolivia, the United Provinces of Central America, and Haiti (which then controlled also the region that later became the domain of the Dominican Republic). These mining companies and their capitalization are listed in Table 2.

Although two or three of the firms that participated in the flotation of Latin-American government bonds also took part in selling the stock of the mining associations, the latter securities were distributed in the main by a different group of merchant-bankers; and perhaps less manipulation of the market occurred. But adequate sales devices were employed. Besides the glowing prospectuses and the glib

General Survey

Table 2. British Mining Associations Formed to Operate in Latin America, 1824–1825 *

Name	Capital Authorized	Paid In
Anglo-Chilian	£1,500,000	£120,000
Anglo-Mexican	1,000,000	750,000
Anglo-Colombian	1,500,000	75,000
Anglo-Peruvian	600,000	30,000
Bolaños	200,000	87,500
Bolívar	500,000	50,000
Brazilian	2,000,000	20,000
Castello	1,000,000	50,000
Chilian	1,000,000	75,000
Chilian and Peruvian	1,000,000	50,000
Colombian	1,000,000	150,000
Famatima	250,000	50,000
Guanajuato	400,000	6,000
General South American	2,000,000	100,000
Haytian	1,000,000	50,000
Imperial Brazilian	1,000,000	200,000
Mexican	1,000,000	150,000
Pasco-Peruvian	1,000,000	150,000
Potosí–La Paz	1,000,000	50,000
Real del Monte	400,000	325,000
Río de la Plata	1,000,000	75,000
Tarma	200,000	5,000
Tlalpuxahua	400,000	120,000
United Chilian	500,000	50,000
United Mexican	1,240,000	775,000
United Provinces	1,500,000	15,000
Total	£24,190,000	£3,508,500

* Compiled from data supplied by English in his *General Guide to the Companies formed for Working Foreign Mines* and his *Complete View of the Joint Stock Companies*.

palaver of promoters, there were two devices which deserve special mention: Latin Americans were members of the boards of directors of ten of the companies (surely no free stock was given as an inducement!) and members of the British Parliament served on nineteen (the MP's played no part, of course, in securing the charters!).

In general, however, the promoters appear to have been reasonably honorable and firmly resolute. They sent out negotiators, managers, mining experts, several skilled miners, and almost every kind of tool, implement, vehicle, and machine to the leading Latin-American mining districts.[20] If the associations failed, it was not for lack of effort. They were frustrated by the British financial panic, Latin-American geog-

Early Imprudence and Vexation, 1822–1880

raphy and temperament, and remoteness of the field of operations. Englishmen lost two or three million pounds sterling,* but some of them climbed a good many mountains, viewed a lot of gorgeous scenery, and showed the natives, the coyotes, and the condors a fine assortment of the latest mechanical inventions.[21] They failed; but their sons and grandsons would try and try again and a good many of them would finally succeed.[22]

Readjustment and Resumption of Investment

The British investment boom of the 1820's was short, quickly interrupted by deflation and serious capital losses. The total nominal investment in Latin America amounted to between £25 million and

Table 3. British Investments in Latin America, End of 1880

Country	Total Nominal Investment	Government Bonds	Economic Enterprises
Argentina	£20,338,709	£11,233,700	£9,105,009
Bolivia	1,654,000	1,654,000	.....
Brazil	38,869,067	23,060,162	15,808,905
Chile	8,466,521	7,765,104	701,417
Colombia	3,073,373	2,100,000	973,373
Costa Rica	3,304,000	3,304,000	.....
Cuba	1,231,600	.....	1,231,600
Dominican Republic	714,300	714,300	.....
Ecuador	1,959,380	1,724,000	135,380
Guatemala	544,200	544,200	.....
Honduras	3,222,000	3,222,000	.....
Mexico	32,740,916	23,540,800	9,200,116
Nicaragua	206,570	.....	206,570
Paraguay	1,505,400	1,505,400	.....
Peru	36,177,070	32,688,320	3,488,750
Uruguay	7,644,105	3,519,220	4,124,885
Venezuela	7,564,390	6,402,800	1,161,590
General	10,274,660	.....	10,274,660
Total	£179,490,261	£123,078,006	£56,412,255

Nominal Capital in Various Economic Enterprises

```
34 railways .................................. £34,437,051
24 public utilities ............................  11,070,395
18 mining enterprises .........................   3,398,305
 8 banking and other finance ..................   3,013,560
 5 real estate enterprises ....................     493,579
 7 shipping and miscellaneous companies .......   3,999,365
```

---

* The extent of their losses is not definitely known. Some of the capital paid in was returned to the investors; but the list of companies in Table 2 is probably incomplete.

General Survey

£30 million at the end of 1826. Very little English capital flowed into the region during the next quarter of a century. Perhaps as much was taken into Latin America by British emigrants as was exported to it by those who maintained their residence in the British Isles. The emigrants went mainly to Argentina, Uruguay, and Chile. But the trickle of British investments of the 1830's and 1840's became a fairly large stream during the next three decades, branching out into at least seventeen countries. The face value of the capital exceeded £179 million by the end of 1880, distributed as set forth in Table 3.[23] Although Cuba was not yet an independent republic, I have included the Cuban investment. Panama, where Englishmen held some bonds of a railroad controlled by citizens of the United States, was, of course, a part of Colombia at this time, and there were not any significant British investments in Haiti or El Salvador.

The Investment in Government Bonds, Old and New

Table 3 shows that approximately two thirds of the British investment in Latin America at the close of 1880 was in government bonds. That was unfortunate. The debt record of most of the governments had not only been bad; it was still bad. With the exception of Brazil, the Latin-American governments that had defaulted on the loans they had floated in London between 1822 and 1825 continued in default for many years. It will be recalled that the face value of their flotations during that period was £21,129,000. Brazil resumed payments on its £3,200,000 in 1829, issuing £400,000 in 5 per cent bonds to cover accrued interest; but it was half a century before the last of the other defaulters began to meet their obligations.

Although the Mexican national government was fairly prompt in negotiating an adjustment on its £6,400,000, issuing £1,584,495 in 5 and 6 per cent bonds in 1831 to pay overdue interest, the bonds soon fell into default again. An issue of £434,350 in 5 per cent securities in 1837 to clear up arrears was followed by further defaults and refunding operations, until Ferdinand Maximilian finally issued £4,864,800 in 3 per cent securities in 1864 to cover accrued interest.

The record of the Central American countries, which had inherited the small debt of £163,000 contracted by the Central American Confederation, was no better. Costa Rica paid off its share — £13,608 — at 85 per cent of par in 1840, failing, however, to pay accrued interest

Early Imprudence and Vexation, 1822–1880

The other republics were even more remiss. Guatemala did not meet its obligations to the British bondholders until 1856, and then only in bonds, an issue of £100,000 in 5 per cent securities in exchange for its share — £68,741 — of the old debt and accrued interest thereon. El Salvador paid off most of its portion — £27,217 — at 90 per cent of par in cash, without accrued interest, in 1860, but failed to redeem the remnant until 1877. The government of Honduras postponed action until 1867, when it issued £90,075 in 5 per cent securities to cover principal and accrued interest on its share — £27,217 — of the old Confederation's debt. Nicaragua failed to make any adjustment until 1874 and, even then, paid only the principal amount — £27,717 — at 85 per cent of its face value.

The first of the defaulting South American countries (after Brazil) to effect a settlement with the British bondholders was Venezuela. Its share of the old debt contracted by La Gran Colombia — £6,750,000 — was 28.5 per cent, according to an agreement reached by the three successor states in 1834. The Venezuelan government redeemed the principal sum and paid off the accrued interest in 1841 with an issue of £3,776,793 in new securities having an interest rate beginning at 1 and 2 per cent and gradually rising to 5 per cent on half of the total and 6 per cent on the rest. This arrangement was followed by further default in 1847 and another settlement, followed soon by still more defaults and readjustments.

Colombia, then called New Granada, refunded its share, 50 per cent, of the old obligations of La Gran Colombia in 1845, with a new bond issue totaling £6,625,950, bearing interest at 1 per cent but gradually rising to 6 per cent. Defaulting again in 1850, the Bogotá government issued £775,500 in 2 and 3 per cent securities in 1861 in payment of accumulated interest.

Ecuador waited until 1855 to begin to service its portion — 21.5 per cent — of the debt inherited from La Gran Colombia. The settlement was rather complicated. The Quito government redeemed the old bonds with £1,824,000 in new securities bearing interest starting at 1 per cent and rising to 3 per cent. Arrears of interest were paid off in land warrants and in Peruvian bonds held in the Ecuadorian treasury. No amortization payments were made on the new paper for many years and a long default on interest payments began in 1868.

Chile resumed service on its old loan of £1,000,000 in 1842, issuing

General Survey

to the British bondholders £750,500 in 3 per cent securities in payment of arrears in interest. The Peruvian government negotiated a settlement with the British bondholders in 1849, refunding the old bonds, £1,816,000, and accrued interest by an issue of £3,776,000 in new securities with rates of interest running from 1 to 6 per cent; and thanks mainly to guano revenues, Peru was able to service its sterling issues without interruption until 1876. The Province of Buenos Aires finally resumed service on its loan of 1824 — £1,000,000 — in 1857. This province and the national governments of Chile, Peru, and Brazil were the only defaulters of the early national period that continued to fulfill their obligations with regularity for any length of time after they had cleared up their original defaults.

In view of this record, one might have expected British investors to shy away from Latin-American government securities. But grandsons seem to profit little from the experience of their grandfathers in the investment field. During the 1860's and early 1870's Englishmen went on another investment spree. It is true that they revealed no enthusiasm for the issues of Colombia, Ecuador, and some of the Central American countries, but they seemed eager to invest in the government paper of most of the others involved in the defaults following the boom of the 1820's.

British investors purchased no Ecuadorian bonds until long after 1880, and they bought only one block of Colombian securities during the thirty-five years following 1845: a small issue of £200,000, with an interest rate of 6 per cent, bought at 86 in 1863. They did not invest in any bonds issued either by the government of Nicaragua or by the government of El Salvador until after 1880, and they purchased only one small issue, £500,000 in 6 per cents, sold to them at 70.5, from Guatemala (1869). They were unable, however, to resist the temptation to buy some £3,400,000 of 6 and 7 per cent bonds offered in 1871 and 1872 by Costa Rica at prices ranging from 72 to 82, and even less did they resist the opportunity in 1867 and 1870 to purchase an aggregate of £3,500,000 in 10 per cent securities offered by the agents of Honduras at 80. In fact, British investors were even induced to take £8,000,000, face value, of a large issue floated by Mexico's Maximilian government in 1864 in Paris and London: 6 per cent bonds offered at 53!

Two Venezuelan issues were sold to British investors in the 1860's.

Early Imprudence and Vexation, 1822–1880

The first was an issue of £1,000,000 in 6 per cent securities offered to the public at 63 in 1862, and the second was an issue of £1,500,000 in 6 per cents sold to investors at 60 in 1864. But Venezuela fell into default in 1867 and was unable to make any flotations in London during the next decade.

Peru sold more government securities in England during this second speculative period than were marketed by any other Latin-American country. Including conversion operations, the aggregate was around £42,482,600. The net, after allowing for old bonds exchanged for the new, was approximately £33 million. It was in 1853, four years after the settlement dealing with the bonds of the early 1820's, that Peru began to offer new paper in London: £2,600,000 in 4.5 per cent securities sold to the public at 85 and £404,300 in 4.5 per cents granted as a subsidy to J. Hegan and Company, the builders of the Arica and Tacna Railway. Next came a consolidation issue of £5,500,000 (£5,288,300 sold in London at 93), 4.5 per cents, marketed in 1862, followed in 1865 by a conversion operation which involved £10 million 5 per cents offered to British investors at 83.5 and in 1869 by £290,000 in government-guaranteed 5 per cent securities for the National Pisco and Ica Railway. The next year a total of £11,900,000 in 6 per cents was sold in England at 82.5, and the year 1872 witnessed the sale of another £15 million of 5 per cents taken by the public at 77.5. Default began on all of Peru's outstanding bonds in 1876.

The Chilean government resumed its sale of securities in the London market in 1858, sixteen years after effecting a settlement of its old debt, marketing an issue of £1,554,800, with interest rate of 4.5 per cent, at 92. After a delay of eight years, further flotations were made at a rapid pace: £450,000 in 6 per cents offered at 92.5 in 1866; £2,000,000, also bearing interest at 6 per cent, taken at 84 in 1867, and a further issue of 7 per cents the same year, of which £626,700 were sold in London at 92; £1,012,700 in 5 per cent securities which sold to investors at 83 in 1870; £2,276,500 in 5 per cents offered to the public at 94 in 1873; and £1,900,000, interest rate also 5 per cent, sold in 1875 to British investors at 88.25. Figured at par, the grand total for Chile in less than twenty years was £9,820,700, of which £7,265,900 were marketed within a decade.

The Brazilian government resumed its flotations in London in 1839, ten years after clearing up its early defaults, selling a small issue,

General Survey

£312,512, of 5 per cents at 78. Another flotation, £732,000, also bearing interest at 5 per cent, was made in 1843, the securities being offered to British investors at 85. Then there was a pause until the next decade, when four issues aggregating £4,443,113 were sold in London: £1,040,600, with interest at 4.5 per cent, taken by British purchasers in 1852 at 90; £1,526,500, interest rate also 4.5 per cent, taken in 1858 at 96; £503,000 in 5 per cents in 1859, a conversion operation; and £1,373,013, bearing interest at 4.5 per cent, sold to English investors at 90 in 1860. The big sales did not begin, however, until 1863, with the flotation of £3,855,300 in 4.5 per cent securities offered to purchasers in London at 88 — mainly a conversion loan. Two years later, with the approach of the Paraguayan War, an issue of £6,963,600 in 5 per cent bonds was sold in London at 74. The next flotation took place in 1871: £3,459,600, with interest at 5 per cent, offered to English purchasers at 89; and in 1875 another 5 per cent issue of £5,301,200 was marketed at 96.5. The nominal value of Brazilian flotations in London between 1839 and early 1875 was £25,067,325, of which £20,952,713 were marketed within fifteen years.

In 1870, more than a decade after adjusting its old debt of 1824, the Province of Buenos Aires sold an issue of £1,034,700, interest rate 6 per cent, in the London market at 88. Another block of £2,040,800, also bearing interest at 6 per cent, was bought by British investors at 89.5 in 1873.

This completes the story of the loans floated in England by the various defaulting states after they had adjusted their old loans of the early 1820's. In addition to these, five Latin-American republics, two or three Latin-American provinces, and one or two Latin-American municipalities marketed loans in London for the first time during the 1860's and 1870's.

The Argentine province of Entre Ríos sold an issue of £226,800, bearing interest at 7 per cent, at 90 to English investors in 1872 and the Argentine province of Santa Fé marketed an issue of £300,000, with 7 per cent coupons, in London in 1874 at 92. Information on a São Paulo loan of £400,000 sold in London in 1865 is scanty. It is not known whether the bonds were issued by the Province of São Paulo or the Municipality of São Paulo. The Municipality of Montevideo floated an issue of £1,000,000 in 6 per cents in London in 1864 at 60 per cent of par.

Early Imprudence and Vexation, 1822–1880

The national government of Argentina marketed its first bonds in London in 1866, a 6 per cent loan of only £550,000, which English investors purchased at 75. Two years later, at the most critical period of the Paraguayan War, a larger issue, £1,950,000, also 6 per cents, was sold to English investors at 72.5. And three additional loans were marketed in London during the early 1870's, all with 6 per cent coupons: £6,122,400 at 88.5 in 1871; £1,225,000 at 76 in 1872; and £357,863 at 80 in 1874. The total was £10,205,263 within a decade.

Bolivia sold its first government bonds in London in 1872, an issue of £1,700,000 in 6 per cent securities which Englishmen bought at 68 and soon regreted their imprudence. The proceeds of the bonds, until they were embargoed in an English bank, were used in a vain effort to build a jungle railway, the Madeira-Mamoré. The Bolivian government ceased to service the bonds in 1875. After a lawsuit, the British investors finally recovered approximately £765,000, about 45 per cent of the face value of the bonds, in the early 1880's, thus suffering a loss of some 23 per cent on their investment.

Paraguay, although just laid waste by a terrible war, was able to float its first issue in England in 1871, an issue of £1,000,000, with 8 per cent coupons, taken by the public at 80. A flotation of £2,000,000, likewise 8 per cents, was attempted in 1872, the securities being offered to the public at 85, but only £562,200 found purchasers. The Paraguayan government began a decade of default in 1874.

The national government of Uruguay sold its first bonds in London in 1872, an issue of £3,500,000, with interest at 6 per cent, which English investors bought at 72. Uruguay defaulted in 1875, but paid the interest arrears in 1878 with an issue of £371,520, bearing 1.25 per cent interest. At the same time, however, the coupons on the securities of 1872 were scaled down to 2.5 per cent for five years.

The government of the Dominican Republic sold an issue of £757,700, bearing 6 per cent interest, in England in 1869, offering the bonds to the public through its agent at 70. A long period of default began in 1872.

Of the total outstanding British investment in Latin-American government bonds at the end of 1880 — some £123 million calculated at par — more than £71 million were in default! (See Table 4.) Venezuela's sterling bonds had been in default most of the time since 1867, but an adjustment had been effected in 1880. And British bondholders

General Survey

Table 4. Latin-American Loans in Default, End of 1880

Defaulting Country	Amount of Default	Date Default Began
Bolivia	£1,654,000	1875
Costa Rica	3,304,000	1874
Dominican Republic	714,300	1872
Ecuador	1,824,000	1868
Colombia	2,100,000	1879
Guatemala	544,200	1876
Honduras	3,222,000	1872
Mexico	23,540,800	1866
Peru	32,688,320	1876
Paraguay	1,505,400	1874
Total	£71,097,020	

would soon force a settlement with Bolivia, as already noted. On the whole, Latin-American government securities had been a decidedly poor investment for nearly sixty years. British bankers and not a few Latin-American governments alike had been scandalously dishonest. English bankers, brokers, and exporters and grafting Latin-American bureaucrats had profited at the expense of British investors.

Capital Ventured in Economic Enterprises

The first British investments in economic enterprises in Latin America had proved unprofitable, as already suggested. Of the some forty-six stock companies organized in the early 1820's to engage in mining, agriculture, pearl-fishing, transportation, and other activities only three or four rewarded their owners. Most of them collapsed before 1840 and nearly all had ceased to exist by 1850. Only three of the eighteen British mining companies operating in Latin America at the end of 1880 had been organized before the middle of the century: United Mexican, St. John del Rey, and Copiapó. Of the other fifteen, no more than six had been organized in the 1860's; nine began operation in the 1870's. The majority of these eighteen mining enterprises, especially those active in Brazil and Chile, were beginning to pay dividends before 1880.

Most of the railway capital brought good returns at the outset. Nearly all of the railway companies had the benefit of government subsidies or guaranties of interest, or both, and were also exempted from certain taxes in many cases. The Latin-American governments

Early Imprudence and Vexation, 1822–1880

usually guaranteed a return of 7 per cent on a stipulated portion of the investment. Capital invested in public utilities likewise brought good returns as a rule. Gas plants and waterworks were sometimes guaranteed a yield of 7 per cent on a large part of their capital, and tramways were also likely to be profitable.

The railway era dawned in the independent countries of Latin America in 1849, with the beginning of the Panama and the Copiapó railroads, but most of the thirty-four companies in which British investors were interested at the end of 1880 had been organized during the preceding decade. Only four of the British-controlled companies — Arica and Tacna, Bahía and San Francisco, Recife and San Francisco, and San Paulo — were set up in the 1850's, and only six — Buenos Ayres Great Southern, Central Argentine, Northern of Buenos Ayres, East Argentine, Lima, and Mexican — originated in the 1860's. British capitalists owned a controlling interest in at least twenty-seven of the thirty-four railroad enterprises in which they had investments in 1880.

Their investment in Latin-American municipal public utilities began in 1858 with the organization of a company to operate a gas plant in Copiapó, Chile. British capital controlled at least ten gas companies at the close of the year 1880, of which six had been established in the 1860's and three during the following decade. (See Appendix A.)

The first British-owned tramway in Latin America started operation in Recife, Brazil, in 1868, and two others were inaugurated during the next decade, both in Buenos Aires. Only four sanitation enterprises were established by British capital in Latin America by the end of 1880, the Valparaiso Drainage Company in that year, the Recife Drainage Company in 1868, the Rio de Janeiro City Improvements Company in 1862, and the Montevideo Waterworks Company in 1879.

The era of the submarine telegraph dawned in Latin America in 1869 with the organization of the West India and Panama Telegraph Company, Limited; and by 1880 British capitalists owned seven submarine telegraph enterprises in the region, all except the West India and Panama enterprise founded in the 1870's, and all except this company and the Cuban Submarine Telegraph Company operating in Brazil and the Río de la Plata countries. The most important of the group was the Brazilian Telegraph Company, Limited. The distribution of the British investment in railways, public utilities, and mining is indicated in Table 5.

Table 5. British Investments in Latin-American Railroads, Public Utilities, and Mining, End of 1880

Country	Railways		Public Utilities		Mining	
	No.	Nominal Capital	No.	Nominal Capital	No.	Nominal Capital
Argentina	6	£7,631,860	4	£1,230,950		
Brazil	11	11,026,090	9	2.917,145	5	£460,104
Chile	4	220,000	2	71,670	2	409,747
Colombia	1	569,800			5	403,573
Cuba	3	1,011,600	1	220,000		
Mexico	1	7,818,395			2	1,381,721
Nicaragua					2	206,570
Peru	4	2,547,500				
Uruguay	3	2,386,805	2	1,142,080		
Venezuela	1	625,000			2	536,590
General			6	5,488,550		
Total	34	£34,437,051	24	£11,070,395	18	£3,398,305

Table 6. British Income from Ordinary Shares in Profitable Latin-American Enterprises, 1880

Company	Nominal Capital	Yield
Amazon Steam Navigation	£606,285	6%
Anglo-Argentine Tramways	200,000	4
Bahía and San Francisco Railway	1,800,000	7
Brazilian Imperial Central Railway	737,500	7
Brazilian Submarine Telegraph	1,300,000	7
Buenos Ayres Gas	270,000	5
Buenos Ayres Great Southern Railway	1,600,000	10
Carrizal Railway (Chile)	20,000	17
Central Argentine Land	106,559	5
Central Argentine Railway	1,850,700	5
Central Uruguay Railway	945,620	6
City of Buenos Ayres Tramways	350,000	7.5
Conde d'Eu Railway	675,000	7
Copiapó Mining	169,747	8
Cuba Submarine Telegraph	160,000	5
English Bank of Rio de Janeiro	500,000	10
Liebig's Extract of Meat	480,000	10
London and River Plate Bank	600,000	10
London Bank of South America and Mexico	250,000	6
Montevideo Gas	541,920	6
Nictheroy Gas	88,920	4.5
Pará Gas	166,870	5.5
Rio de Janeiro City Improvements	1,000,000	6
Rio de Janeiro Gas	750,000	10
St. John del Rey Mining	253,000	25
San Paulo Gas	80,000	10
San Paulo Railway	2,000,000	10
Santa Bárbara Gold Mining	20,000	10

Early Imprudence and Vexation, 1822–1880

Residents of the British Isles seem to have owned only five real-estate enterprises of any importance in Latin America in 1880: three in Argentina, one in Uruguay, and one, of doubtful value, in Ecuador. Nearly half of the total investment of £493,579 was in Argentina — in the Central Argentine Land Company, Limited, and in two *estancia* (ranch) companies.

British commercial banking operations, which (with the exception of Argentina, where English residents had founded an unsuccessful bank in the 1820's) began in Latin America in the 1860's, centered in Argentina, Brazil, Peru, and Mexico. The most important British shipping enterprises operating in the region were the Pacific Steam Navigation Company, Limited, founded in 1840, and the Amazon Steam Navigation Company, Limited, established in 1853 and reorganized in 1872. Liebig's Extract of Meat Company, Limited, organized in 1865 and operating at Fray Bentos, Uruguay, was probably the first successful manufacturing plant inaugurated by Englishmen in South America. It is not surprising that they had a large investment in Peruvian guano, £825,000 in one enterprise. Their objective was a monopoly of this much-esteemed fertilizer.

Although less than half as large as the British investment in Latin-American government securities, this direct investment yielded a larger aggregate income in 1880 than the investment in government bonds, since only £52 million of the government securities were serviced that year and some of these yielded less than 4.5 per cent. A sample of the highest returns from British economic enterprises is exhibited in Table 6.

Several of these companies had outstanding debentures which yielded 5 or 6 per cent, some had preferred shares that paid from 6 to 10 per cent, and in a number of instances a part of the capital consisted of capitalized reserves. Only a few of the ninety-six enterprises in which British funds were invested failed to pay ordinary dividends in 1880 and almost none failed to service any outstanding bonded debt. The average return from this direct investment of over £56 million, figured at par, was probably not less than 6 per cent. Income from Latin-American sterling government bonds averaged approximately 2 per cent on the face value of the securities.

⇋ III ⇌

TWO DECADES OF BRISK INVESTMENT AND AN INTERVENING DEPRESSION

The Boom of the 1880's

British investors, with the titled aristocracy in the van as company promoters and managers, sent large sums to Latin America during the decade following the year 1880. In no other period of equal length, with the exception of the ten years following 1902, did they invest a larger volume of capital in the region. English capital in government securities expanded by more than £71 million in spite of reductions in several countries, especially Costa Rica, Mexico, Peru, and Bolivia. The number of economic enterprises in which Englishmen had investments increased from 96 to at least 289 and the aggregate capital in such enterprises mounted from £56.4 million at the end of 1880 to £231.2 million at the close of 1890. The most remarkable expansion in this direct investment occurred in Argentina, Brazil, Chile, Uruguay, and Mexico. Nominal capital in both government securities and economic organizations added up to nearly £426 million at the end of the decade; and this total does not include insurance companies, trading firms, transoceanic steamship lines, several mining companies, most of them small, listed in the *Mining Manual* for 1891 but not in the *Stock Exchange Year-Book* for that year, the holdings of individual Englishmen and English partnerships, or some companies launched in 1890 but not yet in full operation. The approximate distribution of this capital (par value) is shown in Table 7.[1]

Some of the figures in Table 7 are based upon estimates, to which I have been compelled to resort in computing the totals for government securities of Argentina, Brazil, Cuba, and Mexico, and for economic enterprises in Chile, the Dominican Republic, Mexico, and Venezuela. The statistics for Mexico are more tentative than for the other coun-

Brisk Investment and a Depression

Table 7. British Investments in Latin America, End of 1890

Country	Total Nominal Investment	Government Securities	Economic Enterprises No.	Economic Enterprises Nominal Capital
Argentina	£156,978,788	£72,000,000	62	£84,978,788
Bolivia	503,003	.....	3	503,003
Brazil	68,669,619	37,009,593	47	31,660,026
Chile	24,348,647	9,535,852	36	14,812,795
Colombia	5,399,383	1,913,500	23	3,485,883
Costa Rica	5,140,840	2,000,000	4	3,140,840
Cuba	26,808,000	24,412,000	7	2,396,000
Dominican Republic	1,418,300	714,300	2	704,000
Ecuador	2,189,480	1,824,000	2	365,480
El Salvador	294,000	294,000	..	.....
Guatemala	922,700	922,700	..	.....
Honduras	3,888,250	3,222,000	5	666,250
Mexico	59,883,577	20,650,000	39	39,233,577
Nicaragua	411,183	285,000	3	126,183
Paraguay	1,913,424	828,300	3	1,085,124
Peru	19,101,315	.....	7	19,101,315
Uruguay	27,713,280	16,159,395	15	11,553,885
Venezuela	9,846,219	2,668,850	15	7,177,369
General	10,297,702	.....	16	10,297,702
Total	£425,727,710	£194,439,490	289	£231,288,220

Nominal Capital in Various Economic Enterprises *

93 railways	£146,902,563
42 public utilities	19,979,145
69 mining enterprises	12,581,341
20 nitrate	5,391,000
22 real estate	7,866,209
7 commercial banks	3,625,000
7 shipping and port facilities	5,258,332
13 manufacturing	3,626,340

* This list is incomplete; for more complete enumerations, see Tables 8, 9, 10, and 12.

tries mainly because of uncertainties with respect not only to government securities but to railroads, mining, and real estate as well. Doubt regarding the total for Mexican government securities does not apply to the Maximilian bonds repudiated by subsequent Mexican governments. These are omitted; but allowance is made for British holdings of Mexican domestic issues of silver-peso bonds and the precise value of these holdings is unknown. Similarly, more than the normal uncertainty exists regarding the exact amount of British holdings of Argentine government-guaranteed mortgage-bank cédulas, which were issued in both gold and paper currency; but it is likely that Englishmen held

General Survey

the equivalent of around £21 million in these cédulas as well as nearly £51.5 million in national, provincial, and municipal bonds. The securities listed for Cuba are a refunding issue of 1886, and it is not definitely known whether British investors had all of the outstanding portion of the bonds in their portfolios in 1890. Without entering into further detail it should be observed that neither Bolivia nor Peru is credited with any outstanding sterling issues. Neither, in fact, had redeemed its bonds. English bondholders, as previously noted, had impounded the proceeds of the old Bolivian issue of 1872 and recovered a part of their investment, and Peru had canceled its sterling debt by surrendering most of its railways to British bondholders or their agents.

The default situation had taken a decided turn for the better during the decade. In contrast with the year 1880 when ten of the Latin-American governments were in default to the extent of over £71 million, there were only four defaulters in 1890: Colombia, £1,913,500; the Dominican Republic, £714,300; Ecuador, £1,824,000; and Honduras, £3,222,000. The total sum involved was £7,673,800, less than 4 per cent of the aggregate British investment in the government securities of the region.

The 1880's were a period of great enthusiasm for railway investment in Latin America, especially in Argentina, Brazil, Chile, Venezuela, and Mexico. British railway investments at the end of 1890 — actually larger than the nearly £147 million shown in Table 7 because the Peruvian Corporation's investment in railroads could not be accurately separated from its investment in other enterprises — were scattered through thirteen countries, as revealed in Table 8.

The figures given for Chile, Mexico, Peru, and the Dominican Republic must be accepted with reservations. In both Chile and Mexico, British capitalists had investments in the shares and bonds of some lines which they did not control, so that the exact amount of their holdings in these railroad enterprises is difficult to ascertain; in the Dominican Republic the Samaná and Santiago Railway was built in the early 1880's, and the par value of its total paid-in capital may not have reached £600,000 by 1890. Including the approximate railroad capital of the Peruvian Corporation, the aggregate British investment in Latin-American railways at this time, figured at face value, was probably in the neighborhood of £164 million in one hundred different

Brisk Investment and a Depression

Table 8. British Investments in Latin-American Railways, End of 1890

Country	No. of Enterprises	Nominal Capital
Argentina	22	£64,617,926
Brazil	25	26,037,900
Chile	9	8,000,000(?)
Colombia	5	1,792,800
Costa Rica	1	2,869,560
Cuba	5	1,846,600
Dominican Republic	1	600,000(?)
Honduras	1	16,250
Mexico	7	28,955,290(?)
Paraguay	1	882,930
Peru	9	18,112,180(?)
Uruguay	7	9,013,758
Venezuela	7	4,157,369

Table 9. British Investments in Latin-American Public Utilities, End of 1890

Country	No. of Enterprises	Nominal Capital
Argentina	13	£9,534,655
Brazil	12	3,256,540
Chile	3	696,670
Costa Rica	1	110,000
Cuba	1	220,000
Nicaragua	1	35,703
Uruguay	4	1,640,000
General	6	4,345,577

organizations (instead of ninety-three as shown in Table 7 and contrasted with thirty-four enterprises in 1880). Moreover, Englishmen held government bonds secured by several other railroads in the region, although they did not control twenty-two of the companies in which their money was invested.

British capital in Latin-American public utilities — mainly submarine cable, gas plants, waterworks, telephones, and tramways — was operating in at least seven countries, as indicated in Table 9, but mainly in Argentina, Brazil, Chile, and Uruguay. The six enterprises listed under the "general" heading are submarine-cable companies; and their capital, if it could be accurately allocated, would, of course, raise the aggregate in some of the countries.

General Survey

The *Stock Exchange Year-Book*'s data on British mining companies are incomplete because the securities of many of these were not quoted on the London Exchange. The *Mining Manual* for 1891, which, for the most part, contains data for the previous year, lists 150 mining companies in Latin America in which British capital amounting to some £23 million was invested, but quite a few of these were of little consequence. Table 10 shows the distribution of this capital in mining ac-

Table 10. British Investments in Latin American Mining Enterprises, End of 1890

Country	No. of Enterprises	Nominal Capital
Argentina	4	£360,869
Bolivia	3	503,003
Brazil	4	836,489
Chile	4	725,125
Colombia	18	1,693,083
Costa Rica	2	161,250
Dominican Republic	1	104,000
Ecuador	1	249,350
Honduras	4	650,000
Mexico	18	4,796,080
Nicaragua	2	90,480
Peru	1	150,000
Uruguay	1	260,692
Venezuela	6	2,000,000(?)

cording to the listing of the *Year-Book*, an aggregate of 69 enterprises with British capital amounting to a nominal total of £12,581,341 invested in 14 countries. The size of the investment in Venezuelan mines is uncertain for two reasons: the Aroa copper capital was tied in with a railway, and it was impossible to ascertain the exact size of the British investment in the famous El Callao Mine, which was then controlled by Frenchmen.

The British investment in corporate real-estate enterprises was mainly in Argentina and Mexico, where residents of the British Isles owned around 20 million acres of agricultural, grazing, and timber lands and some urban properties; but British capitalists also owned, or claimed in accordance with contracts connected with the settlement of defaults on public debts, several million acres in Ecuador, Paraguay, and Peru and had investments in at least two large estates in Uruguay. Excluding the holdings of the Peruvian Corporation, the extent of

Brisk Investment and a Depression

which is uncertain, the nominal capital invested in real estate at the end of 1890 was as follows:

Argentina	11 enterprises	£2,852,464
Mexico	7 enterprises	perhaps £4,600,000
Uruguay	2 rural estates	£159,435
Ecuador	1 enterprise	probably £116,130
Paraguay	1 organization	£138,180

These twenty-two investments with a nominal capital of nearly £8 million do not include the holdings of small firms which traded no securities in the London Stock Market or of individual Englishmen residing in the various countries or elsewhere (both excluded from this investigation). Nor do they take into consideration the thousands of acres held by some of the railways, or the holdings of commercial banks and mortgage, loan, trust, and development companies, many of which had investments in urban and rural lands. Omitting two companies organized in 1890 but not yet fully established, there were twenty-one of these financial enterprises with a total nominal capital of £9,721,395. As noted in Table 7, £3,625,000 were invested in seven commercial banks, whose capital, if it could be precisely distributed by countries, would increase the totals for Mexico, Chile, Peru, Uruguay, Argentina, and Brazil, especially the last two. There were also two general financial companies other than commercial banks with an aggregate capitalization of some £950,000. The other twelve financial organizations were distributed as follows: Mexico, seven, with a nominal capitalization of £882,207, possibly more; Argentina, four, aggregating £3,750,174; and Paraguay, £64,014 in a single enterprise.

British capital in Latin-American manufacturing plants, as pointed out in Table 7, aggregated £3,626,340 in thirteen establishments. These included a brewery in Peru; tobacco factories (all controlled by a single company) in Cuba; an establishment producing extract of meat in Uruguay; two sugar refineries, a hide and extract of meat factory, and flour mills (owned by a single organization) in Brazil; and a brewery, a sugar refinery, and four plants engaged in the processing of meat in Argentina.

Such were the magnitude and character of the British investment in Latin America a decade before the close of the nineteenth century: a nominal aggregate of nearly £426 million, slightly more than 45 per cent of the total in government securities and slightly less than 40

General Survey

per cent in railroads. A net of almost 60 per cent of this £426 million had been invested since the end of 1880, over £71 million in government securities and (including the transfer of Peruvian government bonds to railway securities) nearly £130 million in railways. This railroad investment, along with the rush of capital into mining in various countries and the production of nitrates in Chile, was the most outstanding phase of the British capital movement into Latin America during this decade. Argentina, Brazil, Chile, Uruguay, Mexico, and Cuba were conspicuous recipients of British capital. If the capital in commercial banks, submarine-telegraph enterprises, and certain other general organizations could be accurately distributed among them, the aggregate for some of the republics would be increased. The total for Argentina, for instance, would probably be in the neighborhood of £160 million.[2] The Latin-American investment of British subjects was now well established, the main categories clearly defined. The next forty years would be characterized mainly by irregular expansion in the fields already entered. Only three new fields of much significance would attract their capital: rubber and coffee plantations, electric utilities, and petroleum.

Rates of Return for the Year 1890

Returns on the British investment in Latin-American government bonds in 1890 were higher than usual, averaging not far below 5 per cent; but the year was not remarkable for yields from the investment in many of the economic enterprises. Only nine of the sixty-nine mining companies described in the *Stock Exchange Year-Book* paid dividends on their ordinary shares and only three of the twenty nitrate companies.* Among the causes for such meager returns two stand out: (1) most of the mining and nitrate organizations were new, only twenty-nine of the former and only three of the latter having been founded before 1888; and (2) deflation was on the point of setting in after a ten-year inflation. It requires considerable time to bring mines into profitable production; and although Argentina was suffering worse from the depression than were most of the other countries of the region, all of the mining areas were beginning to be affected. Only three of

---

* The only ordinary dividends paid in 1890 by the nitrate companies were as follows: Rosario, 7.5 per cent on £600,000; San Jorge, 10 per cent on £375,000; San Pablo, 2.5 on £160,000.

Brisk Investment and a Depression

the British-owned mining enterprises active in Latin America were conspicuous for the dividends they paid on ordinary shares in 1890:

Colombian Hydraulic Mining Company, Ltd.	20 per cent on £75,000
Copiapó Mining Company, Ltd.	15 per cent on £200,000
Javali Company, Ltd.	25 per cent on £10,480

The last of the three was working gold mines in Nicaragua; the second was extracting copper in Chile; the first was operating a gold mine in Colombia.

Approximately three fourths of the British-owned public utilities returned dividends on their ordinary shares in 1890, but only a few paid more than 6 per cent. Among the most prosperous were the following:

Brazilian Submarine Telegraph Company	7.5 per cent on £1,000,000
Cuba Submarine Telegraph Company	16 per cent on £160,000
Bahía Gas Company	16 per cent on £100,000
Ceará Gas Company	9 per cent on £30,000
San Paulo Gas Company	10 per cent on £161,205
Rio de Janeiro City Improvements	7 per cent on £1,000,000

None of the seven commercial banks owned by British investors failed to pay dividends. Two of them paid 10 per cent, two 5 per cent, one 15 per cent, one 9.5 per cent, and one 12.

Less than half of the British-owned land companies in Latin America paid dividends on their ordinary shares in 1890. The highest returns came from Las Cabezas Estancia Company (Argentina), 10 per cent on £80,000; Pranges Estancia Company (Uruguay), 6 per cent on £116,000; and Uruguay Land and Development Company, 12 per cent on £13,335. None of the seven British land companies in Mexico paid dividends on its ordinary securities. They were all recently organized and highly speculative.

Five of the thirteen investments in manufacturing enterprises yielded no returns on ordinary shares in 1890. The highest dividends were paid by Biechert's Brewery Company (Argentina), 11.5 per cent on £200,000; Liebig's Extract of Meat Company (Uruguay), 17.5 per cent on £480,000; River Plate Fresh Meat Company, 10 per cent on £200,000; and Backus and Johnston's Brewery Company (Peru), 8.5 per cent on £100,100.

General Survey

Only one of the seven investments in shipping and port facilities failed to make a return on its ordinary shares in 1890, but yields were low. The best dividend was paid by the Amazon Steam Navigation Company, 7 per cent on £505,237. The other major enterprise under this category, Pacific Steam Navigation Company, returned only 3.6 per cent on £1,477,125.

So far, the "results," as the *South American Journal* was accustomed to say, were not particularly gratifying. But, by and large, the returns were good on the big railway investment, if one excepts the Peruvian Corporation's holdings. More than three fourths of the railway organizations in which Englishmen had investments in the form of ordinary shares returned dividends in 1890, and thanks mainly to government guaranties, apparently none failed to service its preferred shares or debentures, which paid interest at nominal rates ranging from 4.5 to 10 per cent. Table 11 contains a list of the British railroad companies paying the highest dividends on their ordinary shares.

Returns on investments in government securities and railways in 1890 counterbalanced the low average yields in mining, the nitrate business, shipping, and real estate. Total British income from the some £426 million they had invested in Latin America was around £19 million, an average nominal rate of approximately 4.5 per cent. But this was probably poor consolation for those who had ventured their capital in mining or real-estate speculation or in any other unsuccessful activity. Not a few investors could starve to death on good average yields! Unless most of those who had their money in ordinary shares also held preference shares and debentures in the same or other companies, as many residents of the British Isles went without returns

Table 11. British Income from Certain Railway Ordinary Shares, 1890

Company	Nominal Capital	Dividend
Buenos Ayres and Rosario	£2,252,000	7%
Buenos Ayres Great Southern	5,000,000	10
Central Uruguay of Montevideo	1,360,000	7.5
La Guaira and Caracas	350,000	7
Minas and Rio	1,000,000	7
Nitrate Railways	1,380,000	20
North-West Argentine	200,000	7
Rio Claro–San Paulo	600,000	7.25
San Paulo	2,000,000	14
Venezuela Central	125,000	7

Brisk Investment and a Depression

from their Latin-American investments in the year 1890 as were enriched by them.

The Lull of the 1890's and the Rapid Investment of 1902–1913

British investments in Latin America decidedly moderated their pace during the ten or twelve years following 1890. Expansion during the 1890's amounted to hardly more than a nominal £114 million. The par value of the capital, which had stood at some £426 million in 1890, was slightly less than £540 million at the end of 1900 (excluding transoceanic steamship lines, some trading firms, a few other enterprises whose capital has not been ascertained, and a number of small mining organizations). Nearly £312 million of the total for 1900 were invested in economic enterprises and a little more than £228 million in government and government-guaranteed securities, the major part of the latter being securities issued by Argentina, Brazil, Chile, Uruguay, and Mexico. The major investments in economic enterprises were distributed as follows (capital in millions):

£200.3 in 90 railways	£9.2 in 25 nitrate companies
30.3 in 50 public utilities	5.0 in 17 manufacturing firms
10.8 in 30 real-estate firms	3.5 in 7 commercial banks
10.4 in 59 mining companies	8.2 in 9 other financial firms

Other investments brought the total number of economic enterprises up to about 303. Omitting several general organizations which cannot be assigned to any particular country, the distribution of these enterprises among the nations which accounted for most of them was as follows: Argentina, 67; Brazil, 48; Chile and Mexico, 45 each; Colombia, 22; Uruguay, 14; Venezuela, 9; Peru and Cuba, 8 each. Argentina had more than 40 per cent of the aggregate investment in such enterprises and almost 40 per cent of the total investment in both economic activities and government securities. Brazil's share of the total capital was a bit less than 17 per cent and Mexico's hardly 12 per cent. Nearly half of the railway capital was in Argentina; most of the rest was invested in Brazil, Mexico, Peru, Uruguay, and Chile (in descending order).

English capital moved rapidly into Latin America during the opening years of the new century, however. The nominal £540 million of late 1900 increased to nearly a billion by the last days of 1913. The in-

General Survey

vestment had not yet reached its peak but the number of enterprises financed by British funds probably attained its maximum in that year or shortly thereafter. A fuller analysis of the investment at the end of 1913 is reserved for the next chapter; attention will now be directed to the story of the investment in mining and the extraction of nitrate of soda.

The Investment in Mining

British investment in Latin America's mines was sluggish after the boom and collapse of the 1820's. Most of the companies organized during this early period were unsuccessful, as already noted, and comparatively few new enterprises were created for mining operations in the region during the fifty years that followed. It was not until the early 1880's that the movement of British capital into the mining areas of Latin America began to increase its speed. In fact, the acceleration was rapid, and before the end of the decade it had attained the velocity and magnitude of a second boom.[3]

The *Mining Manual*, which presents a more complete listing than the *Stock Exchange Year-Book*, reveals that Englishmen had investments in at least 150 mining enterprises in Latin America by the end of 1890 (excluding several that were in process of organization or liquidation) and that their total paid-up capital had a par value of some £23 million. Only eighteen of these companies were established before 1880, and four of these were soon reorganized. The total paid-in capital of the older companies was hardly £3.5 million in 1880, and was probably considerably less in 1879. It is likely that around £20 million of English funds flowed into the Latin-American mining regions during the 1880's, including enterprises organized and liquidated during the decade.

Of the 131 new companies founded during the period — omitting 4 reorganizations — 104 came into existence during the years 1886 to 1890, inclusive. The peak of the boom was reached in 1889, with the organization of 42 companies. The capital movement then slowed down rapidly; only 25 enterprises were completely organized during the year 1890, and nearly half of these were insignificant. The boom was over before the general economic depression of the 1890's reached its climax.

This swift movement of English money into Latin-American mines was motivated in part by the quest for copper, a quest stimulated by

Brisk Investment and a Depression

the new electric industries; but eagerness for the precious metals seems to have been a more important factor. The Latin-American mining regions have not experienced since that time another influx of British capital of such size and velocity.

Mexico, with a total of forty-seven companies having an aggregate nominal capital of over £8.5 million at the end of 1890, was the recipient of the lion's share of British funds. Over half of these enterprises were large; seventeen of the forty-seven were capitalized at £200,000 and more. The capitalization of the United Mexican Mining Company, Limited, organized in 1862 but based upon an enterprise founded in the 1820's, was £1,008,862; La Trinidad, Limited, organized in 1884, and Venturas Silver and Gold Mines, Limited, which came into existence in 1890, had a capitalization of £500,000 each. British mining companies were scattered all over Mexico, from Sonora and Sinaloa to Chiapas.

Venezuela stood next to Mexico, with twelve British-financed mining enterprises having an aggregate nominal capitalization of only slightly less than £5.3 million. Two big companies, the largest English-financed mining enterprises existing in Latin America at this time, accounted for nearly half of Venezuela's total. These were the famous El Callao Mining Company, organized in 1870, with considerable French and other Continental investment, and the Quebrada Railway, Land, and Copper Company, Limited, established in 1883 but stemming from British enterprises dating back to a much earlier period, one of them initiated in the 1820's. The paid-up capital of the first of these large companies was no less than £1,288,000; the capital of the second was £1,213,386. Each of the other British organizations, with one exception, was capitalized at £150,000 or above. The British investment in Venezuelan mining in the 1880's might almost be described as a gold rush to Guiana. Besides the Quebrada Company, there was only one other British copper enterprise: Venezuela Copper Company, Limited, organized in 1883, with a capitalization slightly exceeding £400,000 in 1890.

Colombia, with twenty-nine British mining enterprises having an aggregate capitalization of some £2.9 million par value, was not far behind Venezuela, taking into consideration the larger number of British companies active in Colombia's mining districts. Most of these enterprises were comparatively small; only thirteen of the twenty-

General Survey

nine had a capitalization of £100,000 and above; but Englishmen had a more continuous mining record in Colombia than in most Latin-American countries. Their oldest mining organization operating in Colombia in 1890 dated back only to 1864; but four others still active were organized in the 1870's. A few of the companies were mining silver and one was mining emeralds; the rest were panning and dredging gold and platinum, mostly from the rivers and streams of Antioquia and the Chocó.

Chile, with nine British-financed companies capitalized at a total of slightly more than £1.1 million, trailed some distance behind Colombia. The main objectives of British mining enterprises in Chile, of course, were copper and nitrates. The oldest of the group of metal mines was the Copiapó Mining Company, Limited, organized in 1836 and capitalized at £200,000 in 1890. The paid-up capital of the Panucillo Copper Company, Limited, founded in 1864, was £225,000. Tocopilla, nine years old in 1890, was capitalized at £128,893; Camarones Copper Mining and Smelting Company, Limited, established in 1888, had a capital of £250,000.

The British investment in the mines of Honduras at the end of 1890 may have been larger than the British investment in the metal mines of Chile. The 1880's witnessed a gold rush in Honduras; thirteen English enterprises were operating there at the close of the decade, but it has been impossible to ascertain the amount of capital actually paid in. The authorized capital of eight companies aggregated £1,075,000, and the total paid-in capital of four others was £675,554.

Brazil followed next, with six British mining companies having a total nominal capitalization of some £770,000, most of it in two of them. One of the two, the St. John del Rey Mining Company, Limited, with a capital of over £245,000, founded in 1830, was the oldest British mining enterprise in existence in Latin America in 1890. The other, already well known in the mining world, was the Ouro Preto Gold Mines of Brazil, Limited, capitalized at £320,000 in 1890 and organized six years before as an Anglo-French undertaking. A third enterprise of significance was the Santa Bárbara Gold Mining Company, Limited, with a capital of £70,000, organized in 1868. Englishmen were in search of gold in Brazil, but no gold rush occurred there in the 1880's.

The rest of the story will contain a few surprises for those not ac-

Brisk Investment and a Depression

quainted with British mining in Latin America. Englishmen had more money in mining enterprises in Argentina in 1890 than they had in the mines of Peru and Bolivia, and more in the mines of Ecuador and Uruguay than they had in the mines of El Salvador, Nicaragua, and Costa Rica.

British investors controlled eight mining enterprises in Argentina, with an aggregate nominal capitalization of approximately £567,000, and none of them was organized earlier than 1886. They were a part of a general investment boom in Argentina that ended in a panic in 1890. Englishmen also controlled eight mining companies in Peru, only two of them established before 1886, but the aggregate capitalization — slightly above £533,000 — was smaller than in Argentina. Their Bolivian investment was about the same as their Peruvian, around £527,000 in five enterprises, the major part of it in the Royal Silver Mines of Potosí, Bolivia, Limited, capitalized at £339,500. The precious metals were the main objective of British search in all three countries. Interest in Bolivian tin was not yet manifest.

Nearly all of the English mining investment in Ecuador was in a single enterprise, Zarumá Gold Mining Company, Limited, with a nominal capital of over £337,000; organized in 1887, it was a reconstruction of a British company founded in 1881. All of the British mining capital in Uruguay — £260,692 — was in a single company, Gold Fields of Uruguay, Limited, organized in 1888. The total British investment in El Salvador was also confined to a single company founded in 1888, Divisadero Gold and Silver Mining Company, Limited, capitalized at £218,479. Nicaragua and Costa Rica had three British mining companies each, one of the three in each case being larger than the other two combined. The important English enterprise in Nicaragua in 1890 was Chontales Mines, Limited, established in 1886, a reorganization of an English company organized in 1871. Its capital in 1890 was £101,346; the total British investment in Nicaraguan mining at that date was £191,826. The major English enterprise in Costa Rica was Costa Rica Mining Company, Limited, with a capital of £102,000, established in 1887; the other two, organized in 1889, had a combined capitalization of scarcely more than half of that sum.

Only one British mining company was active in the Dominican Republic in 1890. Created in 1888, it was reorganized two years later, with a nominal capital of £93,600. Englishmen seem to have had no

General Survey

mining investment at this time in Cuba, Guatemala, Haiti, or Paraguay.

Table 12 presents a summary of the analysis attempted in the preceding pages. In general, the investment figures represent nominal capital, but in the cases of twenty-four companies they represent authorized capital because the amount of capital paid up was not available. The difference is not of great importance, excepting Honduras, already alluded to in this narrative, and even there the figure is partially adjusted by virtue of the fact that one of the thirteen Honduran companies included had no fixed capital. The authorized capital of the twenty-four companies whose paid-in capital could not be determined was £2,844,855. The paid-up capital of the other companies was £20,367,564. If the capital of the companies organized and liquidated during the period approximately equaled the difference between the authorized and the paid-in capital of the twenty-four whose authorized capital is included, then the aggregate investment given in Table 12, minus the capital of the eighteen companies in existence in 1879 — say between £3 million and £3.5 million — is not far from the total nominal British investment in Latin-American mining during the decade. Some £19 million to £20 million of English money thus poured into the mining areas of the region from the beginning of 1880 to the

Table 12. British Investments in Latin-American Mines, End of 1890

Country	No. of Companies	Total Nominal Investment
Argentina	8	£567,108
Bolivia	5	527,763
Brazil	6	770,027
Chile	9	1,131,748
Colombia	29	2,912,449
Costa Rica	3	154,375
Dominican Republic	1	93,600
Ecuador	2	337,630
El Salvador	1	218,479
Honduras	13	1,750,554
Mexico	47	8,544,870
Nicaragua	3	191,826
Peru	8	533,737
Uruguay	1	260,692
Venezuela	12	5,277,771
General	2	40,000
Total	150	£23,212,419

Brisk Investment and a Depression

end of 1890. It was a considerable sum, probably larger than the aggregate that flowed in from all other European countries and the United States combined.[4]

The full significance of this investment, for British capitalists, for Latin America, and for the world's electric industries and marts of trade — at about the time when the Populists and William Jennings Bryan in the United States, and not a few writers and politicians elsewhere, were beginning an agitation for expansion of the medium of exchange, and shortly before they were overwhelmed by their opponents and Latin-American, Klondike, and South African gold — is a subject which will not be considered here. This summary is primarily concerned with the velocity and magnitude of British investments in mining in a particular region during a boom period preceding a depression. Without doubt, mining was stimulated in Latin America and profits were made — and losses suffered. The safest and soundest investments, for this period and for some years following, were those placed in Chile, Brazil, Colombia (in spite of frequent revolutions), and Mexico. Those ventured in Argentina, Uruguay, and the Dominican Republic must have been courageous or illusory, considering the scarcity of copper and precious metals in these countries. Those ventured in disorderly Honduras, Nicaragua, and Ecuador were highly speculative and therefore hazardous. Nor were returns as certain as the movement of the planets in Peru, Bolivia, Venezuela, Costa Rica, and El Salvador. But what sane economist or historian has ever contended that mining is not a risky business, or that it is never accompanied by exaggerated optimism and a little deception and fraud?

The industrial and commercial world needed its metals in the 1880's and British promoters sent emissaries into Latin America after them. The story of their achievements and failures may be discovered in the mining journals and mining manuals and in the records of international trade and the stock exchanges.[5] In order to be complete and accurate this story must be based upon a consideration of the record of each company — its output, its capitalization, its dividends, its management, and its labor policy. The full story cannot be told here. Only investment trends and a few dividend records will be dealt with in this rapid survey of British investments in Latin America.[6]

The mining investment of Englishmen in this region actually shrank during the decade following 1890. The total number of companies

General Survey

stood at only 121 at the end of 1900, compared with 150 at the close of 1890, while the aggregate nominal investment was £12.27 million in contrast with £23.3 million. The first decade of the new century however, witnessed a rapid expansion. In fact, the British investment in Latin-American mines reached its peak by the end of 1911, with a total of 185 companies and an aggregate nominal investment of approximately £25.7 million. British mining capital was £3.5 million less than this at the end of 1913, smaller by over £3.2 million at the close of 1929, and only a little above a total of £10 million during the last days of 1945. With apologies to the reader for a plethora of detail, a rapid country-by-country inspection of the investment as of 1911 will now be offered.

Nearly half of the British capital in Latin-American mining at the close of 1911 was in Mexico — a nominal investment of almost £12 million in sixty-five enterprises. Most of the companies were small, the majority having a capital of less than £60,000 each. Among the largest organizations were the Santa Gertrudis Company, Limited, with a paid-in capital of £1,368,000; El Oro Mining and Railway Company, Limited, with £1,147,500 paid up; Esperanza, Limited, with £454,993; Palmarejo and Mexican Gold Fields, Limited, with £413,121; and Mazapil Copper Company, Limited, with £401,660. English enterprises were active in almost every mining district in the country except in the region from Chiapas southward.

The second largest British investment in Latin-American mining in 1911 was in Brazil, where the total nominal capital was more than £3,100,000 in eighteen organizations; but well over a third of the investment was in a highly speculative enterprise, the Itabira Iron Ore Company, Limited, with a nominal capitalization of £1,246,889, founded in 1911. The oldest and soundest investments were in two gold-mining companies: St. John del Rey Mining Company, Limited, with £714,21 paid in, and Ouro Preto Gold Mines, Limited, with £136,634.

Colombia followed next, with thirty-five British-financed mining enterprises having an aggregate nominal capitalization of £2,375,642 and with most of the total in nine enterprises capitalized at from £100,00 to more than £300,000 each. The investment was about equally divided between placer gold and platinum and other types of gold and silver mining, but British capitalists owned one large enterprise engaged in extracting emeralds.

Brisk Investment and a Depression

Excluding nitrates, the British mining investment in Chile aggregated nearly £2,200,000, par value, in 1911 and included eight enterprises. Most of these were mining copper; but one large organization was a subsidiary of the huge English borax trust, Borax Consolidated, Limited, and a small company was extracting sulphur.

The English mining investment in Bolivia included twelve companies, with an aggregate nominal paid-in capital of £1,613,338, but Englishmen had only minority holdings in the two largest enterprises; namely, Aramayo Francke Mines, Limited, and Corocoro United Copper Mines, Limited. With a nominal paid-in capital of £596,590 and £673,607 respectively, these big companies accounted for about three fourths of the investment in the Bolivian group.

Peru, with sixteen British-financed mining organizations having a total nominal capital of £1,348,580 paid up, followed closely after Bolivia. Aporoma Goldfields, Limited, with over £266,000 paid in, represented the largest British investment in Peruvian mining. Next in size were Peru Mines and Estates, Limited, and a subsidiary of the British borax trust, each with around £150,000 paid up. The Chimbote Coal and Harbour Syndicate, Limited, had a larger capitalization than either of these — slightly more than £180,000 — but a considerable part of this investment was not in mining.

Most of the English mining capital in Argentina was in the Famatima Development Corporation, Limited, with £734,325 paid in, but there were two other enterprises, one of them fairly large. The total nominal investment in Argentina was £935,272.

The British investment in Venezuelan mines at the end of 1911 included five enterprises with an aggregate nominal capital of slightly above £636,000, the major part of it in the Guiana region. The largest enterprise was El Callao General Gold Mining Company, Limited; another, El Dorado Rubber, Balata, and Gold Mining Company, Limited, attracts attention because of the diversity of its aspirations.

Three British companies having an aggregate nominal capitalization of £232,582 were in search of gold in Uruguay. There were apparently no English mining enterprises operating in either Paraguay or Ecuador at this time.

In Central America, Honduras was no longer a magnet attracting British funds. Only one small English company was operating there. The main centers of English mining operations were Nicaragua, with four enterprises and an aggregate nominal capital of £394,944, and Panama, with two enterprises capitalized at £626,276, mostly in the Darién Gold Mining Company, Limited; but there were also two British-financed enterprises in El Salvador.

Unless some of the nine small enterprises listed in the handbooks with no indication of where they were operating were active in Costa Rica, Ecuador, Guatemala, Haiti, the Dominican Republic, and Paraguay, no English companies were engaged in mining in these six countries at this time. Two British companies, however, were operating in Cuba.

Such, in brief, were the size, character, and distribution of these mining investments at the close of the year 1911 and at their peak. Most of the 185 active companies had been organized or reorganized since the year 1900. Mining enterprises are characterized by a high death rate in Latin America as in most other regions. Only 26 of the 185 organizations in operation in 1911 were more than ten years old; 37 of the total were founded in 1911, 29 in 1910, and 32 in 1909. A "graveyard" list in the *Mining Manual* for 1912 contained 95 companies described as dormant, in process of liquidation, or of little public

Table 13. British Investments in Latin-American Mines, End of 1911 *

Country	No. of Companies	Nominal Capital (Paid Up)
Argentina	3	£935,272
Bolivia	12	1,613,338
Brazil	18	3,123,360
Chile	8	2,185,620
Colombia	35	2,375,642
Cuba	2	323,202
El Salvador	2	120,562
Honduras	1	5,500
Mexico	65	11,688,714
Nicaragua	4	394,944
Panama	2	626,576
Peru	16	1,348,580
Uruguay	3	232,582
Venezuela	5	636,087
General	9	81,525
Total	185	£25,691,504

* No investments in Costa Rica, the Dominican Republic, Ecuador, Guatemala, Haiti, and Paraguay.

Brisk Investment and a Depression

interest. Few of them had survived for more than a decade or so. These 95 are, of course, not included in this survey; but they provoke reflection on things ephemeral and enlarge one's view of British mining operations in this part of the world. Table 13 presents a summary of the active British investment at its zenith.

Tables 14 and 15 — extending the data beyond the general limits set for this chapter — show the trend in British mining investments from the last days of 1890 to the end of 1945. The investment under this category was only some £3.4 million in eighteen companies in 1880, and probably was never much more than that sum at any previous time.

These tables indicate that British enterprises had usually been most numerous in Mexico, Brazil, Colombia, and Peru and that the largest investments, at one time or another, had been in Mexico, Venezuela, Brazil, and Colombia. The tables also emphasize the insignificance of the capital in most of the countries and the further facts that the investment had been most uniform in six of them: Chile, Colombia, Mexico, Peru, Bolivia, and Brazil, and that while the total had varied

Table 14. Number of British Mining Investments in Latin America at Selected Dates, Showing Trends *

Country	1890	1900	1911	1913	1929	1945
Argentina	8	3	3	3	..	..
Bolivia	5	3	12	10	6	5
Brazil	6	11	18	16	10	3
Chile	9	15	8	8	4	2
Colombia	29	31	35	19	16	6
Costa Rica	3	..	..	..	..	..
Cuba	..	1	2	1	..	..
Dominican Republic	1	..	..	..	..	..
Ecuador	2	..	..	1	..	..
El Salvador	1	1	2	2	..	..
Honduras	13	..	1	5	..	..
Mexico	47	39	65	50	19	7
Nicaragua	3	7	4	7	1	1
Panama	..	..	2	3	3	2
Peru	8	5	16	12	7	5
Uruguay	1	..	3	2	..	..
Venezuela	12	3	5	4	5	3
General	2	2	9	1	1	..
Total	150	121	185	144	72	34

Source: *Mining Manual*, 1891–1930, *Stock Exchange Year-Book*, 1882–1946, and *South American Journal*, 1882–1947.

* No investments in Guatemala, Haiti, and Paraguay.

General Survey

Table 15. Par Value (in Millions) of Capital Paid Up in British Mining Investments in Latin America at Selected Dates, Showing Trends *

Country	1890	1900	1911	1913	1929	1945
Argentina	£0.57	£0.20	£0.93	£1.69	..	..
Bolivia	0.53	0.41	1.61	1.61	£1.93	£1.16
Brazil	0.77	1.51	3.12	2.51	3.62	0.85
Chile	1.13	1.76	2.19	1.96	1.48	1.10
Colombia	2.91	2.05	2.38	1.76	3.43	0.49
Costa Rica	0.15	..	..	..	..	..
Cuba	..	†	0.32	†	..	..
Dominican Republic	0.09	..	..	..	..	..
Ecuador	0.34	..	..	0.10	..	..
El Salvador	0.22	0.15	0.12	0.17	..	..
Honduras	1.75	..	‡	0.26	..	..
Mexico	8.54	5.02	11.69	8.60	7.68	2.75
Nicaragua	0.19	0.45	0.39	0.63	0.03	0.03
Panama	..	..	0.63	0.12	1.86	1.64
Peru	0.53	0.46	1.35	1.18	0.81	0.66
Uruguay	0.26	..	0.23	0.18	..	..
Venezuela	5.28	0.26	0.64	0.41	1.28	1.40
General	0.04	§	0.08	§	0.35	..
Total	£23.30	£12.27	£25.68	£22.18	£22.47	£10.08

Source: *Mining Manual*, 1891–1930, *Stock Exchange Year-Book*, 1882–1946, and *South American Journal*, 1882–1947. Since the figures for capitalization in this table are rounded, the grand totals will not be exactly the same for the years 1890 and 1911 as those in Tables 12 and 13.

* No investments in Guatemala, Haiti, and Paraguay.
† The investment in Cuba was £2,287 in 1900 and £15,000 in 1913.
‡ The investment was £5,500 in Honduras in 1911.
§ The investment in Latin America in general was £2,356 in 1900 and £15,000 in 1913.

considerably from decade to decade in all the countries, the most marked oscillations had occurred in Honduras and Venezuela. The oscillations in Honduras were caused by reckless speculation and political disorders; those in Venezuela resulted mainly from domestic disorders and the foreign policies of the Cipriano Castro dictatorship. It is likely that the capital of the Panama enterprises included considerable water.

Although available data are far less complete for investments of United States citizens than for British subjects, statistics published by the United States Bureau of Foreign and Domestic Commerce reveal that American mining investments in Latin America had been much larger than British investments since the late 1920's. Citizens of the United States had $732,053,000 invested in 152 mining enterprises in Mexico, the West Indies, and South America at the end of

Brisk Investment and a Depression

1929 and $512,432,000 in a somewhat reduced number at the end of 1940. The major part of their mining capital in both years was in Chile and Mexico, but fairly large sums were in Peru, Bolivia, Central America, and Cuba, and they also had small holdings in Argentina, Brazil, Venezuela, and Ecuador. The aggregate for South America in 1929 was 31 enterprises capitalized at $480,383,000; in 1940 there were 29 enterprises operating in South America with a total capital of $329,563,000.[7]

Compared with British mining investments at any time since 1825, or with the mining properties of citizens of the United States in the region since shortly after 1900, the mining capital of Continental European nations in Latin America had been of minor significance — although French holdings were second only to British in some countries until the end of the nineteenth century. Lumped together, foreign mining operations in Latin America, from the 1820's until the 1940's at least, usually overshadowed the mining operations of native investors. Latin Americans had not shared very largely in the profits — and losses — of mining ownership and management. Businessmen from the outside had organized companies which had gone into the region and taken out such metals and minerals as the external world desired, paying whatever wages they had to pay in order to attract labor and whatever taxes and other levies the Latin-American governments exacted from them.

The Story of the Investment in Chilean Nitrates

Such were the oscillations of British investments in the mines of Latin America: around £3.5 million in 1880, some £23.3 million in 1890, less than £12.3 million in 1900, nearly £25.7 million at their peak in 1911, almost £22.5 million in 1929, and only a little over £10 million in 1945. The history of English activities in the extraction of nitrates was different in at least two respects: operations were confined mainly to one country, Chile, and the flow of capital was somewhat more constant. As in the case of mining, the story will be extended beyond the chronological limits set for this chapter and deal briefly with the period following 1913.

Large-scale British investment in the nitrate region of South America's Pacific coast began in the early 1880's shortly before the termination of the "War of the Pacific" (1879–1883). Between 1882 and 1896

General Survey

more than thirty joint-stock companies were founded in England for the purpose of engaging in the nitrate business.[8] Their aggregate paid-in capital had a par value of nearly £12.5 million. Most of the British companies destined to dominate the Chilean nitrate industry for more than a quarter of a century were established during this period. The total number in operation, including some nitrate service companies, was twenty-three at the end of 1890 and twenty-five at the end of 1896. At the peak of the trade in nitrate of soda some twenty years later, before synthetic nitrates became a factor in world markets, not more than thirty-six British-controlled joint-stock enterprises were engaged in the industry. At the end of 1900 there were twenty-nine British companies; in 1913 the number was thirty-five or thirty-six; at the close of 1918, thirty-three; and at the end of 1930, as the Guggenheims were starting their plunge into the Chilean nitrate industry, the total was only nineteen. In later years, the production and distribution of Chilean nitrates and iodine were dominated by five huge organizations financed by a complex combination of British, United States, and Chilean capital.[9]

The chief promoters of the joint-stock phase * of British investment in the Chilean nitrate industry were John Thomas North — known as "Colonel" North and the "Nitrate King" — and his intimate associates, especially Robert Harvey, for a time general inspector of nitrates for both the government of Peru and the government of Chile; John Dawson, for several years the manager of the British bank in Iquique; G. M. Inglis, apparently connected with an English trading firm (Inglis and Company) in the nitrate region; and the members of the large Lockett family.† Indeed, it would hardly be an exaggeration to assert that North was mainly responsible for founding all of the British joint-stock companies organized over a period of fourteen years for the purpose of engaging in the production, transportation, and sale of

---

* British firms domiciled in Chile or Peru had been engaged in the nitrate industry for several years before any joint-stock companies were floated (see Miguel Cruchaga, *Salitre y Guano* (Madrid, 1939), *passim*), and they had participated earlier in the closely-allied guano business.

† North's associates can be identified by a careful scrutiny of the boards of directors of the nitrate companies listed in the *Stock Exchange Year-Book*, 1887–1897. North's daughter married George Alexander Lockett (*South American Journal*, Vol. 41, July 11 1896, p. 49) and one of North's two sons, who also became interested in nitrates, may have married a Lockett. Gamble North, a brother of John Thomas, was likewise prominent in the industry.

Brisk Investment and a Depression

nitrate of soda. Companies which he did not himself establish were founded by his close associates or by men who were swept into the business by the stimulation of his activities and by reports of the profits that he and his associates were harvesting.*

Born of poor parents in the village of Yorkshire, near Leeds, on January 30, 1842, North managed somehow to obtain an education in engineering. He had barely reached forty when he organized the Nitrate Railways Company, Limited (August 24, 1882), the first of his joint-stock promotions; but he had spent nearly ten years on South America's Pacific coast during a speculative, chaotic, and violent period, and his ingenuity and bold aggressiveness had enabled him to accumulate a small fortune. By close personal observation and through information obtained from Robert Harvey, John Dawson, and others he had acquired a detailed and accurate knowledge of the Chilean nitrate deposits, especially in the rich province of Tarapacá. With inside information regarding the nitrate policies to be adopted by the Chilean government after it had completed its conquests, and quick to recognize a bargain at a turbulent period when bargains were numerous, North had laid the foundations for spectacular profits, which his financial wizardry enabled him to reap without delay. Within eight years after the founding of his first joint-stock enterprise he was known as the Nitrate King, not only in Chile and the United Kingdom, but also in the United States, Egypt, and most of the countries of Western Europe. Before death ended his brief and sensational financial career on May 5, 1896, he had been connected, at one time or another, either as director or as shareholder, with more than two thirds of the English joint-stock enterprises operating in northern Chile.[10]

British enthusiasm for nitrate investments reached its peak in 1888–1889. No fewer than eighteen enterprises were founded during these two years, seven in 1888 and eleven in 1889. Increased production, fall-

---

* Examination of the directorates of the nitrate companies listed in the various issues of the *Stock Exchange Year-Book* results in the general impression that, until around 1913 at least, only five prominent groups of British capitalists were involved: the North-Harvey group; financiers connected with the London Bank of Mexico and South America (established in 1864 and reorganized in 1877); members and associates of the Gibbs family (Antony Gibbs and Company was a firm earlier active in the guano trade); members of the trading firm of Balfour, Williamson and Company; and the English branch of the Grace family (headed by Michael Grace, who was a brother of W. R. Grace and related by marriage to the Eyres). It may be noted in passing that "Colonel" North also controlled a company, the Arauco Co., Ltd. (1886), in southern Chile, engaged in operating a railway and coal mines.

Table 16. Early British Companies Operating in the Chilean Nitrate Districts

Company	Year of Organization	Nominal Capital (Thousands)	
		1890	1896
Nitrate Railways Co., Ltd.*	1882	£3,581.9	£3,381.8
Liverpool Nitrate Co., Ltd.*	1883	110.0	110.0
Colorado Nitrate Co., Ltd.*	1885	160.0	160.0
Primitiva Nitrate Co., Ltd.*	1886	200.0	...‡
London Nitrate Co., Ltd.	1887	160.0	160.0
Tarapacá Waterworks Co., Ltd.*	1888	400.0	450.0
Anglo-Chilian Nitrate and Railways Co., Ltd.	1888	625.0	1,070.8
San Pablo Nitrate Co., Ltd.†	1888	160.0	160.0
Taltal Nitrate Co., Ltd. (consolidated with Julia Nitrate Co. in 1894)	1888	80.0	
Santa Luisa Nitrate Co., Ltd. (absorbed by Lautaro Nitrate Co. in 1892)	1888	250.0	
San Jorge Nitrate Co., Ltd.†	1888	375.0	375.0
Bank of Tarapacá and London, Ltd.*	1888	500.0	500.0
Julia Nitrate Co., Ltd. (consolidated with Taltal Nitrate Co. in 1894)	1889	150.0	
Tarapacá Nitrate Co., Ltd. (had £80,000 invested in Paccha and Jazpampa Nitrate Co.; liquidated in 1891)	1889		
Lautaro Nitrate Co., Ltd.	1889	300.0	630.0
Nitrates Provision Supply Co., Ltd.†	1889	100.0	100.0
Lagunas Syndicate, Ltd.*	1889	162.8	1,100.0
San Donato Nitrate Co., Ltd.†	1889	160.0	160.0
San Sebastian Nitrate Co., Ltd.†	1889	143.8	143.8
Rosario Nitrate Co., Ltd.	1889	1,250.0	1,175.0
Santa Rita Nitrate Co., Ltd.	1889	96.3	96.3
Santa Elena Nitrate Co., Ltd.†	1889	107.9	107.9
Paccha and Jazpampa Nitrate Co., Ltd.*	1889	360.0	360.0
New Tamarugal Nitrate Co., Ltd.† (reorganization of Tamarugal Nitrate Co., Ltd., founded 1889)	1890	650.0	650.0
Consolidated Nitrate Co., Ltd.	1893		140.1
Lagunas Nitrate Co., Ltd.	1894		900.0
Nitrate Producers' Steamship Co., Ltd.†	1895		62.5
Amelia Nitrate Co., Ltd.	1896		155.0
New Julia Nitrate Co., Ltd. (reorganization of Julia-Taltal Nitrate Co., Ltd.)	1896		
Salar del Carmen Nitrate Co., Ltd.	1896		109.5
Total nominal capital (paid in)		£10,082.9	£12,437.7

* Organized by North himself.
† Founded by North and his close associates.
‡ Liquidated in 1896.

Brisk Investment and a Depression

ing prices, the Chilean revolution in 1891,[11] and the financial panic of 1893 slowed down the movement of capital. Only nine companies were established from 1890 through 1896, three of these reorganizations of earlier companies. Two old companies — Tarapacá Nitrate Company, Limited, and Primitiva Nitrate Company, Limited — were liquidated during the period and one new company survived less than two years. It was not until around 1900 that brisk investment started again.

Table 16, based upon *Stock Exchange Year-Book*, 1883–1897, presents a chronological list, with nominal paid-up capital for those in existence at the end of the years 1890 and 1896 respectively, of the early British joint-stock companies engaged directly or indirectly in the nitrate business.

On the whole, British investments in Chilean nitrate enterprises were fairly remunerative, as indicated by Table 17. The objective of the promoters and managers was handsome profits, to be obtained by manipulation of the stock market or by cartelization, with restricted production under a quota system and with controlled prices presumably made possible by monopolization of a rare product; and while they never succeeded in attaining their goal over long periods, the domination which they managed to exercise was sometimes sufficient to bring them large dividends — until the appearance of synthetic nitrates shortly after 1915 ushered in a new and depressed epoch in the industry. The most profitable years in the natural nitrate business covered two periods of equal length, 1887–1896 and 1904–1913, but returns were fairly high also during the course of World War I. The two flourishing decades mentioned produced British nitrate millionaires and raised some of them to knighthood.[12] To identify them and measure their fortunes is, however, a task which, at the moment, transcends my capacity; I aspire to nothing more than a suggestive introduction. An analysis of the dividend records of the companies founded by the Nitrate King and his coadjutors, with incidental attention, for comparison or contrast, to other enterprises, will be sufficient, it is hoped, to achieve this purpose.

Before beginning the analysis, two special sources of profits should be mentioned: overcapitalization and trading in the securities of controlled companies. To determine the profits of nitrate-company directors who bought and sold the securities of their own concerns would require access to records not available to me; but one may safely

General Survey

Table 17. Most Profitable British Nitrate Companies Operating in Chile

Company	No. of Years Calculated	Year Begun	Nominal Annual Average Return	Par Value of Ordinary Shares At Beginning of Dividend Period	Par Value of Ordinary Shares At End of Dividend Period
Aguas Blancas	21	1909	24.8%	£210,000	£375,000
Alianza [a]	31	1899	20.1	500,000	500,000
Angela	28	1902	14.6	70,000	70,000
Anglo-Chilian	23	1902	16.0	150,000	350,000
Colorado	32	1886	0.2	160,000	160,000
Lautaro	41	1889	10.5	300,000	8,000,000 [e]
Liverpool	45	1885	50.7	110,000	526,000 [f]
Loa	22	1908	17.1	450,000	1,300,000 [g]
London	38	1888	35.2 [b]	50,000	200,000 [h]
New Paccha and Jazpampa [c]	29	1901	12.8	41,000	68,700
New Tamarugal [d]	24	1906	11.5	195,000	1,000,000 [i]
Pan de Azugar	26	1904	11.3	110,000	110,000
Salar del Carmen	31	1898	17.8	109,500	220,000
San Lorenzo	17	1903	15.0	120,000	24,000
Santa Catalina	29	1901	19.5	79,000	79,000

[a] Succeeded company of same name, organized in 1895.
[b] There is uncertainty regarding the exact dividends of this company for the years 1888, 1889, 1903–1905.
[c] Succeeded Paccha and Jazpampa, organized in 1889.
[d] Reorganization of Tamarugal, established in 1889.
[e] Distributed a share bonus of £150,000 in 1923; further capital expansion to acquire additional property.
[f] Share bonus of £219,206 in 1922.
[g] Share bonus of £650,000 in 1922.
[h] Share bonus of £80,000 distributed in 1912.
[i] Share bonus of £273,000 in 1926; additional £450,000 issued in payment for properties of London Nitrate Co. These various bonuses have not been considered in calculating rates of return, which are for cash dividends only.

assume that profits were made. Shady manipulations by North in the case of the Primitiva Company were strongly suspected, for shareholders charged that he knew this enterprise was in bad condition but nevertheless puffed its prospects until he could unload his holdings on the uninitiated after having received dividends amounting to 80 per cent in two years.[13] Profits from watered stock can be illustrated by reciting some of the activities of North and Harvey, who, in almost every instance, owned the properties that formed the basis of the stock companies they floated and controlled. North is said to have bought the securities, amounting to a par of £1,850,000, of the Nitrate Railways at a discount of around 86 per cent, but the English company

Brisk Investment and a Depression

he organized to take them over was capitalized at £2,330,000 in 1882 and £3,380,000 in 1888.[14] North and Harvey paid £5,000 for the Pampa Ramírez nitrate plant and sold it to the Liverpool Nitrate Company, which they organized, controlled, and capitalized at £110,000.[15] North purchased the Laguna property for £210,000 or less, and transferred it to two companies which he promoted, and dominated for a time, with a combined capitalization of £2 million.[16]

Except for the Primitiva Company, which ceased to return dividends after paying 80 per cent on its nominal capital and went into liquidation in 1896, most of the enterprises founded by North and his close associates yielded high — sometimes enormous — dividends on their inflated securities. Dividends from the ordinary shares of the Nitrate Railways Company, £1,380,000 at par, totaled 174 per cent during the eight years beginning in 1888, an annual nominal average of nearly 22 per cent. Returns for the same period on the ordinary shares, £110,000 par, of the Liverpool Nitrate Company amounted to 306 per cent, an annual nominal average of over 38 per cent. Returns on the ordinary shares of Colorado Nitrate Company, with face value of £160,000, aggregated 72 per cent during 1886–1896. The ordinary shares of the Lagunas Syndicate, £1,100,000, yielded a nominal 100 per cent in 1895. San Jorge's capital of £375,000 returned 107.5 per cent in eight years starting with 1889. Paccha and Jazpampa did not do so well; dividends on its £360,000 averaged only 6.5 per cent annually during the five years beginning with 1890 and no payments were made in 1895 or 1896. San Pablo was a little more prosperous; the nominal return on its £160,000 from 1888 through 1895 averaged 7.5 per cent per annum, but no dividend was paid in 1896. The dividend records of some of the other producing companies of the North-Harvey group were poor.

Most of the enterprises of the outsiders were just getting under way in 1896. The records of their older companies will be examined for comparative purposes. Julia and Taltal were practically failures. San Donato paid only 5 per cent on its £160,000, par value, by the end of 1896; Santa Elena only 17.5 on its £107,875; and Anglo-Chilian nothing on its ordinary shares. Other companies did better. Santa Rita's nominal £96,300 yielded a total of 48 per cent in eight years (1889–1896). Lautaro's nominal £75,000 in ordinary shares, raised to £150,000 after the taking over of Santa Rita in 1892, received total dividends

General Survey

of 50 per cent in 1889–1896. London Nitrate Company, during a period of nine years (1888–1896), not only paid 95 per cent on a nominal £100,000 in preferred shares but also managed to return a total of 892 per cent on its nominal £50,000 in ordinary shares![17]

The nitrate services companies, excepting the Nitrate Railways, paid no more than moderate dividends. Bank of Tarapacá and London averaged less than 5 per cent annually; Tarapacá Waterworks Company yielded from 6 to 10 per cent per annum; Nitrates Provision Supply Company paid only a single dividend of 5 per cent.[18]

Some of the early British nitrate companies expired during the lean years following 1895, but most of the survivors began to enjoy another era of prosperity shortly after 1900. During the ten-year period 1904–1913 Colorado's ordinary shares yielded a nominal aggregate of 142.5 per cent, Paccha and Jazpampa's (now called New Paccha and Jazpampa) a total of 251, and Liverpool's a total of 560! New Tamarugal, however, and the two Lagunas companies, each averaged only some 5 per cent annually. The three surviving nitrate service companies organized by North and Harvey — one had ceased to exist and one had been absorbed by another British corporation — returned dividends averaging from 5 to 8 per cent annually. Among the early rival companies still in existence, Rosario paid during the ten-year period a total of 92 per cent in dividends on the par value of its ordinary shares; Santa Rita, 117.5; Lautaro, 143; Anglo-Chilian, 150; London, 210; Salar del Carmen, 287.5. Of the new British companies founded around the turn of the century, Alianza, Limited, paid during this prosperous decade a nominal aggregate of 151 per cent on its £500,000 ordinary; Angela Nitrate Company, Limited, 127.5 on its £70,000; and Santa Catalina, Limited, 195 on its £79,000. Of the thirty-five or thirty-six British joint-stock companies active in the Chilean nitrate industry in 1913, only eight, some of them heavily weighted with debentures or preferred stock, failed to pay dividends on their ordinary shares that year. Fourteen paid 10 per cent or more; five paid from 20 to 35 per cent; and the Liverpool Nitrate Company returned 150![19]

World War I hampered the nitrate business for several months, but conditions greatly improved by the end of 1915. During the next three years New Paccha and Jazpampa returned from 7.5 to 15 per cent annually on the par value of its ordinary shares, New Tamarugal an average of 15 per cent annually, Liverpool from 100 to 140 per cent

Brisk Investment and a Depression

per annum; and although the two Lagunas enterprises were not prosperous, the North-Harvey service companies yielded good dividends, Nitrate Railways paying an aggregate of 19 per cent on its ordinary shares during the three years, Tarapacá Waterworks more than 40, and Nitrate Producers' Steamship Company a total of 85. Among other British nitrate enterprises, at least eight yielded handsome profits during 1916–1918: Alianza, a nominal total of 95 per cent; Angela, an aggregate of 75 per cent on the par value of its ordinary shares; Anglo-Chīlian, 70; Lautaro, 60; Loa, 100; Salar del Carmen, 55; Santa Catalina, 70; and San Lorenzo, 75. Only five of the thirty-three British-controlled nitrate enterprises failed to return any dividends on their ordinary shares during the war years.[20]

This summary should be sufficient to indicate that some British investors drew big profits from the Chilean nitrate industry. Table 17 exhibits the dividend records of their most profitable companies. All told, however, there were twice as many British-controlled nitrate enterprises which returned either very modest dividends or almost none.

Several Chileans with funds to invest obtained considerable wealth from the nitrate business,[21] and the Chilean government secured a good part of its revenues from tariff levies on nitrate exports;[22] but Chilean workers and other laborers who joined them from Peru and Bolivia rarely earned more than a bare subsistence from their toil in the nitrate fields and the sweltering nitrate ports. Their wages were seldom more than the equivalent of two or three dollars a day, often much less, and they had to buy their food and supplies at high prices from company stores. Protests and strikes, at least in the early days of the industry, were sternly suppressed; sometimes strikers were shot down by the Chilean army.[23]

⇋ IV ⇌

AN ANALYSIS OF INVESTMENTS AT THE END OF 1913

British investments in Latin America began with a boom in the 1820's, tapered off sharply during the next twenty-five years, slowly expanded during the 1850's, increased more rapidly during the twelve years following 1860, slowed down during the depression of 1873–1879, boomed a second time during the following decade, with knights, earls, lords, and viscounts playing a conspicuous role as promoters, decidedly moderated their pace in the course of the decade beginning with 1890, and resumed their swift flow during the opening years of the new century, when large investments were made not only in mining and in the extraction of nitrate but in many other enterprises as well.

Magnitude, Character, and Distribution of the Investment

The nominal £540 million of late 1900 increased to nearly a billion by the last days of 1913. The investment had not yet attained its peak in size, but the number of enterprises financed by British funds probably reached its maximum in 1913 or shortly thereafter and the average nominal rate of return was unusually high, probably higher than it had ever been or would ever be again during the period dealt with in this volume. Nor would the relative position of British investors grow any stronger during the years ahead; rather it would become weaker because of the handicaps of two global wars and the flood of competitive dollars flowing into the region from the United States.[1]

According to the estimates of the *South American Journal*, which are too high for some of the countries, especially Mexico and Brazil, the par value of English capital invested in Latin America as of the end of 1913 was £999,236,565: government bonds, £316,404,207; economic enterprises, £682,832,358, with £457,822,726 in railways, £18,514,537 in commercial banking, £15,363,230 in transoceanic shipping,

Investments at the End of 1913

Table 18. Distribution and Rates of Return on British Investments in Latin America, 1913 *

Country	Total Nominal Investment	Average Return (By Country)
Argentina	£357,740,661	4.9%
Brazil	223,895,435	4.8
Mexico	159,024,349	3.5
Chile	63,938,237	5.9
Uruguay	46,145,393	4.6
Cuba	44,444,618	4.8
Peru	25,658,298	2.7
Guatemala	10,445,220	1.4
Venezuela	7,950,009	3.3
Costa Rica	6,660,060	4.0
Colombia	6,654,094	3.4
Honduras	3,143,200	nil
Paraguay	2,995,730	1.9
Ecuador	2,780,974	5.0
El Salvador	2,224,700	5.2
Nicaragua	1,239,100	5.0
Bolivia	419,720	4.0
Banking	18,514,537	13.4
Shipping	15,362,230	6.2
Total	£999,236,565	4.7

* This table is taken from *South American Journal*, whose editors based their estimates upon the par value of securities involving Latin America quoted on the London Stock Exchange at the end of the year. Although Englishmen did not own all the securities thus quoted, they held securities listed on other exchanges and unquoted securities presumed to make up the difference, so that the figures roughly correspond to the amount of the investment in each of the Latin-American countries, with the exception of Mexico, Guatemala, Brazil, and Cuba, for each of which the *Journal*'s estimates are too high. Note also that Panama, Haiti, and the Dominican Republic are omitted. The investments in banking and shipping are set off from the rest because the country-by-country distribution of this capital could not be accurately determined.

and £191,132,865 in miscellaneous activities. The major part of this last sum was invested in public utilities, mining, nitrate, petroleum, agricultural, pastoral, and forest lands, and mortgage and loan companies. Table 18 gives the distribution of the investment among the various countries and the average rate of return for each country as well as the average for the total capital.

Englishmen had investments in the government bonds of sixteen Latin-American nations in 1913. Their major investments in this cate-

General Survey

gory, however, were in the securities of Brazil, Argentina, Chile, Uruguay, and Mexico. Their capital in these bonds exceeded their railway investment and even their capital in all economic enterprises in seven different countries, but only by a very small margin in five of the seven. Table 19 presents a comparative view of the capital in government securities and economic activities and includes a special column for railways alone. The table reveals that more than two thirds of the nominal aggregate investment was in economic enterprises and that railways bulked large among these.[2]

The railroad investment was by far the most important British investment in Latin America at the close of 1913. It represented ap-

Table 19. British Capital in Government Bonds and Economic Enterprises in Latin America, End of 1913 *

Country	Total Nominal Investment	Government Bonds	Economic Enterprises	Railways Alone
Argentina	£357,740,661	£81,582,186	£276,158,475	£215,001,961
Brazil	223,895,435	117,363,470	106,531,965	52,348,848
Mexico	159,024,349	28,596,510	130,427,839	103,729,939
Chile	63,938,237	34,676,865	29,261,372	20,462,219
Uruguay	46,145,393	25,552,548	20,592,855	15,352,963
Cuba	44,444,618	9,687,000	34,757,618	25,842,398
Peru	25,658,298	1,742,280	23,916,018	461,058
Guatemala	10,445,220	1,445,220	9,000,000	9,000,000
Venezuela	7,950,009	4,228,720	3,721,289	2,746,000
Costa Rica	6,660,060	2,005,460	4,654,600	3,363,500
Colombia	6,654,094	3,388,874	3,265,220	3,265,220
Honduras	3,143,200	3,143,200		
Paraguay	2,995,730	752,800	2,242,930	2,242,930
Ecuador	2,780,974	183,974	2,597,000	2,597,000
El Salvador	2,224,700	816,000	1,408,700	1,408,700
Nicaragua	1,239,100	1,239,100		
Bolivia	419,720		419,720	
Banking	18,514,537		18,514,537	
Shipping	15,362,230		15,362,230	
Total	£999,236,565	£316,404,207	£682,832,358	£457,822,726

* This table, taken from *South American Journal* because it would be very difficult to compile more reliable statistics, is incomplete. Haiti, the Dominican Republic, and Panama are not included in the *Journal*'s estimates, although Englishmen certainly had some capital in the second and the third, and the figure for Bolivia is too small. Nor does the *Journal* include mining and other miscellaneous capital in Central America and Colombia. (The editors later raised the 1913 estimate for Colombia to £6,794,094.) But, as I have pointed out in the footnote to Table 18, the *Journal*'s estimates for Mexico, Brazil, Guatemala, and Cuba are too high. The investments in banking and shipping are set off from the rest because the country-by-country distribution of this capital could not be accurately determined.

Investments at the End of 1913

proximately 46 per cent of the total nominal capital and nearly 64 per cent of the nominal aggregate in economic enterprises. It included investments in some 118 railroad organizations in sixteen countries: * Argentina, 19; Brazil, 18; Mexico, probably 20; Chile, 10; Uruguay, 11; Cuba, 5; Peru, 8; Venezuela, 4; Costa Rica, 1 or 2; Colombia, 11; Ecuador, 2; Bolivia, 3; the Dominican Republic, Guatemala, El Salvador, and Paraguay, 1 each. There were also two organizations of an international character, † a railway bridge across a river forming part of the boundary between Brazil and Uruguay, and a railroad construction company. British capital was dominant in the railway systems of Argentina, Uruguay, Peru, and Colombia and occupied a strong position in Brazil, Chile, Venezuela, Mexico, Cuba, Costa Rica, Guatemala, and El Salvador; and Englishmen also controlled the only common carrier in Paraguay and Bolivia's railway outlets to the Pacific.

British capital in other economic enterprises, although far less than their capital in railroads, was also of considerable significance, much more important than indicated by a mere statement of their nominal value, which aggregated a total of £225,009,632, including £33,876,767 for banks and shipping. (But the Peruvian Corporation's investment in railways, probably some £20 million, should be subtracted from this £225 million.) Economic enterprises other than railways numbered around 500 at the end of 1913: 45 engaged in shipping or operating port facilities of one kind or another; 112 public-utility organizations; 115 mining companies; 35 or 36 engaged in the nitrate business; 23 or more extracting and distributing petroleum and its products; 77 active in farming, ranching, urban real estate, and related enterprises; 27 in commercial banking and other finance; 43 in manufacturing and trading; and 12 others of a miscellaneous type.

The investment in shipping included twenty oceanic lines engaged in Latin-American foreign trade; steamboats on Lake Titacaca and on the Amazon, the Magdalena, and the Plata river systems; and facilities for handling maritime and fluvial cargo in ten or twelve countries.[3] British capital was thus strongly entrenched in the Latin-American water-borne carrying trade.

---

* The railway investment was actually larger than Table 19 indicates; eight Peruvian organizations and one Dominican are not included in the total.

† The Antofagasta and Bolivia Railway, connecting the Chilean port of Antofagasta with the leading mining towns of Bolivia, was likewise international, but its capital is listed with the Chilean railroads.

General Survey

Public utilities financed by capital from the United Kingdom were operating in practically every country. British capitalists had investments in telephone exchanges in Argentina, Brazil, Chile, Uruguay, Colombia, Venezuela, Peru, and perhaps in Ecuador and one or two other republics. They also owned gas plants, public markets, waterworks, or sewer systems in Argentina, Brazil, Chile, Colombia, Uruguay, and Costa Rica, and British-financed electric utilities — power stations, tramways, and lighting systems — were operating in ten or more countries.* Moreover, Englishmen controlled the submarine-cable outlets of most of the region [4] as well as several wireless stations, especially in Peru.

More than half of the some 115 [5] British-financed mining enterprises were operating in Mexico and Colombia, 46 in the first and 22 in the second. Most of the other 47 were working mines in Chile, Peru, Bolivia, and Venezuela. Only 1 was active in Argentina, but 9 (evidently not included in the *South American Journal*'s calculation) were operating in the Central American states: Nicaragua, 4; Panama and El Salvador, 2 each; and Honduras, 1.

The British investment in nitrate companies requires little comment. Capitalists of the United Kingdom, as already observed, had been dominant in the Chilean nitrate fields since Chile acquired them from Peru in the early 1880's. Until after 1913 competition by others — Chileans, Germans, capitalists of the United States — was of minor significance.

Although petroleum products had been marketed in Latin America for half a century, chiefly by the Standard Oil group, exploitation of the oil resources of the region itself had scarcely begun by the end of 1913, except in Mexico and Peru. Some twelve of the twenty-three or more [6] organizations financed by British capital were operating in Mexico. Cuba and Peru had at least three each; at least two were operating in Venezuela and one or two in Ecuador; and the Royal Dutch–Shell combine was exploring, producing, or selling in most of the countries.

The boom in rubber planting accounted for twenty-two of the seventy-seven British-financed companies owning, developing, and specu-

---

* British capitalists, including Canadian, had investments in well over 50 electric enterprises; their largest properties were in Rio de Janeiro, São Paulo, Buenos Aires, and Mexico City (see Appendix B).

Investments at the End of 1913

lating in real estate. Among the other fifty-five were enterprises engaged in farming, ranching, extracting forest products, and buying and selling urban and rural lands in Argentina, Brazil, Uruguay, Paraguay, Chile, Peru, Ecuador, Costa Rica, Guatemala, Mexico, and Cuba — twenty-six of them in Argentina,* seven each in Brazil and Mexico, and three each in Uruguay, Chile, and Ecuador.

British investments in financial institutions active in Latin America in 1913 embraced nine commercial banking firms and sixteen † trust, mortgage, loan, and investment companies. The latter were concentrated mainly in Brazil and the River Plate republics; the former were operating in practically every Latin-American country.

Most of the British-financed manufacturing and trading companies were engaged primarily in manufacturing and processing,‡ but they included important mercantile houses in Argentina, Brazil, and Chile. Packing houses and meat-extract plants in Argentina, Uruguay, and Brazil were significant in the manufacturing group; but it also embraced breweries, grain mills, match factories, salt works, textile mills, and tobacco factories; large establishments turning out tanning materials, lumber, dyes, and other forest products; at least one cement plant; one enterprise making jewelry, glassware, cutlery, and silverware; and one large plant in Argentina manufacturing various metal products.

Still other investments were a loan to the Benedictine Order at Rio de Janeiro; bonds of a Mexican company formed to promote irrigation and agriculture; a large corporation owning meat-extract factories and ranches and herds in Argentina; a company engaged in pearl-fishing; and two or three big engineering firms. And more important than these were the Ecuadorian Corporation, Limited, with a variety of investments in Ecuador; the Peruvian Corporation, Limited, with capital in Bolivian and Peruvian railways, steamboats on Lake Titicaca, and lands in eastern Peru; and the Cuba Company, a New Jersey corporation owning sugar plantations and railroads in Cuba.§

* In addition, one company was operating in both Argentina and Paraguay and two were operating in both Argentina and Chile.
† I suspect that the *South American Journal* did not take account of these sixteen in its estimated total of £18,514,537 invested in banking.
‡ The list of trading companies with sales organizations in Latin America is probably far from complete; they are not easy to identify from the descriptions in the manuals.
§ Englishmen probably held a large block of its securities.

General Survey
Rates of Return, 1913

It is likely that rates of return on British capital invested in Latin America were higher in 1913 than they had been in most previous years and larger than they would be in the years ahead. The average rate on the par value of the total investment was 4.7 per cent, as indicated in Table 19. The highest rates were returned from the following countries: Chile, 5.9 per cent; El Salvador, 5.2; Ecuador and Nicaragua, 5 each; Argentina, 4.9; Brazil and Cuba, 4.8 each; Uruguay, 4.6.

Income from government bonds averaged 4.4 per cent on the face value of the securities. Only Honduras and Guatemala were in default; and although they were in default on all of their issues, the aggregate amount outstanding, according to the *South American Journal*, was slightly less than £4.6 million. The best average yields on government bonds were these: El Salvador, 6 per cent; Peru, 5.3; Nicaragua, 5; Chile and Cuba, 4.8 each; Brazil, 4.5; Argentina, 4.3. Omitting Honduras and Guatemala, the lowest yields were Paraguay and Venezuela, 3 per cent in each case, and Colombia, 3.8. Almost half of the Latin-American issues, however, were paying lower rates than the original loan contracts stipulated, many of the downward adjustments having been made since the financial troubles of the 1890's.

Income from capital in Latin-American railways was at a lower rate than income from government bonds. The average nominal return was 4.2 per cent, and would be somewhat smaller still if the railway investment of the Peruvian Corporation were taken into account. Excluding this corporation, an aggregate of over £60.6 million, around 13 per cent of the nominal total in railroads, paid no dividends in 1913, most of the investment bringing no returns being in Mexico, but small sums in eight other countries. The best nominal average yields on the railway investment were: Chile, 5.6 per cent; Ecuador, 5.1; Cuba, 4.9; Argentina, 4.8; Brazil and El Salvador, 4.7 each; and Uruguay, 4.6. The lowest average return came from the Peruvian railways, which are not included in the general average, the rate for the British-owned Peruvian lines probably averaging a little more than 2 per cent. Considerable water had been pumped into this railway capital, although the exact amount has not been determined. If it was as much as 50 per cent of the aggregate, one might still conclude

Investments at the End of 1913

that the returns from these railroads were somewhat short of excessive.* The highest nominal dividends on ordinary shares were paid by the Antofagasta and Bolivia and the San Paulo, the first paying 11 per cent on a nominal £2 million and the second 14 per cent on £2.4 million. Another railroad that yielded rather high returns in 1913 was the Samaná and Santiago in the Dominican Republic, also an enterprise not included in the *South American Journal*'s calculations, which paid 10 per cent on its ordinary stock (some £425,000), 8 per cent on its preference, and 3 per cent on its debentures. Its total nominal capi-

Table 20. Some High Yields on the Ordinary Shares of British Enterprises Operating in Argentina and Brazil, 1913

Company	Nominal Capital	Yield
River Plate Trust, Loan and Agency	£ 500,000	20%
River Plate Land and Farming	40,000	20
Mortgage Company of the River Plate	200,000	18
Forestal Land, Timber and Railways	1,540,449	15
River Plate and General Investment Trust	500,000	11
New Zealand and River Plate Land Mortgage	350,000	10
River Plate Electricity	150,000	10
Las Cabezas Estancia	160,050	9
Primitiva Gas	1,299,900	8
Rio de Janeiro Flour Mills and Granaries	608,001	20
St. John del Rey Mining	546,265	10
Ceará Gas	30,000	10
City of Santos Improvements	625,000	7.5
San Paulo Gas	275,000	6

Table 21. British Income from the Ordinary Shares of Eleven Nitrate Companies, 1913

Company	Nominal Capital	Yield
Liverpool	£ 56,800	150%
New Paccha and Jazpampa	57,250	35
Alianza	500,000	30
Anglo-Chilean	550,000	30
London	160,000	25
San Lorenzo	24,000	25
Angela	70,000	20
Rosario	600,000	20
Lautaro	550,000	19
Salar del Carmen	109,500	17.5
Aguas Blancas	210,000	15

* Many of the railway companies owned subsidiaries which may have siphoned out an undue share of the income earned by the railroads.

General Survey

tal, however, was only about £500,000, compared with £10.1 million for the Antofagasta and Bolivia and £5.4 for the San Paulo.

The highest yields for the year 1913 came from the shipping and banking capital and from enterprises listed by the *South American Journal* under the broad miscellaneous heading. The return on the nominal £18,514,537 in commercial banks averaged 13.4 per cent and none of the investment failed to yield income. Two of the banks, London and Brazilian and London and River Plate, paid 20 per cent each on the par value of their capital. British Bank of South America paid 17 per cent and Anglo–South American paid 12. The average nominal yield for the capital invested in shipping was 6.2 per cent, as indicated in Table 18.

The nominal £191,132,865 invested in the broad miscellaneous category returned an average of 5.5 per cent in spite of the fact that more than 8 per cent of the total investment (mostly capital in the Peruvian Corporation) brought no returns. Numerous enterprises in this group were conspicuous for their high yields. The highest nominal averages came from the following countries: Chile, 11.1 per cent; Uruguay, 7.6; Argentina, 6.1; Brazil, 5.7. The lowest average nominal rate of return was from Peru, where the Peruvian Corporation was mainly responsible for the small yield. The nitrate companies accounted for the high return from Chile. Uruguay's high yield may be attributed largely to dividends paid on the ordinary shares of four British enterprises: Pranges Estancia Company, 25 per cent on £120,000; Liebig's Extract of Meat Company, 22.5 per cent on £500,000; Uruguay United Estancias, 11 per cent on £65,000; and Montevideo Waterworks, 8 per cent on £850,000. The returns from Argentina and Brazil were pushed up by the dividends paid on the ordinary shares of such enterprises as those listed in Table 20. But the rates of return shown in Table 20 seem moderate when compared with the nominal yields on the ordinary shares of some of the British nitrate companies operating in Chile. The best nitrate yields for the year 1913 are listed in Table 21.

Such dividends as those revealed in Tables 20 and 21 may well have caused resentment or jealousy in the countries from which they came; but, in the case of Chilean nitrate profits, it is likely that Chileans were less exploited than the purchasers of this rare commodity in the world outside.

⇌ V ⇌

BRITISH INVESTMENTS AT THEIR PEAK, 1928

British capital in Latin America reached its maximum near the end of 1928.* Although the reduction that followed was by no means rapid until the late 1940's, a gradual contraction began in 1928–1929 with the sale of several public utilities to corporations controlled by capitalists of the United States. The global economic depression of the 1930's, followed by World War II and its distressing aftermath in the British Isles, accompanied by growing prosperity and rising nationalism in Latin America, undermined the British position and reduced British capital to relative insignificance. After more than a century of heavy reliance upon Englishmen, Latin Americans were having to look elsewhere for financial aid and support. The end of an era was at hand.[1]

Size and Character of the Investment

According to the editors of the *South American Journal*, whose figures are probably at least £80 million too high, the nominal total of English capital invested in Latin America at the end of 1928 was £1,211,038,544: government securities, £343,787,427; railroads, £490,-990,928; banks and shipping, £41,852,334; miscellaneous, £334,407,855. The miscellaneous investment was mainly in public utilities, petro-

---

* The statistical series presented by the editors of the *South American Journal* indicates that the English investment reached its peak in 1931, with a nominal total of £1,221,639,882, but I feel certain that this figure is too high and that considerable contraction had occurred since 1928. The *Journal's* editors included large blocks of securities owned by Canadians or citizens of the United States merely because they happened to be quoted at the end of the year 1931 on the London Stock Exchange, and thus exaggerated the investment to a greater extent than usual. Already the English nitrate investment had been reduced by the participation of Chilean capital and the investment of the Guggenheims; already Electric Bond and Share and International Telephone and Telegraph Corporation had decidedly pared down the British capital in telephone systems and electric utilities. The slight expansion in the petroleum investment after 1928 was not sufficient to compensate for this vast shrinkage in British nitrate and public-utility capital.

General Survey

leum and mining enterprises, nitrate companies, real estate, manufacturing plants, port works, and mortgage, loan, and trust companies. The par value of the capital in public utilities probably amounted to not less than £115 million, including submarine cables, telephones, gas plants, waterworks, and all types of electric utilities. The nominal capital invested in petroleum was around £35 million. The nominal investment in mining was in the neighborhood of £22 million and the investment in the nitrate business was almost as large. Next in size was the capital in urban real estate and agricultural and forest lands, followed closely by manufacturing and then by mortgage, loan, and trust companies and port works. Table 22, based upon the *South American Journal's* estimates, shows the distribution of the investment among the major countries and the average rates of return. The capital figures for Brazil, Cuba, and Mexico, particularly the last, are too high.

The par value of the total for these nine countries, according to the *Journal's* estimates, was £1,126,986,663. The nominal aggregate for banking and shipping companies (presumably including only oceanic lines) was £41,852,334, yielding a nominal rate of return of 6.1 per cent, an investment which could not be accurately distributed among the various republics. This leaves £42,199,547 for the other eight republics customarily included in the *Journal's* calculations, which always ignore Haiti, the Dominican Republic, and Panama. But this sum is an overestimate, even if the small British investments in Panama and the Dominican Republic are added to the nominal aggre-

Table 22. Distribution of English Capital among the Major Latin-American Countries, End of 1928

Country	Nominal Capital	Rate of Return
Argentina	£420,375,352	5.6%
Brazil	285,663,034	4.9
Chile	76,907,023	4.9
Colombia	7,548,246	4.0
Cuba	43,829,828	3.7
Mexico	199,029,980	0.8
Peru	26,162,130	3.7
Uruguay	41,098,894	5.1
Venezuela	26,372,176	3.9

Source: *South American Journal*, Vol. 115, p. 621, and Vol. 116, pp. 11, 102, 119, 153, 255, 393, and 423.

British Investments at Their Peak

gate for the other eight.* (Englishmen probably had little or no investment in Haiti.) The investment in Bolivia, approximately £3 million, was mainly in mining, manufacturing, trading, and public utilities. The investment in Paraguay, some £3.8 million, was in government bonds, livestock enterprises, and a railroad. The £4 million in Ecuador were in government bonds, railways, petroleum, public utilities, and land. Panama's £1.1 million were in two highly speculative mining ventures and the Dominican Republic's £663,550 represented the capital of a railroad. English capital in the five older republics of Central America was almost entirely in government bonds, railways, and public utilities: Costa Rica, about £5.5 million; Guatemala, between £6 million and £7 million, depending on the amount of British funds invested in the International Railways of Central America; † El Salvador, slightly less than £1.9 million; Honduras, around £2 million; and Nicaragua, nearly £700,000, including a mining company.

Most of the English investment in Latin America in 1928, as in 1913, was in government securities and railways. Englishmen held government bonds of almost every Latin-American country, but Brazil, Argentina, Chile, Uruguay, and Mexico accounted for the major part of their holdings. Capital in government securities exceeded capital in railways in Brazil, Chile, Uruguay, and El Salvador, and made up almost the entire investments in Honduras and Nicaragua. But in the region as a whole the railway capital was considerably larger than the capital invested in government bonds. Table 23 compares the two kinds of investment in nine of the countries.

Owing mainly to consolidations, the number of railway enterprises controlled by Englishmen in Latin America had decreased since 1913, but the nominal capital invested in them had expanded to the extent of over £37 million, due largely to the injection of water. The number of land companies had also been reduced, chiefly because of the complete failure and collapse of the organizations set up to engage in growing or collecting rubber; and so likewise had the number of

* The two other sources mentioned in note 1 (Ch. V), p. 229 indicate that the total aggregate investment in Bolivia, Paraguay, Ecuador, the six countries of Central America, and the Dominican Republic was somewhat less than £30 million at the end of 1928.

† *South American Journal* seems to list the entire capital of this railroad under Guatemala. A company with headquarters in Chile owns some Bolivian railways, but this capital is ascribed to Chile.

General Survey

Table 23. British Investments in Latin-American Government Bonds and Railways, End of 1928

Country	Par Value of Total Investment	Government Bonds	Railways
Argentina	£420,375,352	£ 65,482,478	£251,411,571
Brazil	285,663,034	164,964,319	49,536,427
Chile	76,907,023	29,208,583	20,497,861
Colombia	7,548,246	2,093,962	2,652,903
Cuba	43,829,828	6,189,400	29,929,666
Mexico	199,029,980	38,784,430	99,932,690
Peru	26,162,130	2,899,940	18,000,000
Uruguay	41,098,894	21,256,263	14,819,691
Venezuela	26,372,176	1,487,080	3,437,520

Source: Except for the figure for Peruvian railways, the statistics in this table are taken from the *South American Journal*, Vol. 115, p. 621, and Vol. 116, pp. 11, 102, 119, 153, 255, 393, 423. The *Journal's* estimates for Brazil and Mexico are too high, about £55 million too high in Mexico's case and £9 million in Brazil's. The £18 million listed for Peru's railroads are meant to include the Peruvian Corporation's investment in this category, but the exact amount is uncertain.

mining and nitrate enterprises. But there had been little diminution in the number of enterprises engaged in manufacturing or operating public utilities,* and petroleum companies were larger and more numerous than in 1913.

Rates of Return, 1928

Although the year 1928 was at the height of an economic boom, the average rate of return on the English investment in Latin America was slightly lower than in 1913, brought down mainly by the slump in Chilean nitrates and the scant returns from Mexico and Cuba. The nominal average rates for the two years were as follows: for the total investment, 4.7 per cent in 1913 and 4.4 per cent in 1928; government bonds, 4.4 and 4.2; railways, 4.2 and 3.9; banks and shipping, 10.1 and 6.1; miscellaneous investments, 5.5 and 5.1. The average nominal rate of return for Chile in 1913 was 5.9 per cent, but it was only 4.9 in 1928, the rate from miscellaneous capital, in which the nitrate investment bulked large, having fallen from 11.1 per cent to 3.9. The average nominal rate of return from Mexico, according to the *South American Journal*, which magnifies the decline by including a large sum of unprofitable railway capital not actually owned by Englishmen, dropped from 3.5 per cent to 0.8 per cent, Mexican government

---
* See Appendix B for a list of electric utilities.

British Investments at Their Peak

bonds paying no interest in 1928, Mexican railways returning only a nominal 0.2 per cent, and English miscellaneous investments in Mexico yielding only 2.6. The average nominal rate of return from Cuba had also declined since 1913, from 4.8 per cent to 3.7; but the average nominal rate had increased from nearly all the other countries: Argentina, from 4.9 per cent in 1913 to 5.6 per cent in 1928; Brazil, from 4.8 to 4.9; Colombia, from 3.4 to 4; Peru, from 2.7 to 3.7; Uruguay, from 4.6 to 5.1; and Venezuela, from 3.3 to 3.9. The total income received by Englishmen from their Latin-American investment in 1913 was approximately £47.7 million, compared with slightly less than £53.7 million from a considerably larger nominal investment in 1928.*

Income from the English investment in government bonds can be described as rather high in 1928. The average nominal return, as already noted, was 4.2 per cent. Only Mexico was in complete default; even Ecuador made some payments. The best average yields were from Peru, 6 per cent, and from Chile and Colombia, 5.3 per cent in each case. Brazilian bonds averaged 5 per cent, Argentina's 4.4, Uruguay's 4, Venezuela's 3, and Cuba's 4.8.

Nominal returns on the somewhat inflated railway capital were low. The average for the fifteen republics in which it was invested was only 3.9 per cent, according to the *South American Journal's* rather pessimistic estimates. Returns were fairly good in only four of the countries: 5.5 per cent in Argentina; 5.1 in Uruguay; 5.2 in Chile; and, surprisingly enough, 5.6 per cent in Colombia. In Mexico, as already noted, the English railway investment yielded almost nothing. In Cuba the nominal yield was only 3.8 per cent; in Brazil, 3.3; in Peru and Costa Rica, about 3 in each case; in Venezuela, Paraguay, El Salvador, and Guatemala, about 2.8; and almost nothing again in Ecuador and the Dominican Republic. By including quoted securities not owned by Englishmen the *Journal* depressed the averages for Mexico and Brazil. A proper adjustment in the capital involved would raise Mexico's average to around 2 per cent and Brazil's to at least 3.5.

The most profitable railroad owned by Englishmen in Latin America was the San Paulo.[2] The return on its total nominal capital of £6 million was 8.3 per cent in 1928; its £3 million in ordinary shares

---

* According to the *South American Journal's* tabulations, the highest annual income ever received by Englishmen from their investments in Latin America was paid in 1929, a total of over £55.5 million.

General Survey

yielded 12 per cent. The rate of return on the nominal capital of the Buenos Ayres Great Southern, the most profitable British-owned railroad in Argentina, was 6.2 per cent, and the par value of the capitalization of this company was nearly £69 million! Its ordinary shares, with a par value of £32 million, paid a dividend of 8 per cent in 1928. The Antofagasta and Bolivia Railway, with a nominal capitalization of more than £11.3, all listed as a Chilean investment by the *South American Journal,* yielded 6 per cent on its total capital in 1928 and paid a dividend of 7 per cent on its more than £6.4 million in ordinary shares. The Dorado Railway, perhaps the most profitable railroad ever owned by Englishmen in Colombia, returned 7.4 per cent on a nominal capital of £945,153. On nearly two thirds of this capital, £604,347 in ordinary stock, the yield was 8 per cent.

The average rate of return on English capital invested in commercial banks and shipping, with a combined par value of over £41.8 million, was 6.1 per cent, as previously stated. The banking capital was more profitable than the investment in shipping, which really should not be accredited entirely to Latin America. The Anglo–South American Bank paid a dividend of 10 per cent on a nominal £5,632,670. Bank of London and South America yielded 11 per cent on a nominal £3,540,000. British Bank of South America paid 10 per cent on £1 million. Nitrate Producers' Steamship Company paid 10 per cent on £156,300, the par value of its paid-up capital. Argentine Navigation Company, operating a line of steamers on the rivers flowing into the Río de la Plata, returned 10 per cent on a nominal £2 million. Buenos Ayres Southern Dock Company rewarded its English shareholders with an average of more than 6.5 per cent on a nominal investment of £2.2, paying 7 per cent on its £1.2 million in ordinary shares.

At least four of the British-owned mortgage, loan, and trust companies yielded handsome profits. Dividends paid on their ordinary shares in 1928 were as follows: New Zealand and River Plate Land Mortgage (no longer active in New Zealand), 8 per cent on a nominal £1 million; River Plate and General Investment, 20 per cent on a nominal £275,000; River Plate Trust, Loan and Agency, approximately 15 per cent on a nominal £1.5 million; Rio Claro Investment (in Brazil), 10 per cent on a nominal £788,750.

Rates of return on most of the public utilities owned by Englishmen in Latin America were rather low in 1928. The smaller enter-

British Investments at Their Peak

prises of an earlier day had in many instances fallen under the control of giant holding companies and capitalization was often enormously inflated. Some of the most profitable independent companies are listed in Table 24. Recent share bonuses had also inflated the capital of most of these.

The majority of the English land and ranching companies returned only moderate dividends in 1928, some none at all. A few, however, yielded rather large dividends, the most profitable being those in Argentina and Uruguay. Their capital, as a rule, was entirely in ordinary shares. Table 25 lists nine which must have pleased their owners in 1928.

The days of big profits in the Chilean natural nitrate business had almost gone by the end of 1928. The synthetic product was flooding the markets. Machinery was idle in the nitrate fields. The larger Eng-

Table 24. British Income from the Ordinary Shares of the Most Profitable Latin-American Utility Companies, 1928

Company	Nominal Capital	Dividend
Bogotá Telephone	£258,493	10%
Chili Telephone	900,000	6
La Plata Tramways	250,000	7.5
Montevideo Gas and Dry Docks	675,000	7
Montevideo Waterworks	1,300,000	8
Province of Buenos Aires Waterworks	454,400	6
Rio de Janeiro City Improvements	1,431,330	10
River Plate Electricity	450,000	11
Tarapacá Waterworks	160,000	10
United River Plate Telephone	6,080,000	8
Venezuela Telephone	136,975	8

Table 25. British Income from the Ordinary Shares of the Most Profitable Ranching Companies, 1928

Company	Nominal Capital	Dividend
Argentine Southern	£545,000	8%
Espartillar Estancia	120,000	15
Estancias and Properties	110,000	10
La Concordia	72,000	33.3
Las Cabezas	160,050	20
Río Negro	300,000	10
South American Cattle Farms	300,000	10
Tecka	200,000	10
Uruguay United Estancias	65,000	10

General Survey

lish companies were trying to save themselves by swallowing the smaller ones, and some had folded up. Only two or three paid dividends. The Angela Nitrate Company probably surprised its owners when it sent them a dividend of 25 per cent on their nominal £70,000

Not more than a fifth of the English-financed mining companies operating in Latin America in 1928 — there were more than seventy of them — made returns on their ordinary shares, but almost half of these paid high dividends. Compagnie Aramayo de Mines en Bolivie in which British capitalists had a minority investment, perhaps amounting to a par of £300,000, paid 20 per cent; Exploration Company, Limited, 12.5 on £359,255; Patiño Mines, in which Englishmen may have had as much as £1 million invested, 15 per cent; Pato Mines (Colombia), 125 per cent on £100,000;[3] St. John del Rey, 10 per cent on £546,265 in ordinary shares and the same on £100,000 in preference shares; San Francisco Mines of Mexico, 37.5 on £751,979; Santa Gertrudis (Mexico), 15 per cent on £1,553,400. The average nominal rate of return on the English mining investment in Latin America in 1928 in spite of these lush dividends, was less than 5 per cent.

Most of the English oil companies active in the region were engaged in exploration or in buying and selling leases and concessions. Only a few were producing petroleum, but most of these were enriching their owners. Lobitos, operating in Peru, returned 10 per cent on a nominal £1 million; Venezuelan Oil Concessions Holding Company paid 22.5 per cent on nearly £5.4 million; and Venezuelan Oil Concessions, Limited, 111.5 per cent on £1 million! Mexican Eagle failed to pay a dividend on its ordinary shares in 1928, but some of the profits of this prosperous enterprise were probably siphoned off by the Royal Dutch–Shell combine, and Mexican Eagle paid 8 per cent on an equivalent of £1.9 million in preference shares.*

Available records indicate that about half of the some twenty-five or thirty English manufacturing enterprises in Latin America were prosperous in 1928. Only one of the British-controlled meat-packing firms, the Smithfield and Argentine, was in financial straits. It is true that three of the other five failed to pay dividends on their ordinary shares; but these had a heavy load of high-income preference share

* Royal Dutch paid a dividend of 24 per cent on its ordinary shares in 1928 and Shell Trading and Transport paid 25 per cent. Rates of return have been calculated on the par value of paid-up capital.

British Investments at Their Peak

and debentures, so that the average nominal return on the total investment was in no instance less than 4.1 per cent and was better than 5 per cent for two of the three. Union Cold Storage, the most profitable of the Argentine group, returned a dividend of 10 per cent on a nominal £1 million in ordinary shares. Liebig's Extract of Meat Company, with headquarters in Uruguay, paid 16 per cent on £2 million, the face value of its ordinary securities. English-owned breweries and wineries did not fail to reward their stockholders. Backus and Johnston's Brewery, operating in Peru, paid 7 per cent on ordinary shares having a part value of £110,000; Biechert's Brewery, in Argentina, returned a nominal 15 per cent on £610,000; and Cinzano, Limited, a winery busy in Argentina and Chile, paid a nominal 7.5 per cent on £644,815. Still more prosperous were three other enterprises. Rio de Janeiro Flour Mills and Granaries returned 20 per cent on ordinary shares with a par value of £1,364,838. Havana Cigar and Tobacco Factories, Limited, serviced 7 per cent preferred with a face value of £270,000 and paid a dividend of 35 per cent on a nominal £250,000 in ordinary shares. Henry Clay and Bock did even better. This company, also operating in Cuba, serviced £170,000 in 8 per cent preferred, an equal sum in 6 per cent debentures, and returned a dividend of 75 per cent on ordinary shares with a par value of £160,000! *

Such were the rates of return from some of the most profitable British enterprises in Latin America in 1928. It is well to recall, however, that the 1920's were, for the most part, an unusually prosperous period, that the nominal average rate of return on the entire English investment was only a little more than 4.4 per cent in 1928, and that the annual nominal average for the eight years beginning in 1923 and ending in 1930, possibly as high as for any period of equal length in the long history of English investments in Latin America, was not much above 4.2 per cent.† And the prospect soon darkened. The annual average during the next eight years was around 2 per cent.

* Havana Cigar and Tobacco and Henry Clay and Bock were under the control of the American Tobacco Company, but Englishmen held large blocks of their securities.

† So the statistics published by the *South American Journal* indicate. Elimination of the unprofitable non-English capital included in its calculations might raise the average a few points, perhaps to 4.5 or 5 per cent. Removal of the water might push the rate up to 6 or 7 per cent, if capital losses are ignored. There were some capital losses even during the most prosperous periods, and heavy losses during the twenty years following 1930, especially in Mexico and Brazil.

⇋ VI ⇌

A DECADE OF RAPID CONTRACTION

"Our compilations show that during the ten years that have elapsed since the outbreak of the second world war . . . the amount of British capital invested in Latin America has been nearly halved." So wrote the *South American Journal* in its issue for January 21, 1950.[1]

Extent and Nature of the Shrinkage

The *Journal*'s estimate for the end of 1949 was £560,364,102. Its estimate for the close of 1939 was £1,127,904,305. The capital was thus *more than halved*. The shrinkage was gradual rather than precipitate during most of the period, but rapid considering the decade as a whole. Although slight increases were recorded by the *Journal* for the years 1943 and 1944, these seem to have been the result of more complete listing and a minor change in method. The major contractions occurred in 1941 and 1948, £172.5 million and £277.3 million respectively. Table 26 presents the statistics, country by country, together with approximate rates of return on the nominal investment.

The *South American Journal*, as usual, omitted the Dominican Republic, Haiti, and Panama. No English capital of any importance was in the last two. The only British investment of significance in the Dominican Republic was the capital in the Samaná and Santiago Railway, and this investment, a par of £663,550, was liquidated in 1949 Remarking that Nicaragua's sterling debt of "about £338,600" — in fact, only £324,490 — was not quoted on the London Exchange, the *Journal* did not include any capital for that country in its estimate for late 1949. The *Journal*'s figures for the investments in Brazil, Mexico, and Guatemala were too high for both years, in spite of the omission of Guatemala's sterling securities in 1949. It will be observed that the largest reductions in capital occurred in the countries that

A Decade of Rapid Contraction

Table 26. A Decade of Decline in British Investments in Latin America

Country	Nominal Investment		Average Annual Return	
	End of 1939	End of 1949	1939	1949
Argentina	£428,518,172	£69,428,083	2.6%	3.4%
Bolivia	4,481,469	3,070,817	7.3	20.8
Brazil	260,790,683	170,525,640	0.4	3.2
Chile	85,878,232	45,277,707	1.7	2.1
Colombia	5,797,087	5,280,917	1.3	3.9
Costa Rica	4,701,600	4,459,960	2.5	0.9
Cuba	34,403,941	24,345,029	1.1	0.7
Ecuador	4,363,609	4,363,609	3.8	4.0
El Salvador	1,105,240	1,698,690	..	1.6
Guatemala	10,738,300	9,796,829	1.9	1.2
Honduras	1,728,400	889,820	..	..
Mexico	172,573,838	140,048,494	0.3	0.9
Nicaragua	416,220	......	4.0	..
Paraguay	3,185,080	3,300,290	1.7	0.4
Peru	29,321,862	25,094,134	1.1	1.4
Uruguay	39,281,186	26,624,198	2.8	4.7
Venezuela	18,888,408	11,882,017	7.3	0.6
General				
Shipping	12,753,348	10,237,868	4.6	6.9
Commercial banks	8,977,630	4,040,000	2.2	6.0
Grand total	£1,127,904,305	£560,364,102	1.7	2.5

had long been the main recipients of British funds: Argentina, Brazil, Chile, and Mexico. Small expansions were recorded for El Salvador and Paraguay, the result of a new issue of government securities in the first and of an increase in the capital invested in lands in the second.

Although contraction occurred during the decade in nearly all types of British investments in Latin America, the major reductions took place in the capital involved in government bonds, railways, and commercial banking. According to the *South American Journal*, the nominal capital in government securities shrank from £324,149,858 in 1939 to £174,607,126 in 1949, the nominal aggregate in railways from £477,765,391 to £160,777,164, and the nominal total in commercial banks from £8,997,630 to £4,040,000. There was also considerable contraction in the *Journal*'s broad miscellaneous group, especially in municipal public utilities. The *Journal*'s nominal total for these miscellaneous investments was £304,258,078 at the end of 1939 and £210,701,944 at the close of 1949.

General Survey
Inspection of Capital Losses and Decline in Yields

Surprising as it may well seem, British income from Latin-American investments, despite this sharp reduction in the nominal principal, did not greatly diminish during the decade. The world had climbed out of the economic depression so that yields on some direct investments were better; several of the governments cleared up their defaults on foreign loans; and British capitalists sold or otherwise liquidated many of their least profitable investments. Income for 1949 was £14,291,151, excluding interest received from Nicaraguan government bonds, while it was only £19,010,329 in 1939, including interest on the Nicaraguan securities. For all but four years of the decade the total income was higher than in 1939. It was £25,902,717, for example, in 1946, the peak year for the period, and £25,208,743 in 1945. The annual average nominal rate of return slowly rose from approximately 1.7 per cent in 1939 to 2.5 in 1949, reaching its highest point, however, in 1948, with a yield of 2.9 per cent.

There was, as already suggested, a decided contraction during the decade in the segment of the investment that yielded no income. This portion of the nominal capital decreased from £698,077,803, or nearly 62 per cent of the total, in 1939 to £246,425,946, or less than 44 per cent of the aggregate, in 1949. But there were wide variations in this shrinkage among the major types of investment, as an examination of Table 27 will disclose.

A marked decrease is evident in the percentage of the capital yielding no returns in three of the categories, running from 100 per cent for both commercial banking and shipping to nearly 62 per cent for government bonds. Little change in percentage occurred in the broad

Table 27. Categories in Which British Investment in Latin America Yielded No Income, 1939 and 1949

Type of Investment	Nominal Capital		Percentage of Total Investment	
	1939	1949	1939	1949
Government bonds	£210,891,798	£5,457,460	65.0%	3.1%
Railways	336,032,299	145,791,450	70.3	90.6
Commercial banks	4,937,630	nil	55.0	nil
Shipping	1,417,054	nil	11.1	nil
Miscellaneous	144,799,022	95,177,036	47.6	45.2
Total	£698,077,803	£246,425,946	61.9	43.9

A Decade of Rapid Contraction

miscellaneous group, but the unprofitable segment expanded by 20.3 per cent in the railway investment. This expansion should be attributed, however, not so much to failure in earnings as to withholding of income pending negotiations for the sale of several railroads and arrangements for the distribution of the proceeds, and the same circumstance also accounts for a decline in income under the railway category from 1.2 per cent in 1939 to 0.3 per cent in 1949. In the four other classifications the rate of return increased: government bonds, from 1.2 to 2.1 per cent; commercial banks, from 2.2 to 6 per cent; shipping, from 4.6 to 6.9; and miscellaneous, from 2.9 to 4.3.

Changes in the size and percentage of the investment bringing no returns also varied widely among the various republics. Table 28 presents these variations and the ten-year trend in each of the countries. Although the percentage of the aggregate investment returning no income actually expanded in nine of the seventeen states listed in this table — Argentina, Bolivia, Chile, Costa Rica, Cuba, Guatemala, Paraguay, Peru, and Venezuela — this expansion was more than offset by the large contractions that occurred in the profitless segments in several of the other states, particularly Brazil, Colombia, El Salvador,

Table 28. Country-by-Country Breakdown of British Investments in Latin America Yielding No Income, 1939 and 1949

Country	Nominal Capital		Percentage of Total Investment	
	1939	1949	1939	1949
Argentina	£188,762,997	£34,453,358	44.0%	49.6%
Bolivia	720,817	720,817	16.0	23.4
Brazil	233,574,950	30,760,877	89.5	18.0
Chile	15,139,349	9,905,344	17.8	21.9
Colombia	4,065,038	953,074	70.1	18.0
Costa Rica	1,628,900	3,804,960	34.6	85.3
Cuba	27,150,361	22,495,629	78.8	83.9
Ecuador	2,236,380	2,236,380	51.2	51.2
El Salvador	1,105,240	752,100	100.0	44.2
Guatemala	6,300,000	6,288,228	58.6	64.1
Honduras	1,728,400	889,820	100.0	100.0
Mexico	162,494,546	99,962,492	94.1	71.5
Nicaragua	nil	nil	nil	nil
Paraguay	2,235,080	2,809,280	73.3	85.1
Peru	22,059,100	18,916,000	75.2	75.4
Uruguay	13,199,149	675,000	17.8	2.5
Venezuela	9,222,812	10,802,587	48.8	90.9
Total	£691,723,119	£246,425,946	62.5	45.1

General Survey

Mexico, and Uruguay, so that the percentage of the aggregate capital that yielded no returns declined by 17.4, excluding the undistributed investment in nine of the countries. The annual average rate of return in 1949 was larger than in 1939 in ten of the seventeen, including four — Argentina, Bolivia, Chile, and Peru — of the nine which showed an expansion in the portion of the investment that returned no profits. Omitting Nicaragua because its share of the capital was not quoted in London, only five of the republics paid British investors a smaller rate on their investment in 1949 than in 1939. These were Costa Rica, Cuba, Guatemala, Paraguay, and Venezuela; and in Venezuela's case the reduction was caused by loss of identity of a profitable petroleum company through sale to the Royal Dutch–Shell group (which, of course, was part English).

In the process of reducing the unprofitable segments of their capital, particularly in selling or otherwise disposing of their railway investments, British capitalists suffered heavy losses during the decade.* Owners of the ordinary shares of the railways sold to the Mexican, Argentine, and Uruguayan governments seldom recovered more than a very small fraction of the face value of their securities and sometimes got no compensation whatever. Owners of preference shares had to be satisfied with much less than par, and occasionally holders of bonds and debentures recouped less than 100 per cent. Having liquidated most of their railways, British investors now owned a comparatively larger number of profitable enterprises in Latin America. If their entire investment had been as profitable as the portion that returned income, the yield for the year 1949 would have been almost 4.5 per cent instead of 2.5. If their total Argentine investment had been as profitable as the half that yielded interest and dividends, their income from Argentina would have been at the rate of 6.8 per cent. If all of their capital in Ecuador had been as profitable as the segment that brought returns, the yield would have been above 8 per cent instead of merely 4; and if the rate of profits had been as high on the aggregate Bolivian investment as it was on approximately three fourths of it, the return would have been 27 per cent.

Samples of companies whose ordinary shares yielded large dividends for the year 1949 are listed in Table 29. Here are twenty-seven enter-

---

* Their losses depended, of course, on what they had paid for their shares. In some cases this was little or even nothing, the shares having been issued as bonuses.

A Decade of Rapid Contraction

Table 29. Dividends Paid on Certain Ordinary Shares of British Capital in Latin America, 1929

Company	Nominal Capital	Nominal Yield
Montevideo Waterworks	£1,625,000	8%
Telephone Properties (Venezuela)	410,932	7
Cambuhy Coffee and Cotton Estates (Brazil)	420,000	15
City of San Paulo Improvements and Freehold Land Company	393,238	16.6
Forestal Land, Timber and Railways (Argentina)	3,708,837	12
Las Cabezas Estancia (Argentina)	160,050	8
Tecka Land (Argentina)	200,000	11
Backus and Johnston's Brewery (Peru)	110,000	14
Ecuadorian Corporation *	1,200,000	10
Havana Cigar and Tobacco	250,000	35
Henry Clay and Bock (also Cuba)	159,990	35
Liebig's Extract of Meat	2,000,000	10
Rio de Janeiro Flour Mills and Granaries	1,364,838	8
Rio Clara Investment Trust (Brazil)	788,750	10
River Plate Electricity	356,250	8
River Plate and General Investment	275,000	12
Moorside Trust (Argentina)	300,000	10
Lobitos Oilfields (Peru)	1,000,000	17.5
Anglo-Ecuadorian Oilfields	1,500,000	7.5
Fresnillo Mining (Mexico) *	400,000	131
Frontino Gold Mines (Colombia)	190,573	10
Pampa Mining (Peru)	70,000	7.5
St. John del Rey Mining Company (Brazil)	546,265	7.5
Patiño Mines and Enterprises (Bolivia) *	2,600,000	20
Pato Consolidated Gold Dredging (Colombia) *	1,230,000	15
San Francisco Mines of Mexico	1,028,406	50
South American Gold and Platinum (Colombia) *	790,000	30

* Firms in which the English investment cannot be precisely determined; all but the Fresnillo Company were controlled by either Canadians or citizens of the United States. Their capital has been converted into sterling for convenience.

prises which paid dividends of 7 per cent and above on the par value of their ordinary shares. Among the one hundred and fifty or more economic organizations in which Englishmen had their capital invested in 1949 it would be difficult to find many others making such high returns, and British investors had only minority interests in four or five of these. Railway companies are conspicuously absent. The only railroad enterprise owned by British investors in Latin America that paid dividends of as much as 6 per cent on its ordinary shares in 1949 was the Dorado Railway Company, Limited, a short line running along the rapids of the middle Magdalena River in Colombia. As of late 1949, the date set for the end of this investigation, it appeared

General Survey

that the sooner Englishmen could rid themselves of their railroads in this region the better, and that they would probably dispose of all their holdings under this category within the next few years. But unless the railway business in Latin America should take a remarkable turn in favor of the British owners, it would not be easy to dispose of them without suffering further losses of capital. The Costa Rica Railway, the Salvador Railway, the International Railways of Central America, the lines controlled by the Peruvian Corporation, the Guayaquil and Quito Railway, the Paraguay Central, and minority holdings in the Mexican National Railways would not be easy to sell in the circumstances that prevailed at the beginning of the year 1950. The era of profitable railroading in Latin America appeared to have ended, to have given way to the era of the omnibus, the truck, and the airplane.

After selling all of their railways and a good part of their municipal public utilities, however, British investors seemed likely at mid-century to have fairly profitable holdings left in Latin America. But, as the editors of the *South American Journal* remarked in their issue for January 21, 1950, "it has . . . been getting more and more difficult to compile" statistics on this subject. The arrival of the era of the branch plant, the subsidiary, and the holding company had greatly complicated the task. Investment manuals no longer revealed sufficient data on capitalization and yields, and stocks without par value caused further confusion. The investigator would have to depend largely on official tax records and the archives of corporations. Among enterprises belonging to this new type of investment the following may be mentioned: Brazilian Traction, Light and Power, with at least nine subsidiaries, jointly owned by Englishmen, Canadians, and citizens of the United States; Sidro, a Belgian corporation controlled by capitalists of the British Isles and Continental Europe and owning part of the securities of several electric companies in Central Mexico; Sodec, a similar internationally-controlled organization incorporated in Luxembourg which owned the assets of Compañía Hispano-Americana de Electricidad in Argentina; the Royal Dutch–Shell combination with its many subsidiaries; the Ecuadorian Corporation, representing Canadian, English, and United States capital; and both Patiño Mines and the South American Gold and Platinum Company, representing these three Anglo-Saxon and probably other national groups. Purely British

A Decade of Rapid Contraction

companies with branches in one or more of the Latin-American countries (and often in many other parts of the world as well) are illustrated by the British Match Corporation, Dunlop Rubber Company, Crosse and Blackwell, Maple and Company, Mappin and Webb, Courtlands, Associated Portland Cement, Eno Proprietaries, and Imperial Chemicals, none of which, in all probability, was included in the reckoning of the *South American Journal*.

But British investments in Latin America had not been "all washed out" [2] by World War II and its aftermath; at any rate, not before 1949. Their future would depend upon tax and other policies in the British Isles, the attitudes of the several Latin-American nations, and the possibilities of world peace rather more perhaps than upon British capitalists themselves, who were still more numerous and prosperous than many in the United States suspected. Barring some major catastrophe, it seemed likely that British investments in Latin America would be maintained for an indefinite period at some point between £300 million and £400 million, if transatlantic shipping companies and agencies of British trading firms are included, and that most of their capital would be invested in manufacturing, petroleum, mining, finance, and the extraction of forest products.

PART TWO

Country-by-Country Inspection of the British Investment

⇋ VII ⇌

MEXICO: A STORY OF BONANZAS AND HEARTBREAKS

Growth and Character of the Investment

It is not likely that even the nominal total of English capital invested in Mexico at any time between 1901 and 1950 will ever be determined with a satisfactory degree of accuracy. Shortly after the turn of the century English, Canadian, and United States capitalists all began to invest in several of the leading Mexican utility companies, and within a few years the confusion was worse confounded by the injection of Continental capital and the organization of giant holding companies. Beginning with the year 1904, Mexican bond issues, whether in sterling, dollars, francs, or pesos, were sold in all the great markets of the world, and the same was true of the securities of the Mexican National Railways (Ferrocarriles Nacionales) after 1908. The following estimates of the total nominal investment are offered with some hesitation, after considerable investigation, computation, and meditation:[1]

End of 1880	£ 32.7 million
End of 1890	59.8 million
End of 1900	67.4 million
End of 1910	98.4 million
End of 1924	159.4 million
End of 1949	85.4 million

Residents of the United Kingdom began to risk their capital in Mexico in the early 1820's, as noted in Chapter II, purchasing government bonds having a par value of £7 million and organizing seven mining associations with an aggregate nominal capital (paid up) of over £2.2 million. But they soon suffered for their enthusiasm and learned a lesson which they did not forget until the era of Ferdinand Maximilian and the stable years of the Porfirio Díaz period. The par value of the English investment in Mexican government bonds was in the neighborhood of £23.5 million at the end of 1880, some £20.6 million at the close of 1890, and approximately £25 million at the end of the nineteenth century; and according to the *South American Journal*'s estimates, which are somewhat too high for the more recent years, the nominal total was £30.3 million in 1910, approximately £43.2 million at its maximum in 1924, and over £29.1 million at the end of 1949.*

Reckoned at par, the British investment in Mexico's railways, which began around 1860, amounted to some £7.8 million by the end of the year 1880 and rose to more than £30.6 million by the close of the century. The size of the investment in subsequent years is very difficult to determine, owing to uncertainty with reference to the amount of English capital involved in the Mexican National Railways, but the estimates tabulated by the *South American Journal* — £93.7 million at the end of 1910, £103.7 million at the end of 1913, more than £109.4 million at the peak in the last days of 1924, and still over £73.1 million at the end of 1949 — are certainly far too high. The par value of the investment of Englishmen in Mexican railways probably never rose much above £51.1 million, the approximate total for 1924. It may have stood near the same figure in 1913, and the nominal total was perhaps somewhat above £42.5 million in 1910; but it could hardly have amounted to more than a nominal £25 million at the end of 1949.†

Other English investments in Mexico, classified as miscellaneous by the *South American Journal*, were of minor significance compared with the capital in government securities and railways until after 1900, when they were rapidly expanded by the investment in petroleum, mining, and public utilities. The nominal capital under this miscellaneous category was less than £1.4 million in 1880 and no more than £12 million at the termination of the century, but it rose to £26.8 million by the end of 1910 and, according to the *Journal*'s exaggerated estimates, rocketed to £63.7 million by the last days of 1924 and was

* The figures for the years following 1890 include some peso and franc bonds. After 1942, sterling bonds began to be redeemed at less than a third of their face value!

† The English-controlled railroads were sold to the Mexican government in 1945–1946 for less than £3,000,000, about 12 per cent of their nominal capitalization! Thereafter the English investment in common-carrier lines was confined to Ferrocarriles Nacionales and United Railways of Yucatán.

Mexico: Bonanzas and Heartbreaks

still as high as £37.7 million at the close of 1949.* There were two periods of brisk investment in Mexican mines, as already noted, the 1880's and the first decade of the twentieth century. The par value of English capital invested in Mexican mining organizations was in excess of £8.5 million at the end of 1890 and almost £11.7 million at the end of 1911; but the mining investment had shrunk to less than £3 million by the last days of 1949.² The size of the English stake in public utilities, difficult to estimate because of the international character of the capitalization of many of the Mexican utility companies, was certainly insignificant until 1898, but it probably amounted to as much as £12 million at its peak in the 1920's and to some £3 million or £4 million at the end of 1949. The Mexican oil boom at its height may have involved a nominal capitalization, no doubt considerably inflated, of as much as £25 million.† The investment in real estate seems to have reached its maximum around 1910, with a nominal capital in excess of £5.1 million, only about £500,000 more, however, than the nominal total for 1890. Most of this investment was highly speculative, made with the hope of developing plantation rubber or profiting from rising land values. Capital invested in manufacturing never exceeded £3 million, most of it involved in a jute mill,‡ two salt factories, a packing house, and a cement plant.

Low Average Returns

On the whole and over the long period since the 1820's, the English investment in Mexico turned out to be less profitable than that in any other major Latin-American country and almost as unremunerative as British investments in Central America, Ecuador, and Paraguay. This was especially true of the capital invested in government bonds, railroads, real estate, and public utilities.

* At least £20 million should be subtracted from the *Journal*'s figure for 1924, and £30 million would amply cover the investment at the end of 1949, including the debt contracted by Mexico, by an agreement of 1947, in compensation for the expropriation of English oil properties.

† The major investment was made by Mexican Eagle Oil Company. The Mexican government agreed in 1947 to pay this company the sum of $81,250,000 (U.S. currency) for its expropriated properties, in 15 equal annual installments beginning in September 1948.

‡ The jute mill, called Santa Gertrudis, was a very private enterprise belonging to the Lord Cowdray group. It published few reports on dividends, but it seems to have been a success (see p. 102). The other manufacturing establishments paid almost no dividends on their ordinary shares.

Country-by-Country Inspection

According to the editors of the *South American Journal*, whose estimates are too low because they included too much unremunerative capital not owned by residents of the United Kingdom, the average nominal annual rate of return on the entire investment was no more than 4.1 per cent in 1910 and 3.1 per cent in 1913, and declined sharply thereafter, so that the annual average for the quarter of a century beginning with the year 1924 was less than 1 per cent. The rate of return was certainly somewhat higher for the years indicated. It is unlikely, however, that the nominal annual average ever rose far above 5 per cent even during the most prosperous years of Don Porfirio's dictatorship or that the average nominal yield was much above 2 per cent for any year following 1913 (even excluding consideration of losses of capital).

In the course of a century and a quarter after the first English investment in them, Mexican government securities were in default at least half of the time. There were two long periods — 1867 through 1885 and 1914 through 1943 — when Englishmen received no income from their Mexican bonds. The annual nominal average for the twenty-eight years starting with 1886 was approximately 4.5 per cent, but it was only a little better than 1 per cent for the six years beginning in 1944, and such income as had been received was eventually more than offset by large reductions in the principal. Income from the investment in Mexican railways seldom reached a nominal 6 per cent annually at any time. It was 3.2 in 1910, less than 3 in 1931, less than 2 per cent annually between 1914 and 1934, and nothing whatever from 1935 through 1949!

As in most of the other Latin-American republics, the average nominal rate of return from the English miscellaneous investment in Mexico was higher than from the capital invested in either government bonds or railways. The average nominal rate was 5.3 per cent in 1910 and 4.9 in 1913, and it had not often been less than 5 per cent during the fifteen years preceding 1910; but the recent revolutionary period in Mexico and the world economic depression that followed brought the rate down to a nominal annual average of slightly less than 3 per cent for the thirty-six years starting in 1914.[3]

There were a number of unprofitable investments in this miscellaneous group, including especially nearly all of the real-estate and public-utility enterprises, most of the manufacturing concerns, and

Mexico: Bonanzas and Heartbreaks

the majority of the mining companies. Now and then, however, a few Englishmen were cheered by mining bonanzas, and Weetman Dickinson Pearson and his associates were immensely enriched by the exploitation of Mexico's petroleum.

A Sample of Profitable Enterprises

Before inspecting the records of the prosperous mining and oil companies, brief notice will be given to the returns from commercial banking and other financial firms. London Bank of Mexico and South America, Limited, owned for more than two decades a controlling interest in a flourishing subsidiary in Mexico which operated under the name of Banco de Londres y México, founded in 1889. On a nominal paid-up capital averaging about £350,000 during the period, this branch returned an average annual dividend of 12.8 per cent. International and Mortgage Bank of Mexico, founded in 1888 under the control of English capital, did not do so well at the outset, returning an average annual dividend of only 4.25 per cent for the sixteen years beginning in 1890. During the following decade, however, the annual average was slightly more than 10 per cent. Its nominal paid-up capital was £350,000. Banco Nacional de México, a French-controlled firm in which Englishmen owned a minority interest, paid an average dividend of approximately 15.7 per cent annually for the three decades starting in 1883, on a nominal capital of £1,600,000 until 1905 and £3,167,510 thereafter.[4]

Not more than a tenth of the many mining enterprises organized by Englishmen for the purpose of operating in Mexico, at least a hundred all told, were notable for big dividends. Real bonanzas were very few.

Quintera Mining Company, Limited, perhaps more French than English, made a rather poor start, but paid good dividends for at least a decade. On a nominal paid-in capital of £52,000 the annual rate of return from 1898 through 1907 was almost 15 per cent.

El Oro Mining and Railway Company, Limited, organized in 1899, paid fairly high dividends only now and then. During the four decades starting with the year 1900 the average annual return on a nominal capital of £1,147,500, reduced to £286,875 in 1929, with some loss to stockholders, was approximately 8.5 per cent, and for two of the four decades it was 9.4.

Country-by-Country Inspection

Income from Mazapil Copper Company, Limited, founded in 1896, was intermittent. Unprofitable at first, Mazapil returned an annual average dividend of 10.6 per cent on its ordinary capital — a par of £281,660, raised to £422,920 in 1912 and to £600,000 in 1920 — during the decade starting in 1908 and paid a share bonus of 50 per cent besides. During the next two years the average was 15 per cent, but after a 20 per cent share bonus in 1920 dividends almost ceased until a return of 2.5 per cent was made in 1943. The next year the dividend was 7.5 per cent and for the five subsequent years the annual average was 12 per cent.*

Available records indicate that the Santa Gertrudis Company, Limited, organized in 1909 to work gold and silver mines in the famous Pachuca district, was only moderately profitable. The company paid an annual average of 7.25 per cent on a nominal paid-up capital of £1,275,000 during the twenty years beginning in 1912.

San Francisco Mines of Mexico, Limited, established in 1913 to work gold, silver, lead, copper, and zinc mines in Chihuahua, may be described as a near bonanza. With an average nominal capital of approximately £900,000 over the years, all in ordinary shares, it yielded its owners no income during its first decade of operations; but during the following decade it rewarded them with a handsome annual average of 25 per cent; and then, after ten years of modest earnings — an annual average of only 6.25 — the company paid a yearly average of 27 per cent during the next seven years, the dividend being no less than 50 per cent in 1949.

Far more profitable, although their properties were soon worked out, were two companies operating in the El Oro district of central Mexico: Esperanza, Limited, organized in 1903, and Mexico Mines of El Oro, Limited, established the next year, with large French participation. Capitalized at £455,000, all in ordinary shares and all called up, Esperanza yielded an annual nominal average of no less than 50.7 per cent during the decade beginning in 1904! The return then dropped to 5 per cent in 1914 and never recovered. Reorganized in 1923, the company was finally dissolved in the early 1930's. Its highest annual payment, 160 per cent, was made to the shareholders in 1906. Mexico Mines of El Oro, with a paid-in capital of £180,000, par value, during

---

* Mazapil also serviced and redeemed two issues of debentures, £120,000 in 6 per cents, followed by £120,000 in 7 per cents. The company was probably overcapitalized.

Mexico: Bonanzas and Heartbreaks

most of the period of its prosperity, all in ordinary shares, remitted its first dividend, 50 per cent, in 1908 and its highest dividend, 110 per cent, in 1917. For the two decades starting with 1908 its nominal annual average return was 62 per cent! No further payments were made after 1927; the company was dissolved by voluntary resolution in 1930.

English capitalists took control of the Fresnillo Company, a New York corporation organized to work silver, lead, and zinc mines in Zacatecas, in 1919. Its capital, all common stock, amounted to a par of approximately £210,000 ($1,050,000). It was a decade later before the company began to return big dividends. The annual average was 37.5 per cent during the ten years beginning in 1929 and 69.8 per cent for the next decade, after which 131 per cent was paid in 1949 and 87 per cent in 1950![5]

No such dividends were ever paid by any of the English petroleum enterprises operating in Mexico. In fact, few of them paid any cash dividends at all from petroleum production, making their profits, if any, from speculation in oil lands and leases. The outstanding exception and by far the most important English-owned oil concern in the republic was the Mexican Eagle Oil Company, Limited, organized in 1908. Incorporated in Mexico, this company issued its share capital in pesos. The nominal total was 30 million pesos at first, but it was soon expanded, juggled, and contracted, and finally transformed into no-par. The book value of the capitalization was said to have been more than 492 million pesos in 1929, and the company had already issued, serviced, and redeemed 6 per cent debentures with a face value of £1.5 million. For years when rates can be determined without the aid of expert accountants, dividends on ordinary shares were either high or entirely lacking, either as much as 8 per cent on the inflated capital or nothing at all. There were not only ordinary shares but preferred ordinary shares and preference shares, the last issued in 1922. The 7 per cent cumulative preference shares — 17,412,440 pesos at the outset, reduced to 7,771,600 pesos in 1928 — were usually promptly serviced. No payment was made on the ordinary shares until 1914, but after that date they were accorded essentially the same treatment as the preferred ordinary so far as dividends were concerned. The first dividend was paid on the preferred ordinary in 1911. It was 8 per cent that year and for each of the next two years. The average rate of return on both classes of ordinary for the decade ending in 1923 was 23.5 per cent; but few dividends were paid thereafter. The Mexican government expropriated the company's properties early in 1938 and nine years of intermittent negotiations were required to effect a settlement. The government of Mexico finally agreed to pay interest at the rate of 3 per cent annually starting from March 18, 1938, on an indemnity of $81,250,000. The total compensation, principal and interest, would amount to $8,689,258 each year for a period of fifteen years.[6]

Weetman D. Pearson (Lord Cowdray), head of the engineering firm of S. Pearson and Son, Limited, probably garnered larger profits from Mexico than any other man, either during or since the Spanish Conquest, with the possible exception of Edward L. Doheny of California. Mexican Eagle Oil Company bought its leases and concessions from Cowdray's firm, paying a total of 43,167,000 pesos in ordinary shares for them; and S. Pearson and Son, after receiving dividends amounting to nearly 100 per cent of the face value of their securities, sold them, perhaps at a price well above par, to the Royal Dutch–Shell combine during the prosperous era following World War I (1919).[7]

But Weetman Pearson had already made a small fortune in Mexico before his profits began to roll in from petroleum. His engineering firm had been operating there since 1889, draining the valley surrounding Mexico City, building the harbor works at Veracruz, reconstructing the Tehuantepec Railway, erecting huge warehouses and dredging ports on each side of the Tehuantepec Isthmus, establishing a jute mill, building power plants, organizing electric-utility enterprises, constructing or operating short railways in and around Veracruz, and organizing a terminal company in that city. The Díaz government paid his organization no less than £9 million for its construction work around Mexico City, in Veracruz, and on the Isthmus of Tehuantepec. Pearson transformed his engineering firm into a public corporation in 1897, capitalizing it at slightly more than £1.5 million, all except £500,000 in 5 per cent debentures being owned by the Pearson family itself. Ordinary shares with a par value of £500,000 paid a regular dividend of 10 per cent annually; an equal amount of preference shares received a cumulative 5 per cent.

Santa Gertrudis Jute Mill Company, Limited, established in Orizaba in 1893, rarely failed to return a dividend on its ordinary shares during the first twenty-eight years of its operation. Its goal was 15 per cent annually, but this proved impracticable; the annual nominal average for the period seems, however, to have exceeded 10 per cent. The par value of the shares amounted to approximately £100,000 in 1893 and £152,640 by 1910. Debentures amounting to £129,500, figured at par, paid a regular 6 per cent per annum.[8]

Vera Cruz Railways, Limited, organized in 1900 with a nominal paid-up capital of £500,000, half in ordinary and half in 5 per cent cumulative preference shares, turned out to be a less profitable company, failing to pay any dividends on its ordinary shares. It is possible, however, that Pearson sold his securities before the time of troubles that followed the downfall of Díaz.

Vera Cruz Terminal Company, Limited, created in 1907, managed to pay interest at the prescribed rate of 4.5 per cent annually for almost a decade on debentures with a par value of £800,000, and Pearson may have disposed of his holdings before the payments ceased. The ordinary shares of this enterprise, issued for purposes of control, amounted to only £90.

Cowdray's electric utilities in Veracruz, Orizaba, Córdoba, Puebla, and Tampico were not good income-producers. He was fortunate enough to sell them, however, along with recently acquired electric utilities in Chile, to American and Foreign Power Company for a neat sum. The sale was made just before the crash that put an end to the booming 1920's, and Cowdray's profits were no less than £2,738,793![9]

Weetman Pearson was a man of tremendous influence in Mexico. He knew how to deal with Porfirio Díaz and the coterie which surrounded the Mexican dictator. He employed flattery and every other means a situation seemed to suggest. He named the first dredge he imported into Mexico City in honor of Don Porfirio's beautiful wife. He honored Porfirio, Junior, and other henchmen of the dictator with directorships in his companies and probably paid them well. His immense success is said to have aroused the jealousy of H. Clay Pierce and other powerful businessmen of the United States, and even to have caused uneasiness in government circles at Washington.[10]

But the profits made by Cowdray and his associates and by English owners of securities in some lucky mining companies and a few banks failed to lift the average returns on the British investment in Mexico over the years since the 1820's to a level that can be described as exploitative. Most Englishmen received no more than a meager income

Country-by-Country Inspection

from their Mexican investments and a good many suffered losses. A handful of speculators, bankers, mineowners, engineers, oilmen, and exporters were amply rewarded, but the United Kingdom as a whole could not have greatly benefited. Heartbreaking disappointments were far more numerous than bonanzas.

⇌ VIII ⇌

THE SMALL CARIBBEAN COUNTRIES: A STORY OF MEAGER PROFITS

With the possible exception of Ecuador and Paraguay, no countries of Latin America yielded more trifling rewards to British investors than did the five republics of Central America. English capital ventured in Cuba was not conspicuously remunerative. British investments in Haiti and Panama were so insignificant that they may be ignored, and funds sent to the Dominican Republic often brought almost no returns at all.[1]

Central America

Residents of the British Isles made their first investment of any size in Central America in 1822, when they purchased bonds with a face value of £200,000 from the fictitious Kingdom of Poyais at 80 per cent of par. Three years later they bought an issue of £163,000 from the Central American Confederation at 73. The first gamble resulted in total loss. The second was not quite so unfortunate, but the bonds went into immediate default and half a century passed before the last of the states that succeeded the Confederation resumed payments to British bondholders. The financial irresponsibility, for which the dishonesty of English bondsalesmen and Central American government agents served as an excuse, injured the financial reputations of the new republics; yet they managed, one and all, to sell new issues in the British market before the end of the nineteenth century, some of their later issues likewise accompanied by chicanery and fraud. Guatemala marketed £11,300 in 1863 and £500,000 in 1869. Honduras managed to sell a nominal total of £3,500,000 in 1867 and 1870. Costa Rica sold a nominal aggregate of £1,400,000 in 1871 and 1872. Nicaragua marketed £285,000 in 1886 and El Salvador floated £300,000 in 1889 and £500,000 in 1892.

Country-by-Country Inspection

With the exception of the Guatemalan issues, the purpose of all of these later loans was to finance railways, which were to serve as security for the bonds; but the railroads were not completed and Englishmen soon found themselves in possession of two unprofitable short lines, one in Costa Rica and the other in El Salvador. The few miles of track laid in Honduras were too worthless to justify the troubles of foreclosure.

But Englishmen continued to buy Central American government bonds. The par value of their holdings in 1913 exceeded £8.6 million: Costa Rica, £2 million; El Salvador, £816,000; Guatemala, more than £1.4 million; Honduras, above £3.1 million; and Nicaragua, over £1.2 million. The nominal value of their holdings at the end of 1949 was still some £4.1 million: Costa Rica, in excess of £1.4 million; Honduras, approximately £1 million; El Salvador, £855,690; Guatemala, £426,980; Nicaragua, £324,940.[2]

Although only Honduras failed to service its government bonds in 1913, as it had failed to service them for the preceding forty years, the other four countries had been in default most of the time since the early 1870's; and while only Guatemala was remiss in 1949, all five of the countries had been in default a good part of the time since 1913. Interest rates were scaled down to 3 or 4 per cent, so that bond income was very small even when paid. In fact, all interest on Honduran bonds was erased in 1926 in order to induce Honduras to pay off some of the principal of its bad debt. Central American government securities were a very poor investment for most Englishmen, whatever may have been the gains of bondsalesmen and speculators.

Although Central American railway securities were not much better, Englishmen made a further investment in the railroads of the region shortly after 1900. The exact amount they ventured in the Guatemala Railway, which soon expanded into the International Railways of Central America, is not easy to determine. The *South American Journal* indicates that as much as £9 million of its securities were quoted on the London Stock Exchange and includes this large item in its annual estimates of total nominal capital invested by Englishmen in Guatemala. It is not likely, however, that more than half of this sum was ever invested by Englishmen in the securities of this company. According to the *Journal's* very liberal figures, the par value of the English investment in Central America's railroads at the end

The Small Caribbean Countries

of 1913 was in excess of £13.7 million: Guatemala, £9 million; Costa Rica, £3,363,500; and El Salvador, £1,408,700. The nominal rates of return for that year, better than usual and better than they were likely to be again, except in a few lucky years, were 4.7 per cent for El Salvador's railway, 3.7 per cent for Costa Rica's, and 1.6 per cent for the International Railways, which were listed under Guatemala because most of the property was in that country. The common stock of International Railways, the equivalent of £6 million, paid no dividend that year.

During the period extending from 1913 through 1949 little change occurred in the size of the British railway investment in Central America and no change for the better from the standpoint of English investors. With a nominal capital of £3,055,000 in 1949, of which £1,800,000 were in ordinary shares and the rest in 6.5 per cent debentures, the Costa Rica Railway Company, Limited, organized in 1886, paid interest on only the £600,000 invested in its first-mortgage debentures. The Salvador Railway Company, Limited, created in 1898, paid no dividends on its shares — £250,000 ordinary and an equal amount of preferred — in 1949 and had paid none since 1913. Nor did it service any of its loan capital of £312,100, no income having been received from this presumably sounder part of the investment since 1932. The International Railways of Central America, a New Jersey corporation organized in 1904 as the Guatemala Railway Company but assuming the more pretentious title in 1912, was able in 1949 to pay only the interest on its bonds and return a dividend of 2.5 per cent on its $10 million in 6 per cent preferred. No dividend had ever been paid on its ordinary stock, which had a book value of nearly two thirds of its total capital of some $48 million.[3]

British investments in other economic enterprises in Central America were, on the whole, hardly more profitable than the railway investment. With only one notable exception, which will be examined shortly, capital ventured in mining brought almost no returns, although at one period (the late 1880's) it amounted to a par of more than £2 million. The investment in public utilities yielded income on no capital other than outstanding debentures. Costa Rica Markets and Tramways, Limited, organized in 1886 and liquidated in the early 1940's, never paid a single dividend on its £60,000 in ordinary shares and sometimes failed to service its debentures, which had a par value

Country-by-Country Inspection

of somewhat less than its share capital. Costa Rica Electric Light and Traction Company, Limited, created in 1898, did no better for the owners of its £130,000 in ordinary shares, but usually managed to pay from 5 to 6 per cent annually on debentures which sometimes amounted to twice that sum. This corporation sold its property to American and Foreign Power Company, a subsidiary of Electric Bond and Share, in 1929. Such securities as Englishmen owned in the United Fruit Company yielded good income. Their ventures in commercial banking and other finance did not prosper, however, except in two instances, which will soon be specified. The London Bank of Central America, Limited, for example, which operated under various names from 1893 until it was absorbed by the Anglo–South American Bank in the 1920's never paid an annual dividend of more than 8 per cent on a nominal investment averaging about £100,000 and paid no dividends during half of its thirty-two years of independent existence.

I have been able to discover only three British enterprises operating in Central America that yielded high returns, and only two of these were remarkable for the profits they produced. The Anglo–Central American Commercial Bank, Limited, organized in 1914, paid an average annual nominal dividend of nearly 12.4 per cent on its share capital of £55,002 for the two decades preceding its liquidation in 1936 and an average of 900 per cent annually on its £300 in founders' shares![4] The Mortgage Company of Costa Rica, created in 1911 for the purpose of lending money on coffee, sugar, cacao, and banana lands, paid an average dividend of 10 per cent annually for fourteen years on its paid-up ordinary shares amounting to £10,000, and managed also to service and redeem £200,000 in 6 per cent debentures. The company then paid a share bonus of 150 per cent and further inflated its capital until the nominal total in ordinary shares reached £100,000 by 1928 and its 6.5 debentures amounted to £150,000. This injection of water and the arrival of the world economic depression soon proved fatal to the shareholders. Dividends of 5 per cent annually were paid for the next five years, but only one other return, and this merely 2 per cent, was made thereafter, and the company was finally dissolved in 1948. Butters Salvador Mines, Limited, organized in 1899 to mine gold in El Salvador, seems to have been the most prosperous company ever owned by Englishmen in Central America. With a paid-in capital of £150,000, par value, all in ordinary

The Small Caribbean Countries

shares, it returned a nominal average annual dividend of 52 per cent for the decade starting in 1903 and an annual average of 23 per cent for the next four years.[5]

At this point, however, it is well to recall that the aggregate nominal British investment in Central America seldom yielded an average annual return of more than 3 per cent and that for a good part of a century it yielded less than 2 per cent or even no return at all. The capital of the three companies mentioned composed a very small fraction of the total investment, which, at its peak in 1913 or 1914, aggregated a nominal sum of about £21 million, stood at £7.5 million in 1880, rose to £11.7 million by the end of 1890, amounted to approximately £13 million in 1939, and still stood at around £12 million at the end of 1949.[6]

The Dominican Republic and Cuba

English investments in the Dominican Republic probably never amounted to more than £3 million at any time. They were confined mainly to government bonds, a gamble or two in mining, the misnamed San Domingo Improvement Company (a corporation controlled by New York speculators), and a single railroad. The mining ventures were losing propositions; sterling government securities — amounting to a par of £714,300 from 1872 to 1887, £736,000 in 1890, and perhaps around £1.5 million in 1900 — were in default most of the time; the Improvement Company was liquidated in 1905 or 1906 after a forced reduction in its nominal capital; and the railroad enterprise, Samaná and Santiago Railway Company, Limited, organized in 1888 with a nominal capital that never exceeded £700,000 was profitable for a time, but ceased to pay dividends in the 1920's and was finally liquidated some two decades later.[7]

According to the estimates of the *South American Journal*, which are probably from £5 million to £10 million too high for the thirty-five years preceding 1941, the British investment in the Cuban republic amounted to a nominal total of £31.6 million in 1910, to more than £44.4 million in 1913, to some £45.7 million at its maximum in 1927, and to approximately £24.3 million at the end of 1949. Englishmen began to invest in Cuban railways at an early date, buying the bond issues of companies controlled by Spaniards and Cubans. The par value of these railroad securities exceeded £1.2 million by the end of

1880, amounted to more than £1.8 million a decade later, and was in excess of £7.2 million by the last days of the year 1900. The first Cuban lines came into the possession of capitalists of Great Britain as the result of foreclosures. The peak of this railway investment was reached in 1927, when the nominal capital stood at £30.3 million. Englishmen also invested in Cuban public utilities and port works, in tobacco factories, in speculative enterprises which attempted to extract a profit from asphalt and petroleum, in coastwise shipping, and perhaps in sugar plantations and sugar mills and commercial banking, although their investment in sugar and banking is difficult to trace.

The average annual nominal rate of return on this investment probably never exceeded 5 per cent. It was only 3.8 per cent in 1910 and 4.8 per cent in 1913. It rose to 4.9 per cent in 1924 and maintained the same nominal rate for 1925, but gradually declined thereafter. The rate had dropped to 2.3 per cent by 1931, and the annual average for the eighteen years starting with 1932 was only a little better than 1 per cent.

The large investment in railways was mainly responsible both for the higher and the lower rates of return. The average annual nominal yield on railway capital rose from 3.1 per cent in 1910 to 5.1 per cent in 1923, to 5.3 in 1924, and to 5.6 in 1925, but declined to 1.6 in 1930 and 1.3 in 1931 and continued to shrink thereafter. The average for the period beginning in 1932 and ending in 1949 was less than 0.6 per cent. The next year the Cuban government took control of the British-owned railroads, but negotiations for their purchase had not resulted in a final agreement by the end of 1950.

The size of the English investment in government bonds of the Cuban republic has not been easy to ascertain because none of these securities were sterling securities. Perhaps the total, figured at par, was as high as £4 million or £4.5 million in 1917 and 1918. *South American Journal*, in its estimates for the aggregate British investment in Cuba for the year 1913, includes £9,687,000 for Cuban government securities; but this figure, based upon the aggregate of Cuban government bonds quoted at the end of that year on the London Stock Exchange, evidently covers the whole of the Cuban foreign debt. British holdings probably did not amount to more than £2.5 million at that time. Whatever the size of this portion of the investment, it brought steady returns of from 4.7 to 4.8 per cent over a period of thirty-six years,

The Small Caribbean Countries

until all of the Cuban bonds held by Englishmen were finally redeemed in 1940.

Aside from the companies to be discussed below (and possibly the banking and sugar investment on which financial data have not been found), the capital placed in miscellaneous economic enterprises was not profitable. The Cuban Steamship Company, Limited, organized in 1893 and liquidated in 1915, returned dividends for only a few years. The investment in enterprises established to exploit petroleum and asphalt never reached the dividend stage. Among the public-utility companies, only the Cuba Submarine Telegraph Company, Limited, created in 1870, yielded good returns for more than a decade or so. The average annual nominal rate of return on the £160,000 of ordinary capital invested in this company was 12 per cent for the forty-five years starting with 1880; but the return was only 2.5 per cent in 1926 and no dividends were paid between that date and 1950. There were also £60,000 in 10 per cent cumulative preference shares. (The Direct West India Cable Company, Limited, got control of this enterprise in 1927.)

The Cuban Ports Company, a corporation organized by Norman Davis (American speculator and diplomat) in 1911, turned out to be a fairly profitable investment for Englishmen who bought its bonds. Although they received no income from this capital, $6 million, from 1913 through 1916 because the Cuban government nullified the concession, they were fortunate enough in 1917, thanks to pressure exerted by the United States government, to receive Cuban government securities in exchange for the bonds of this company. The new securities paid 5 per cent annually until the last of them were redeemed in 1931. Havana Marine Terminals, Limited, a Canadian corporation in which Englishmen may have been financially interested, attempted in vain, however, to salvage the recouped assets of the Cuba Ports Company. Organized in 1919, Havana Marine Terminals was never profitable and passed out of existence in the middle 1930's. An English investment of over £700,000 in 5 per cent bonds of the Port of Havana Docks Company, a Maine corporation organized in 1910, was more fortunate. These bonds were serviced regularly and finally called at par in 1941.

Two enterprises engaged in the manufacture of tobacco proved to be the most profitable investments ever made by Englishmen in Cuba.

Country-by-Country Inspection

The first to be organized was Henry Clay and Bock and Company, founded in 1888. The second enterprise, Havana Cigar and Tobacco Factories, Limited, was established in 1898. Control of both was acquired by the Havana Tobacco Company, a subsidiary of the American Tobacco Company, in 1902; but English investors continued to hold some of the ordinary shares and apparently all of the preference shares.

The average annual nominal dividend paid by Henry Clay and Bock on £159,900, face value, in ordinary shares for the three decades starting in 1889 was modest, only 4.9 per cent; but thereafter the profits were spectacular. For the decade beginning in 1919 the annual nominal average was 28.5 per cent; for the following decade it was 22; for the ten years beginning in 1939 it was 26; and the dividend was 35 per cent in 1949 and 50 in 1950! The £170,000 in cumulative preference shares paid a regular 8 per cent annually.

Havana Cigar and Tobacco Factories did little more than service its £270,000 in 7 per cent cumulative preference shares until after 1910; but for the next forty years the returns were very high. The average annual nominal rate of return on the £250,000 invested in ordinary shares was 24 per cent for the four decades, and for two of the four it was 31 per cent and 29 per cent respectively! The highest annual dividend paid was 75 per cent in 1928.[8]

A few more enterprises like these two and the three Central American Companies previously described might have made English investments in the little republics of Middle America profitable. But a diligent search has revealed no others.

IX

RAINBOW-CHASING IN NORTHERN SOUTH AMERICA

A few years ago, while searching through many issues of the *Stock Exchange Year-Book* for British companies interested in Latin America, my eyes fell almost by accident upon this item: "Contractors, Limited. . . . The company was registered February 21, 1900, for the purpose of draining Lake Guatavita, Colombia, and carrying on mining operations on the land thus exposed." This was intriguing! Here was the place where the legend of El Dorado, the Gilded Man, may have originated some four centuries earlier! Here was Lake Guatavitá, the Indian shrine, where the Chibcha chiefs were supposed to have taken their ceremonial baths after anointing themselves with oil and sprinkling gold dust over their naked bodies. Here was the lake into which the Indians were said to have cast their precious religious offerings for centuries. Assuming that these ceremonies had gone on for a thousand years or so, how deep would be the layer of gold at the bottom and how thick the deposit of precious ornaments? Englishmen who founded this company with such an unromantic name were determined to answer these questions and enrich themselves in the process. The company is reported to have gone about the task systematically, draining the lake and bringing in a dredge, probably at very heavy expense owing to the difficult Colombian terrain and expensive means of transport. I traced Contractors, Limited, through numerous issues of the *Year-Book* with intense eagerness, and in the issue for 1927 I read this report: "A few emeralds and some pottery and small ornaments of gold and copper have been found." The company was bankrupt. No rich deposit of gold and no tall heap of golden artifacts were found in the sand and mud at the bottom of Lake Guatavitá. The experience was almost typical of British efforts to

Country-by-Country Inspection

enrich themselves by investments in Colombia, Ecuador, and Venezuela until after 1900.

Summary of Investments and Average Annual Returns

La Gran Colombia, the big nation of Símon Bolívar's dreams, enjoyed great prestige in England during the early 1820's. The reader may remember that Englishmen bought two issues of its government bonds amounting to a total of £6,750,000 at par, organized three mining companies to search for its precious metals and copper, and founded some other enterprises for the purpose of fishing for pearls or engaging in land speculation and colonization.

Disappointment came swiftly. The government defaulted on its securities in 1825. Mining and other enterprises achieved no immediate success. La Gran Colombia soon broke up into three disorderly nations. Several decades passed before capitalists of the British Isles drew any substantial income from this part of the world.[1]

It was not until 1834, four years after the dissolution of La Gran Colombia, that the three states that succeeded it were able to agree upon the apportionment of their sterling debt, and the nineteenth century was more than half gone before the last of them began to meet its obligations to British bondholders. Including accumulated interest, the debt had swollen to £9,806,406 by 1834, and the overdue interest — the rate was 6 per cent — continued to pile up. As stated in Chapter II, Venezuela signed a resumption agreement with the British bondholders in 1840 and Colombia (then called New Granada) reached a settlement with them in 1845, but Ecuador procrastinated until 1855. All three agreements were a good deal alike, although Ecuador's was a bit more complicated. New issues of bonds in each case were exchanged for the old and for the unpaid coupons. The interest rate was reduced to 2 per cent or less, but escalator clauses pushed it up (theoretically) to 5 or 6 per cent within a decade or so. Ecuador paid part of the interest arrears with land and Peruvian bonds. Venezuela's sterling debt stood at £2,794,826 after the settlement. Ecuador's amounted to only £1,824,000. Colombia's was larger than both combined, for the total was £7,089,766; but this was later reduced by another agreement.

These arrangements were hardly worth the effort required to effect them. All three republics suffered from grave disorders during most of

Northern South America

the second half of the century and their sterling bonds were in default a good part of the time. Yet they managed somehow to float further issues in England, either before 1900 or during the early years of the new century. Their outstanding government securities quoted on the London Stock Exchange at the end of the year 1913 aggregated more than £10.3 million: Ecuador, including government-guaranteed railway bonds, £2,780,794;* Colombia, £3,388,874; Venezuela, including bonds recently issued in settlement of claims of British subjects, £4,228,720. The average nominal rate paid by Venezuela for the year 1913 was 4 per cent. Colombia paid an average of 3.8 and Ecuador paid 5 per cent. Without further failure to live up to its obligations — 3 per cent annually, plus small amortization payments — the Venezuelan government finally redeemed all of its sterling issues in 1930. Colombia, after paying an average nominal annual rate of around 5 per cent for nearly twenty years following 1913, fell into default again during the world depression of the 1930's, but paid an average of 3.2 per cent for the eight-year period beginning in 1942. Ecuador soon reverted to its old habits; between 1914 and 1949 its government fulfilled its obligations to British bondholders no more than a third of the time. There was no pot of gold for Englishmen at the end of this rainbow.

But government securities, by and large, made up only a fraction of the total British investment in these three countries, although such securities sometimes amounted to about half the capital invested in Ecuador. In 1923, when the English investment in Colombia reached an all-time peak of £11.3 million, par value, government securities accounted for hardly more than £4.5 million; and government bonds accounted for only £1.4 million of Venezuela's peak investment of £6.3 million in 1928 and for about £2 million of Ecuador's maximum British investment of some £4.3 million in 1939. There seems to have been little reduction in Ecuador's share of British capital during the following decade and little change in the distribution between government bonds and economic enterprises. Aggregate English capital in Colombia and Venezuela at the end of 1948 (reckoned at par) was approximately as follows: Colombia, £5.3 million, with government bonds accounting for £3 million; Venezuela, £18.3 million and no gov-

* Some of the Ecuadorian securities held by English investors were dollar, and not sterling, securities, but these have been given a sterling equivalent for the sake of uniformity.

ernment securities. Englishmen pursued many other rainbows in this region besides the multicolored engraved paper of its governments attractively displayed by investment bankers.

One of them, railways, has already been mentioned in Ecuador's case. But the Guayaquil and Quito Railway was the only important railroad venture of Englishmen in that country, and they had been drawn into it because they were trying to choose the better of two bad prospects. They had traded almost worthless government securities for what they hoped would prove to be sounder government guaranteed railway securities issued by a company engaged in building and then operating the most important line in the republic, the railroad connecting Ecuador's major port with its capital city. Having discovered before long that they had failed to better their position, British capitalists made only one other investment in Ecuador's railways.*

With respect to Colombia and Venezuela the story was different, so far at least as the number of railroad ventures was concerned. Beginning with the purchase in the late 1860's of some bonds of the Panama Railroad, Englishmen invested at one time or another in eleven or twelve Colombia railways; and they ventured their capital in at least seven Venezuelan railroads, starting with an investment made in the 1870's in the Bolívar Railway Company, Limited, which owned a short line in northwestern Venezuela. In both republics, however, they soon discovered that such investments were not very promising. In Colombia's case, they were glad to exchange some of their railway debentures for government bonds. At its maximum around 1890 the English investment in Venezuela's railroads was slightly more than nominal £4.1 million; at its height in Colombia around 1913 it was only a little above £3.2 million. By the end of 1949 this capital had been reduced to some £2.3 million in Venezuela, where negotiations were under way for the sale of all the British-owned lines, and to less than £1 million invested in a single railway in Colombia.

With three possible exceptions, to be discussed later, the British railway investment was not very remunerative in either of these republics. The average return on the nominal capital in 1913 was 2

---

* They invested £200,000 in a short railroad connecting the port of Manta with the town of Santa Ana. The line had the grandiose name of Central Railway of Ecuador although its length was only 40 miles. Its financial record has not been available to me but I doubt that it was a profitable enterprise.

Northern South America

per cent in Colombia and 3.8 per cent in Venezuela. For the year 1923 the average rate was 3.9 for Colombia and 2.5 for Venezuela. For the twenty-seven years beginning in 1923 and ending in 1949 the average annual return on the nominal paid-up capital in Colombian railroads was 2.6 per cent, and it was less than 2 per cent on the nominal paid-in capital in the Venezuelan railways.

The English investment in various other economic enterprises, classified by the *South American Journal* as miscellaneous, yielded better income, especially during the period following 1922. The average annual nominal rate of return on these investments in Venezuela was 3.47 per cent for the decade beginning in 1923, approximately 7 per cent for the subsequent decade, and 9.7 per cent for the six-year period beginning in 1943, the highest yield being 11.5 per cent in 1948. For Colombia the average annual nominal rates of return were 3.8 per cent for the decade beginning in 1923, almost 6.5 per cent for the subsequent decade, and more than 7.6 for the seven years starting in 1943, the nominal yield for 1949 being 15.4 per cent. The average nominal annual return on miscellaneous English investments in Ecuador was seldom more than 2 or 3 per cent until 1930, but for the next twenty years the annual nominal average was approximately 5 per cent, the highest yields being for the years 1948 and 1949, when the nominal rate of return was at least 8 per cent each year. Somewhere among these investments were a few gold-heaped urns. To track them down will be the task of the second part of this chapter.

Inspection of Companies Recording the Highest Yields

First, however, the most profitable railways ever owned by Englishmen in this part of South America will be examined. Two of these were in Colombia and only one in Venezuela.

The La Guaira and Caracas Railway Company, Limited, was organized in 1882 to build and operate the short line that winds its way through the mountains from Venezuela's leading port up to its capital city. The face value of the company's ordinary shares was £350,000 until this sum was expanded to £472,477 by a stock bonus paid in 1926. Debentures with 5 per cent coupons stood at £370,000 in 1890 and £375,045 in 1950. The company was a profitable enterprise before the completion of a competitive highway and the onslaught of the world depression in 1929. It seldom failed to pay an ordinary dividend until 1931. For the decade beginning in 1884 the average nominal return was 4.5 per cent per annum; for the next decade, owing to political disturbances, the annual nominal average dropped to a little less than 4 per cent. Then there was a decided recovery. For the twenty six years starting in 1904 and ending in 1929 the average nominal yield on the ordinary shares was nearly 6.4 per annum, and for ten years of the period the return was 8 per cent annually. But the end of the lush epoch was near. The dividend for 1931 was only 1.5 and thereafter no dividend was paid. Negotiations for the sale of the railway to the Venezuelan government began in 1949. The price received for its properties in 1950 was £1,011,000.[2]

The two fairly profitable British-owned railroad enterprises in Colombia were the Dorada Railway Company, Limited, and the Barranquilla Railway and Pier Company, Limited, both organized in 1888, the first to build and operate a line around the rapids of the middle Magdalena River and the second to improve and operate a short railroad connecting the city of Barranquilla with a port on the Caribbean Sea. The profits of the two organizations, especially the Barranquilla Railway, will not become evident until share bonuses are scrutinized.

Until some time after it was reorganized in 1905, the Dorado Railway Company was not a financial success. Few, if any, dividends were paid before 1911. For the decade beginning in that year the annual nominal average for the ordinary shares was only 3.75; and it rose to 6.8 during the next decade only to fall to less than 3 per cent during the depression years 1931 through 1940. So far the record does not suggest a profitable enterprise; but note the following facts: debentures with 6 and 8 per cent coupons sometimes amounted to more than the share capital, which was £350,000, par value, between 190 and 1925 and £604,347 by 1950; a stock bonus of 50 per cent was paid in 1926; and the average annual rate of return on the inflated capital in ordinary shares during the nine years from 1941 on was a little better than 4 per cent, the rate being 6 per cent in both 1948 and 1949.

The share bonuses of the Barranquilla Railway and Pier Company are more impressive than its dividends. They began with a stock bonus of 25 per cent in 1913, followed by 20 per cent in 1920, another 20 per cent in 1928, and 50 per cent in 1929, making a total of 115 per cent and raising the ordinary shares from a par of £200,000 in 1912 to very nominal £475,000 in 1930. No dividends were paid until 189

Northern South America

and for the sixteen years beginning in 1897 the average was slightly less than 3 per cent of the face value of the paid-in ordinary shares. For the next eighteen-year period, however, namely from 1913 through 1930, the annual nominal average was almost 7 per cent on this very inflated capital, the return being 8 per cent each year for the last five years of the period. Debentures amounting to £100,000, paying a regular 6 per cent, were issued in 1888 and redeemed by 1930. Finally, in 1933, the company's property was sold to the Colombian government for approximately £330,000, or 165 per cent of the nominal sum actually invested, to be paid in equal installments over the next ten years.[3]

Such is the financial record of three fairly profitable railways out of a total of eighteen or twenty in which Englishmen ventured their capital in this region during the more than eighty years following 1868, when they bought an issue of Panama Railroad bonds. These Panama Railroad securities, paying 7 per cent, together with another issue of 6 per cents which they bought in 1881 and an issue of £120,000, also having 6 per cent coupons, which they purchased from the Cúcuta Railway Company in 1887, were the only profitable investments they ever made in railways controlled by others in northern South America.

British capital invested in the public utilities of the region brought no startling returns. Apparently, residents of the British Isles never owned any gas plants in Ecuador or Colombia or Venezuela; and the Cartagena Waterworks, which they owned and operated from 1905 until they sold this property to the Municipality of Cartagena in 1926 at much less than cost, was their only venture in this field.[4] They specialized in telephones, tramways, and electric-power plants, and some of these ventures seem to have been profitable.

The oldest of the group was the Venezuela Telephone and Electrical Appliance Company, Limited, founded in 1890 to establish telephone exchanges in Caracas and other leading Venezuelan towns. The capitalization of this company expanded rapidly, but no share bonuses were paid. Debentures, most of them paying 5 or 6 per cent but some paying 7, expanded from £70,000 in 1890 to £140,100 by 1925, and were called early in 1931 only to have another issue, amounting to £300,000, substituted for them. Preference shares, cumulative 8 per cents, which amounted to only £8,600 in 1905, increased to £136,975 by 1930 and expanded to £288,528 in 1931, when the company assumed the name of Telephone Properties, Limited. Ordinary shares, which amounted to a par of only £70,000 from 1890 through 1925, were rapidly increased to £273,950 by 1930 and to £410,932 in connection with the reorganization of the next year. In a company thus heavily loaded with loan capital and preferred shares the holders of the ordinary shares often failed to receive any dividends. Although the annual return on their nominal investment in them averaged almost 3 per cent during the first decade and only two dividends were passed, nothing whatever was paid from 1900 through 1923! But better days were ahead. The ordinary dividend was 5 per cent in 1923 and 8 per cent each year for the next seven years; and for the two decades starting in 1931 and ending in 1949 the average nominal annual return was 5.5 per cent, thus bringing the annual nominal average up to 3.35 per cent for the sixty years of the company's existence. Taking the 6 and 7 per cent debentures and the 8 per cent cumulative preference shares into account, this was not a bad financial record.

In spite of the fact that it paid no dividends from 1900, the year it was organized, until 1913, managing to service only its £40,000 in 5 per cent debentures, the Bogotá Telephone Company, Limited, chalked up an even better record. On ordinary shares amounting to a par of £22,607 in 1910 and £258,493 by the end of 1927 the average annual nominal rate of return for the seventeen-year period starting in 1913 was approximately 12.1 per cent, and the shares were then sold to Telephone and General Trust, Limited, at 75 per cent above par, £1 15 *s*. for each £1 share.[5]

Compared with these two telephone companies, the other utility enterprises owned by English capitalists in this region made a poor showing. United Electric Tramways of Caracas, Limited, organized in 1906 to consolidate and electrify the streetcar lines of Venezuela's capital, yielded rather high dividends for a brief period on its ordinary shares, amounting to a face value of £170,000, paid up. From the time the first dividend was paid in 1913 until 1927, the average annual nominal rate was almost 9 per cent. After that year, however, all dividends ceased. The company managed to service its 5 per cent debentures — £169,000 in 1910 and £180,900 (some of the latter having 7 per cent coupons) by 1930 — most of the time; but no further dividend was paid on the ordinary shares after 1927 and the company was finally liquidated twenty years later. The Ecuadorian Corporation,

Northern South America

Limited, established in 1913 and reorganized twice, with considerable Canadian and perhaps some United States capital in recent years, made a poor showing in spite of diversified operations which included banking, brewing, and real estate along with tramways and power plants. It seems to have returned no dividends on its ordinary shares — a par of £283,000 in 1910, £310,000 in 1925, and $3,136,145 (Canadian) in 1937 — until 1928 and almost none thereafter until 1944, when 4 per cent was paid. Afterwards, however, returns were rather high, rising from 5.8 in 1945 to 8 in 1946 and 10 per cent each year for the next three years. Perhaps the explanation of lack of ordinary dividends for the first three decades is to be found mainly in the heavy load of 6 per cent debentures and 8 per cent cumulative preference shares, which together nearly always amounted to more than the par value of the ordinary shares until after the reorganization of 1928.

Capitalists residing in Great Britain continued, of course, to interest themselves in the mines of tropical South America — and also continued to suffer disappointments. But a few of the many mining companies — perhaps not fewer than seventy or eighty in all — which they organized to operate in this region during the course of the century were lucky enough to find bonanzas. They failed, however, to discover any in Ecuador's El Oro Province, where they ought to have found them if a name has any significance. The Great Zarumá Gold Mining Company, Limited, organized in 1881 and repeatedly reorganized thereafter, spent many years vainly searching this jungle.

English capitalists controlled one rich mining district in Venezuela for more than a century and shared the ephemeral profits of another. The district they controlled was the Aroa district, which they are said to have purchased from the Bolívar family. The profits they extracted from it are suggested by the dividends paid by the South American Copper Syndicate, Limited. The total for the nine years from 1909 through 1917 was 1,287.5 per cent on a nominal capital of £15,000, an average of a little more than 143 per cent annually![6] But it seems that the rich veins were finally exhausted. The corporation was reorganized as the South American Copper Company, Limited, in 1928 and was eventually liquidated in 1940 without ever paying another ordinary dividend. The famous El Callao Mining Company, organized under French control in 1870, never even approached such dividends. The annual nominal rate of return for its most profitable decade averaged only 13 per cent. But its capital was enormously inflated: from an equivalent of £4,800 in 1870 to around £13,000 in 1873 and approximately £1,300,000 in 1882.[7]

Eight of the sixty or more British mining organizations active in Colombia at some time during a period embracing a century and a quarter were quite profitable. One of these, the Frontino and Bolivia Gold Mining Company, Limited, established in 1864 and reorganized several times, was among the oldest English mining companies in Latin America; and it enjoyed a long stretch of lush years. From 1888 through 1897 the average annual rate of return on its nominal ordinary capital of around £140,000 was 13.75 per cent; from 1898 through 1907, although dividends were paid for only three of the ten years, it was 6.25; for the two decades starting in 1918 it was above 8.7 per cent on a somewhat larger capital; and the average annual return on a nominal capital of £190,573 from 1938 through 1949 was 7 per cent, the rate being 10 per cent for each of the last two years of the period. Nor is this the complete story. Debentures and preference shares usually amounting to from a fourth to a half of the face value of the ordinary shares received a regular annual 10 per cent from 1905 through 1949. Much more remarkable were the profits extracted by Pato Mines, Limited. Organized in 1909 to work placers in Antioquia, this company made a poor start, paying no returns on an investment of £100,000 in ordinary shares until 1919. But thereafter the profits rolled out. Dividends averaged a nominal 100.5 per cent annually for the following decade and 62.5 per cent annually for the next four years, after which the company began to operate through a subsidiary, Pato Consolidated Gold Dredging, Limited, with a much larger capital — $3,200,000 (Canadian), the equivalent of £640,000, or more — and continued to pay handsome returns. For the decade starting in 1939 the average nominal dividend was no less than 30.2 per cent per annum, and for the years 1949 and 1950 the average was 20 per cent.

It would be interesting to set forth the dividend record of another company engaged in working Colombia's placers; but since British investors never controlled this enterprise (South American Gold and Platinum Company, a Delaware corporation), it will be passed over. It is time to call attention to a pot — rather a lake — of black gold which Englishmen found in Venezuela.

Before bringing up this subject, however, brief notice will be taken of a petroleum enterprise which partially compensated Englishmen for their vain search for gold-filled urns in Ecuador. Anglo-Ecuadorian Oilfields, Limited, a firm founded in 1919, finally began to pay regular dividends in 1929 on its nominal capital of £1,500,000, all in ordinary shares, and the annual nominal average for the next two decades was approximately 7 per cent.

But this was small change if compared with the bountiful yields of Venezuelan Oil Concessions, Limited, organized in 1913. After paying an annual average dividend of 62.2 per cent on its nominal capital of £1 million during the five-year period starting in 1926, this company speedily expanded its capitalization to more than £7.1 million and still continued to pay high dividends: an annual nominal average of more than 12 per cent from 1931 through 1935, rising to 20 per cent for the next thirteen years. It then exchanged its shares for shares of Shell Transport and Trading Company, Limited, at the rate of £2 for each share of 13 s. 4 d., face value.[9]

Englishmen found a few pots of gold in tropical South America to repay them for their long years of rainbow-chasing; but on the average and over the century their rewards were small, and the Englishmen who garnered the best of them were not often those who did most of the chasing. In many instances almost nothing was gained; worse still, actual losses were frequent. It is likely, however, that Latin Americans long remembered the British bonanzas and soon forgot both the numerous losses and the moderate profits.

X

VENTURES, MOSTLY IMPRUDENT, IN PARAGUAY, BOLIVIA, AND PERU

Englishmen who risked their capital in Peru and Bolivia may have been actuated in part by romanticism. These were the lands occupied by the subjects of the famous Inca lords, lands which were supposed to have enriched the Spaniards after becoming the major center of Spanish empire in the New World. But any romantic notions which Englishmen may have held about Paraguay must have had their origin in the accounts of the noted Jesuit missions in this region. Whether impelled solely by the profit motive or by a mixture of cool calculation and sentimental imagination, most British investors who ventured their savings in these three countries were doomed eventually to become the victims of frustration and near futility.

Paraguay and Bolivia

Residents of the United Kingdom made their first large investments in Paraguay in 1871 and 1872, purchasing two issues of Paraguayan government bonds with a total par value of £1,505,400. Their next venture of any magnitude was an investment in a railroad enterprise, the Paraguay Central Railway Company, Limited, organized in 1889, although the inflated capitalization of another organization, a land company registered the previous year, was reported to be in excess of £200,000. Government securities, a railway, and real estate, these were the major types of British investment in Paraguay. The total never amounted to much more than £3.8 million, which was about £500,000 above the nominal aggregate for 1949 and several preceding years.[1]

The first investment of any size ventured by Englishmen in Bolivia was also made in the early 1870's, an issue of government bonds with a face value of £1.7 million purchased in 1872. A few years later they

Paraguay, Bolivia, and Peru

began to buy some of the shares of a mining company controlled by Chileans and Frenchmen. Their railroad investment in Bolivia was made through a corporation, the Antofagasta and Bolivia Railway Company, whose capital is usually attributed to the English investment in Chile. Mines, lands, public utilities, and manufacturing are the main categories of British investment in Bolivia. Very little English money went into Bolivian government securities after 1872. The initial investment, from which heavy losses were suffered, served as an effective warning. Excluding the railroad capital referred to above, total nominal English capital operating in Bolivia probably did not amount to more than £2 million before the middle 1920's or far exceed £3 million at any time thereafter, although the *South American Journal's* estimates for recent years at times reached a nominal aggregate of more than £4.4 million, a sum which probably included the total capitalization of two or three mining companies in which Englishmen had only minority interests. Their most profitable investments in Bolivia were in the shares of such companies. But more about this later.

During the three quarters of a century following Paraguay's default on its sterling bonds in 1874 English capital in that country yielded very little income. A return of as much as 3 per cent on the total nominal investment was unusual. Sterling government securities were in default exactly half of the time and resumption of services always meant a paring down of the interest rate, so that Paraguay rarely paid more than 3 per cent and frequently paid only 1 per cent on its sterling bonds. The Paraguayan Land Company, organized to colonize and make profitable the more than two million acres of land ceded to English bondholders in 1886 in return for the cancellation of interest in arrears, was a failure. After two decades of vain effort to attract immigrants and develop its holdings, the company folded up. The railway investment, which expanded from £882,930 in 1890 to nearly £3 million a quarter of a century later, never paid an ordinary dividend, seldom paid a preference dividend, and soon failed to service more than the first-mortgage debentures, which had coupons of 6 and 7 per cent and a par value of from £600,000 to £750,000. The three big English companies organized in the twentieth century to engage in the livestock business are so closely connected with enterprises with headquarters in Argentina that it is impossible to determine how much of their profits they derived from Paraguay.

Country-by-Country Inspection

The oldest of these ranching enterprises is South American Cattle Farms, Limited, organized in 1910 by the management of Liebig's Extract of Meat Company and closely associated with that prosperous firm. During the two decades starting with the year 1913 South American Cattle Farms, which owned ranches in both Argentina and Paraguay, paid an annual average of 6.4 per cent on its nominal paid-up ordinary shares of £300,000; but no separate report of its earnings was published thereafter in *Stock Exchange Year-Book*. Assuming that its Paraguayan operations were as profitable as those in Argentina, this was probably the most remunerative enterprise ever owned by Englishmen in Paraguay. The other ranching enterprises are Paraguay Land and Cattle Company and Paraguayan Cattle Farms, Limited, both controlled by South American Assets Company, Limited, organized in 1920 to bail out such residents of the United Kingdom as had been captivated by the gigantic Percival Farquhar speculations in several South American republics. This holding company paid no dividend on its ordinary shares, £250,000 at par, during the first thirty years of its existence; but it carried a heavy load of 6 per cent debentures and reduced the nominal aggregate of capital invested in them from £350,000 to £168,393, and it is likely that the income which made this possible was drawn mainly from the two Paraguayan ranching organizations.

Very few economic enterprises operating in Bolivia under the control of investors living in the British Isles were remarkable for their high dividends. Most of the mining companies owned exclusively by Englishmen were near failures. Incomplete data suggest that Berenguela Tin Mines, Limited, organized in 1905 and dropped from the *Stock Exchange Year-Book*'s list after 1930, may have been one of the few exceptions, for during a stretch of twelve years beginning with 1916 this company yielded an annual average of 14.6 per cent on the par value of its paid-in capital, which expanded from £20,000 to £40,000 during this period. Bolivian General Enterprises, Limited, created in 1903 for the purpose of collecting wild rubber and experimenting in plantation rubber, soon turned to land speculation and public utilities. Although still in existence in 1950, it was practically bankrupt. In the course of forty-seven years it had paid only three dividends; but it had managed to earn enough to return to its shareholders half of the principal of their original investment of £275,052.

Paraguay, Bolivia, and Peru

A claim against the Bolivian government for expropriated lands was almost its sole asset in 1950. National Match Factory of Bolivia, Limited, established in 1907, collapsed in 1930 without having paid a dividend on either its ordinary or its 6 per cent preference shares, the first amounting to a nominal £50,000 and the second to a nominal £30,000; nor had it been able to service its 6 per cent debentures — £80,000, figured at par — since 1917. The two Bolivian subsidiaries of International Power Company, Limited, a Canadian holding company set up in 1926 with some English participation, probably did not prosper. At any rate, the record of the parent company, which also owns subsidiaries in Mexico and Venezuela, does not suggest large earnings from any source.

Yet the statistics published from time to time by the *South American Journal* disclose a high nominal rate of return from Bolivia in recent years: 31.6 per cent for 1942; 21.7 for 1943; 35.8 for 1946; 21.9 for 1948; and 20.8 for 1949. What is the explanation? In the first place, too much profitable capital of enterprises in which Englishmen had only minority holdings was listed as British capital merely because it was quoted on the London Stock Exchange. But, in the second place, returns were actually fairly high because investors residing in the United Kingdom owned a good portion, though less than a controlling share, of such capital.

Perhaps the earliest of the profitable companies in which Englishmen held a minority interest was Compañía Huanchaca de Bolivia, organized in 1873 by Chileans and Frenchmen to work silver mines. This enterprise, which financed the construction of the Antofagasta and Bolivia Railway, paid an average annual dividend of 32.5 per cent on a nominal paid-up capital of some £1.5 million during the twelve-year period beginning in 1883. It then ceased to prosper and was soon dissolved.[2]

Another very profitable enterprise with a minority British investment was Compagnie Aramayo de Mines en Bolivie, organized in England in 1906 as Aramayo, Francke and Company, but transferred to Switzerland under its new title in 1916. In addition to share bonuses amounting to 60 per cent, this company, which was engaged mainly in the mining of tin, returned an annual average dividend of slightly more than 22.5 per cent on its nominal ordinary capital — £600,000 at the outset, raised to approximately £1 million in 1928 and then reduced to the equivalent of £800,000 in 1936 — for the twenty years starting in 1910; and after passing four dividends and paying only 2.5 per cent in 1935, entered another prosperous period, returning a nominal 11.25 annually for the next decade and an average of 8 per cent annually from 1946 through 1949.[3]

A third profitable concern with fairly large English minority holdings is Patiño Mines and Enterprises, Consolidated, a Delaware Corporation organized in 1924 with a capital of over $27 million, reduced to $13.5 million in 1937 and to $6.75 million in 1946 without loss to shareholders. Besides large stock bonuses in affiliated companies, this mining corporation paid an annual average nominal dividend slightly in excess of 12 per cent during the first two decades of its operation and an average of 28.8 per cent for the seven years beginning in 1944.[4]

If Englishmen had owned all the capital of the Aramayo and Patiño companies their returns from Bolivia might have been as high at times as the *South American Journal* indicates; but since their holdings probably amounted to no more than a third or a fourth of the total securities of the two companies and since their unremunerative investment in Bolivia was practically as large as this profitable investment, the rate of return will need to be reduced to an annual average of around 12 or 15 per cent for the quarter of a century following 1924 and for the two earliest decades starting in 1890 the average will have to be reduced to about half that nominal rate. Even after making appropriate adjustments, however, it is more than likely that the Bolivian investment was for several decades one of the most profitable English investments in Latin America — profitable in spite of, perhaps even because of, the poverty of the Bolivian people.[5]

Peru

Two striking facts soon become evident in even a cursory inspection of the British investment in Peru: (1) the investment reached its peak in the 1870's and (2) from 65 to 90 per cent of the total after 1890 was tied up in one giant enterprise, the Peruvian Corporation Limited, an unprofitable investment which caused a decided reduction in the average annual returns on the total capital involved. The aggregate nominal English investment in Peru was in excess of £36. million in 1880, but only £19.1 million at the end of 1890. It rose to more than £25.6 million by the end of 1913 and mounted to another

Paraguay, Bolivia, and Peru

peak in 1935, exceeding £30 million by the end of that year, but shrank to a nominal total of £25 million or less by the close of 1949.

The main categories of English investment in Peru, as in many other Latin-American countries, were government bonds and railways. Contrary to what might have been expected, mining did not attract a very large share of English capital, only a little more than £1.3 million at its maximum in 1911;[6] nor did real estate, or public utilities, or manufacturing. But Englishmen were diligent in their search for Peru's petroleum and were finally handsomely rewarded for their efforts.

It will be recalled (see pp. 19–21) that residents of the United Kingdom made their first important investments in Peru in the early 1820's, when they purchased government securities with a par value of £1,816,000 and organized three or four mining companies with a nominal paid-up capital of some £250,000. Heavy losses made Englishmen wary for a time, but the new generation plunged again. After more than twenty years of default, the Peruvian government made a settlement with British bondholders in 1849, and it was shortly afterward that large new issues began to be floated in England. During the two decades beginning in 1853 a grand total of approximately £42.3 million, par value, was marketed in the United Kingdom and on the Continent. It was an epoch of tremendous enthusiasm for railways in Peru and these issues were sold mainly for the purpose of constructing, with Henry Meiggs of New York and California as promoter and supervisor, a number of lines running from the seacoast up into the high Andes. Englishmen had a nominal investment of some £33 million in Peruvian government securities in 1876, when every issue went into complete default. In 1890, after the national government at Lima had failed to service the bonds for a period of fourteen years, the Peruvian Corporation was organized to take over the railroads, which had been hypothecated as security, and bail out the unfortunate bondholders. Having burned their fingers twice, and very badly the second time, Englishmen became extremely cautious regarding Peruvian government bonds. They purchased no more new issues until 1909, and the par value of their holdings was less than £2 million as late as the end of 1913. Later, however, their investment in Peruvian government securities expanded until it reached £6 million, and it was still more than £3 million at the close of the year 1949.[7]

Country-by-Country Inspection

Englishmen began to invest directly in Peruvian railways at an early date, organizing their first enterprise, Arica and Tacna Railway Company, in 1857 and their second, Lima Railways Company, Limited, in 1865. They also bought some bonds issued by two railroad companies owned by the Peruvian government. But their biggest railway investment was thrust upon them in 1890, when they took over seven or eight lines in the process of trying to salvage their extravagant investment in Peruvian government bonds. The nominal value of English capital tied up in Peruvian railroads exceeded £18 million by the end of that year, and little reduction occurred between 1890 and 1950.

The investment of British capitalists in economic enterprises other than railways never amounted to more than a nominal £4 million or £5 million at any time. Their investment in mining, as already noted, was comparatively small. The same was true of public utilities, merely a minority interest in various tramway, gas, and electrical enterprises operating in Lima and an ephemeral investment in a telephone company. Their investment in the cultivation and milling of sugar was likewise small, and they owned only two manufacturing plants of any significance, a brewery and a textile mill. They organized several companies for the purpose of discovering and exploiting petroleum, but their investment in oil enterprises probably never amounted to more than £3 million.

Already I have intimated that the average yield of English capital invested in Peru was small. With the exception of a decade or so around the middle of the nineteenth century, when Peruvian government bonds averaged a regular 4.5 per cent and when the profits returned by the capital invested in the guano business were high, the average nominal annual yield never quite reached 5 per cent. It was only 2.7 in 1913 and 3.4 in 1924. The average for the following six years was almost 4 per cent, but afterwards there was a decided slump which brought the average for the nineteen years starting with 1931 down to a mere 1.6 per cent.

For the period beginning in 1909 and ending in 1930, government securities were, on the whole, the most profitable English investment in Peru. Coupons ranged from 5 to 7.5 per cent, and the nominal average rate of return was approximately 6 per cent during this period. Then began several years of default and a downward adjustment

Paraguay, Bolivia, and Peru

interest rates, so that the average annual nominal yield from 1931 through 1949 was barely 1 per cent.

As previously indicated, British railway capital yielded only meager returns, and this was true for most of the period before 1890 as well as for the decades that followed. Ordinary shares with a par value of £9 million, approximately half of the investment in the Peruvian Corporation, which owned 80 per cent of Peru's railways, never paid a single dividend during the first sixty years of the corporation's existence. For ten years or so during the 1860's and 1870's the rate of return on the railroad investment averaged about 5 per cent; but for the six decades following 1890 the nominal average was less than 3 per cent.

A few of the miscellaneous economic enterprises owned by Englishmen were more profitable. Backus and Johnston's Brewery Company, Limited, founded in 1889, was prosperous for at least half of the first sixty years of its operation. For the decade beginning in 1940 it paid an average nominal dividend of 7.7 per cent annually on its £110,000 in ordinary shares and serviced £65,000 in 7 per cent debentures. The Peruvian Cotton Manufacturing Company, Limited, organized in 1890 and apparently dissolved in 1918, paid an annual average of 7.2 per cent on its nominal capital — £80,183 in 1898, raised to £100,000 in 1915 — for the two decades beginning in 1898. A banking enterprise in which Englishmen had a minority investment, Banco del Perú y Londres, paid an average annual dividend of over 10 per cent on its nominal capital for a quarter of a century (1905–1929).

Nearly all of the some twenty-five or thirty mining companies owned by Englishmen in Peru at one time or another failed to prosper. Anglo-French Ticapampa Silver Mining Company, in which they held only a minority interest, was probably more profitable than any other. Organized in 1903, it paid its first dividend in 1905 and an average of nearly 16 per cent annually down through the year 1919 on a nominal capital ranging from £100,000 to £140,000; but made no further payment to its owners between 1920 and 1950!

Three of the six English companies organized to explore for petroleum in Peru — Peruvian Petroleum Syndicate, founded in 1901; Peru Syndicate, founded in 1919; and Mancora Oilfields, Limited, registered in 1920 — probably made only slim profits, if any; and two others — London and Pacific Petroleum Company, founded in 1889, and Lagu-

Country-by-Country Inspection

nitos Oil Company, organized in 1911 — had to wait several years for the rich harvest. But the sixth enterprise, Lobitos Oilfields, Limited, organized in 1908, began promptly to yield remarkable dividends.

Starting with a nominal paid-up capital of £360,000, all in ordinary shares, which was raised to at least £1 million by 1925, Lobitos returned an annual average of 18.2 per cent during the thirty-eight-year period beginning in 1912. Not a single dividend was passed, and a 40 per cent bonus in the shares of Anglo-Ecuadorian Oilfields, Limited (£160,000, figured at par), was paid to the shareholders in 1919.

More remarkable still was the financial record of International Petroleum Company, Limited, a Canadian corporation organized in 1920 mainly for the purpose of acquiring the holdings of the London and Pacific and the Lagunitos companies. International Petroleum, which also owned producing properties in Colombia, was organized as a subsidiary of Standard Oil of New Jersey, but the two affiliated English companies seem to have traded their holdings for blocks of its shares. For three decades beginning in 1921 International Petroleum paid an average annual dividend of 40 per cent on a nominal capital of approximately $36 million! No year passed without a reward to its shareholders; the return was no less than 100 per cent annually for four consecutive years (1935-1938)! But English investors probably did not own more than a fourth of its securities, perhaps not more than an equivalent of £2 million.[8]

Two or three very profitable investments amounting to only £5 million or so could make no very marked improvement in the average returns on British capital invested in Peru when from £9 million to more than £20 million failed to yield income every year from 1890 through 1950. The capital tied up in the Peruvian Corporation was the dead weight that brought the average earnings down. It is appropriate to conclude with a glance at its recent record. Not only had its ordinary shares with a par value of £9 million never paid a dividend; its preference stock with a par value of £7.5 million had returned no dividend since 1930, and its 6 per cent debentures amounting to nearly £4 million were in arrears, having received only 3 per cent annually in 1947, 1948, and 1949. Average rates of return on the English investment in Peru would continue to be low until this dead capital could be revived or discarded.[9]

⇋ XI ⇌

THE CHILEAN EXPERIENCE

More stable than the average Spanish American republic and as well endowed with natural resources as most of them, Chile soon became a favorite among a few British investors and for many years justified their confidence. The major disappointments came well after 1900, and were mainly the result of conditions in the world outside, over which neither Chileans nor Englishmen could exercise effective control.

A Summary View of the Investment and Rates of Return

More than a hundred years have passed since investors living in the British Isles ventured their first capital in Chile. Their investment was comparatively small, however, until toward the end of the nineteenth century. The nominal total was hardly more than £8.4 million, nearly all of it in government bonds, at the close of the year 1880 and not much in excess of £24 million at the end of 1890. It was somewhat more than £51 million by the end of 1910, some £64 million at the close of 1913, and nearly £79 million at the end of 1926. The investment never rose much higher than this latter sum. A contraction soon set in, which brought the nominal aggregate down to around £45 million in 1949, and all signs indicated that it would shortly be considerably less.[1]

The largest segment of British capital in Chile was nearly always in government bonds. At its maximum in the year 1913 the total in government securities, figured at par, was approximately £34.6 million. The nominal aggregate had been £7.7 million in 1880, £9.5 million in 1890, and more than £25.5 million in 1910; and it was still above £20 million at the end of 1949.

Next in size was the capital invested in Chilean railways, which surely would have been larger if the Chileans had not disclosed a de-

133

cided inclination toward government ownership shortly after 1850. The exact magnitude of the British investment in Chilean railroads is difficult to determine because Englishmen invested in some railways controlled by Chileans, particularly the Aguas Blancas, the Copiapó, the Coquimbo, and the Tongoy, as well as in British-controlled lines. The British investment in railroads was probably in the neighborhood of £8 million by the end of 1890, more than twice that sum in 1910, and near its peak in 1913, when the nominal aggregate stood at £20.4 million.

Crowding close behind the railroad capital was the capital invested in the nitrate business, which exceeded £5.3 million by the end of 1890 and continued to expand until it reached a nominal aggregate of £20 million or more around 1928 before the American Guggenheims plunged into the Chilean nitrate gamble. The capital of some of the nitrate companies was diluted by liberal injections of water.

Englishmen invested in Chilean mining at an early date. Their most important mining enterprise in the country was the Copiapó Mining Company, Limited, founded in 1836; but their investment in this category probably never far exceeded £2 million. Their investment in public utilities, which seems to have begun with the Copiapó Gas Company, Limited, in 1858, was nearly as large. The most important British investment in shipping was in the Pacific Steam Navigation Company, founded in 1840; but since this company operated up and down the Pacific coast to Panama, all of its capital can hardly be ascribed to Chile. The investment in the livestock business was never large. Apparently Englishmen never placed their capital in more than three or four pastoral enterprises of any magnitude, and one of these was partly in Chile and partly in Argentina. The investment in manufacturing, except possibly in a few branch plants, was confined mainly to a munitions factory and a flour mill. The most important enterprise engaged in merchandising was Chilian Stores (Gath and Chaves), Limited, controlled by a British firm in Argentina.

The *South American Journal* lists all of these investments, except those in government securities and railways, under the broad category of miscellaneous, presenting estimates for the years 1910 and 1913 and for each year from 1923 through 1949. For the period beginning in 1931 and ending in 1940, however, the *Journal*'s figures are undoubtedly too high. The British investment in Chile, other than their capital

The Chilean Experience

in government bonds and railroads, amounted to some £6.6 million in 1890, over £11 million in 1900, above £28 million in 1926, and less than £9 million in 1949.[2]

Average rates of return [3] from British capital in Chile were among the highest recorded for the Latin-American countries until 1930, but after that year they slumped until they became almost as low as the yields on the Mexican investment, which was on the whole the least remunerative of all the major British investments in this part of the world. Except for the early 1890's, the average nominal return from British capital invested in Chile rarely fell below 5 per cent until 1931. It was 4.8 in 1910 and 5.9 in 1913, and for the eight years starting with 1923 it averaged almost 6.3 per cent, rising to a maximum of 10.6 in 1926, when the total income from a nominal investment of £78.8 million amounted to £8.4 million. But the lean years were not far off. The average nominal rate of return plunged down from 4.7 in 1930 to 0.3 in 1933, remained below 1 per cent until 1937, and did not rise to 2 per cent again until 1949, when the yield was 2.1. The decline cannot be attributed entirely to default on government bonds, although every Chilean sterling issue went into default in 1932 and service was not resumed until 1936, and even then at an average interest rate of less than 2 per cent (in fact, less than 1 per cent for 1936, 1937, and 1938) for every year except 1939, when the yield was 2.1, and 1949, when it was exactly 2. Neither can the slump be attributed mainly to the diminution in railway earnings, although these dropped to 1.3 in 1932 and never rose to 2 per cent again. Nor can it be ascribed largely to the inflated capitalization and deflated markets for nitrates. The slump was well nigh universal.

Chile defaulted for a period of nearly twenty years on its first sterling loan, an issue of £1 million floated in 1822; but for a period of exactly nine decades thereafter the debt record of the Chilean government approached perfection. This signified that Chilean government bonds were a sound investment calculated to yield steady income, but it also meant that Chile could borrow money at a moderate rate of interest. In fact, the rate ranged from 4.5 to 5 per cent for many years. The average nominal yield on British holdings of Chilean government securities was 4.7 per cent in 1910 and 4.8 in 1913. Owing to new flotations at slightly higher rates, the average annual nominal return was a little above 5 per cent for the nine years starting in

1923. Afterwards came the debacle already described, but a considerable number of Englishmen had already made fortunes in Chile.

The railway investment, until 1931, was more profitable than the investment in government securities, but was equally unprofitable after that time. There were a few years during the 1880's and late 1890's when the nominal railway capital yielded an average of 8 or 10 per cent per annum. The average return was 4.7 in 1910 and 5.6 in 1913, and for the eight-year period beginning with 1923 the annual nominal average was approximately 7 per cent.

Most profitable of all, until 1927, when synthetic nitrates began drastically to force down prices, was the investment described as miscellaneous by the *South American Journal*. Although profits derived by English capitalists from a monopoly of natural nitrate of soda were mainly responsible for the high yields under this heading, companies engaged in other economic activities often paid good dividends, as will be observed when the records of some of them are examined in the pages that follow. Except for three or four years in the early 1890's, these miscellaneous investments returned a nominal annual average of 10 to 15 per cent during the last two decades of the nineteenth century. They yielded 11.1 per cent in 1913 and an annual nominal average rate of approximately 11 per cent for the four years starting with 1923. Thereafter the returns were low, the highest yields after 1926 being 4.4 per cent in 1927 and 4 per cent in 1928.

Dividend Records of Some Profitable Companies

Regarding the dividend records of specific companies, it can be stated at the outset that British manufacturing enterprises in Chile, judged by the information available,* proved rather unprofitable. The Chilian National Ammunition Company, Limited, established in San Bernardo in 1896, paid an annual average return on its approximately £35,000 (par value) in ordinary shares of not quite 6 per cent during the decade starting with the year 1897 and seldom paid a dividend thereafter. Outstanding debentures, ranging from £18,000 to £20,000 over the years, yielded a steady 6 per cent; but unless the share capital was greatly inflated, this was a poor return for the total investment. A venture in the manufacture of textiles, Chilian Mills Company, Limited, organized in 1900, turned out to be a complete failure and was

* Information is scanty for branch plants, if any, of such firms as Dunlop Rubber Company, Limited, Imperial Chemicals, and Eno Proprietaries.

The Chilean Experience

closed down after twelve years of operation. Santa Rosa Milling Company, Limited, established in 1913 to engage in the milling of flour at both Callao, Peru, and Concepción, Chile, with Chile as its main center of operations, yielded an average nominal return of 8.2 per cent annually on its ordinary shares — £262,500 — for a period of sixteen years starting in 1914 and ending in 1929, but paid only three ordinary dividends from 1930 through 1949 (3 per cent in 1931, only 2.5 in 1948, and 5 in 1949). Preference shares, however, amounting to £137,500, usually paid the stipulated noncumulative 7 per cent.

The four British-owned public utilities in Chile were, on the whole, fairly profitable. Available records for the earliest of them, the Copiapó Gas Company, Limited, organized in 1858 and controlled by English capital for a quarter of a century, indicate a steady yield of 7.5 per cent per annum on its nominal capital of £25,000, all in ordinary shares. Valparaíso Drainage Company, Limited, established in 1880, was much more profitable until it was reorganized and overcapitalized in 1905. Starting out with a paid-up nominal capital of approximately £92,000, a little more than half of it in shares * and the rest in debentures (presumably 5 per cents), this company paid an average nominal annual dividend on its ordinary capital of slightly more than 13 per cent for the seventeen years beginning in 1888. Its ordinary capital was then inflated to £150,000, and £100,000 in new debentures with 5 per cent coupons were soon issued; and, as if this watering were not enough, the share capital was raised to £160,000 in 1912, divided equally between 5 per cent cumulative preference and ordinary. It is no wonder that the ordinary shareholders went without dividends most of the time thereafter. They received an average of less than 2.6 annually on the par value of their securities during the next seventeen years and no income whatever thereafter. Even the preference shareholders were deprived of their 5 per cent after 1931, but the debentures were finally redeemed in 1946, and the 21 million Chilean paper pesos (approximately £260,000) in Valparaíso municipal bonds, bearing interest at 7 per cent, which this company was paid for its property in 1948, would perhaps provide a better income. The bonds were guaranteed by the national government.

The dividend record of the Tarapacá Waterworks Company, Lim-

* A few of these shares were deferred ordinary, paying smaller dividends. *Stock Exchange Year-Book* does not reveal the exact amount of capital invested in them.

ited, organized in 1888 to supply water to Iquique and the surrounding communities of that arid region, was excellent. The company skipped only two dividends during a period of more than sixty years (1947 and 1949) and paid an annual average of nearly 7 per cent from 1888 through 1946, while for the twenty years starting in 1908 and ending in 1927 the annual nominal average was better than 9.3. The face value of the ordinary shares was £400,000 at the outset, but this sum was reduced, by repayment from earnings, to £160,000 by 1925. An issue of £50,000 in 5.5 per cent debentures floated in the early 1890's was soon paid off and there were never any preference shares.[4]

The Chili Telephone Company, Limited, established in 1889, was even more profitable if its stock bonuses — £319,000 in all — are taken into account. Its ordinary shares — no preference shares were ever issued — which amounted to a par of £200,000 in 1890 and £220,000 from 1895 to 1909, were expanded to £900,000 by late 1926 by the payment of these paper bonuses and the sale of shares at par to existing stockholders, and the company finally sold its properties in 1927–1928 to the American Telephone and Telegraph Corporation for 160 per cent of the face value of this inflated capital.[5] Dividends averaged only a nominal 3 per cent annually for the decade beginning in 1890, but rose to 6.6 during the following ten-year period, and to 7.7 for the decade starting in 1910, without reckoning with two stock bonuses amounting to a total of over 83 per cent. The annual average for the 1920's was just under 6 per cent in cash, besides a share bonus of 20 per cent paid out in 1924.

The most profitable British mining investment in Chile was the old Copiapó Mining Company, already mentioned. With a par capital of approximately £170,000 in 1880 and £225,000 by 1900, all in ordinary shares, this company's dividends averaged approximately 11 per cent annually from 1881 through 1901. Then its old copper mine played out.

The preceding statistics will at least suggest that the nitrate business was not solely responsible for the high returns on the British miscellaneous investment in Chile during the period before the world economic depression of the 1930's. The profits extracted by some of the British enterprises from the Chilean nitrate beds, however, were very handsome, as pointed out in Chapter III. The *South American Journal* assembled in June 1914,[6] some statistics from the recent reports of fifteen of the larger companies. The average yield on their

The Chilean Experience

nominal capital, including debentures and preference shares as well as ordinary, was 13.4 per cent in 1912 and 16.7 in 1913. And the two most profitable of all the British-owned nitrate companies, the Liverpool and the London, were not among the fifteen. The London Company paid 25 per cent on the par value of its ordinary shares, amounting to £180,000, in both 1912 and 1913; the Liverpool Company paid 125 per cent on its par of £56,800 in ordinary shares in 1912 and 150 per cent in 1913! Such returns were not very unusual for either of these two dividend-coiners, as a short summary of their records will reveal.

The Liverpool Nitrate Company, Limited, was created in 1883. Its ordinary shares were reduced from £110,000 in 1885 to £44,000 in 1905 by the repayment of capital and then gradually raised to £350,000 by 1924. Leaving out of consideration a share bonus of 300 per cent paid in 1922, the average nominal annual dividend for the forty years extending from 1885 through 1924 was 56.3 per cent!

The London Nitrate Company, Limited, was organized in 1898 with a nominal capital of £160,000, of which only £50,000 represented ordinary shares until the preference shares were transformed into ordinary shares in 1905. The share capital was then gradually expanded to £200,000 (all ordinary shares still) by 1920. For the decade starting in 1888 and ending in 1897 the ordinary dividends averaged 89.2 per cent annually! During the next ten years the annual average was 14 per cent; for the decade beginning in 1908 the per-annum average was 20.5 per cent; and for the next eight years (until the company was placed in "voluntary liquidation") the annual average was 12.5.

Salar del Carmen Nitrate Syndicate, Limited, another very profitable nitrate corporation, founded in 1896, was included in the *South American Journal*'s profitable list of 1912–1913. This organization and Alianza Nitrate Company are among the few nitrate firms with dividend records that approached those of the Liverpool and the London companies. With a nominal capital of some £100,000 at the outset and £200,000 by 1918, all in ordinary shares, Salar del Carmen paid an annual average nominal dividend of nearly 20 per cent from 1898 through 1907, an annual average of 18.25 during the next decade, and an average of 21.25 per cent annually from 1918 through 1925. Alianza paid an annual nominal average of 20.4 per cent on £500,000 during a period of twenty-six years (1903–1928).

A few comments on British income from three of the Chilean rail-

Country-by-Country Inspection

ways will conclude this summary. Among the eight or ten railroad enterprises which Englishmen owned at one time or another in Chile, the Taltal Railway Company, Limited, organized in 1881, the Nitrate Railways Company, Limited, established in 1882, and the Antofagasta and Bolivia Railway Company, Limited, incorporated in 1888, were the most important and the most profitable. The first two were in the nitrate region. The third furnished an outlet for ores and other products of Bolivia and Northern Chile.

The £425,000 in ordinary shares of the Taltal Railway Company were increased to £550,000 by 1905, to £900,000 by 1912, and to £1,200,000 by 1920, at least £450,000 of the expansion being the result of the payment of share bonuses. Dividends on this nominal capital averaged only 4.4 per cent annually for the two decades beginning with 1886, but the annual average increased to 7.7 per cent, not including a stock bonus of 20 per cent, for the decade starting with 1906, and to 8.1 per cent for the next ten years, again without including a stock bonus — a new share for every three shares held — in 1924. Moreover, dividends continued to be fairly good until 1931: 5 per cent in 1927 and 6 per cent each year for the next three years. A tremendous slump then occurred. Although all outstanding debentures had been redeemed and no preference shares had ever been issued, the ordinary dividend dropped rapidly to 1 per cent in 1936 and no payment whatever was made from 1939 through 1949.

The Nitrate Railways Company expanded its ordinary shares, mainly by the payment of stock bonuses, from a par value of £1,200,000 in 1886 to £1,380,000 in 1890, to £2,291,670 in 1926, and to £2,365,840 shortly afterward. For the five years beginning in 1888 cash dividends averaged 22 per cent per annum, for the next five they averaged above 10 per cent, and for the thirty-two years starting in 1898 and ending in 1929 they averaged almost 5.5 per cent annually. Then followed the famine decades, with a yield of 2 per cent in 1930, no returns whatever during the next six years, and 1.25 per cent each year from 1938 through 1949,* when the company finally announced its intention to cease operating

The Antofagasta and Bolivia Railway Company's ordinary shares amounted to £1,410,000 in 1890 and £2,200,000 from 1895 through 1905

---

* There were also some deferred ordinary and some preferred shares, but these went through so many permutations and convolutions that it has proved impossible to make definite statements regarding the capital involved or income trends.

The Chilean Experience

(par values). Throughout this early period dividends were held down to a steady 6 per cent by the Huanchaca Mining Company (Compañía Huanchaca de Bolivia), which controlled the railway corporation. After 1903, however, the railway company became independent and profits began to mount. For a period of twenty-six years from 1904 on, ordinary dividends averaged 8.74 per cent annually in spite of a tremendous expansion of capital — mainly through the payment of stock bonuses — which totaled £2,253,744 by 1930. The nominal capital in ordinary shares was £5,578,560 million by 1920 and £6,415,344 by 1930. But there were no ordinary dividends between 1930, when 4 per cent was paid, and 1950. Dividends on the company's preference shares — £2,000,000 — were also somewhat in arrears by 1950. Its debentures — amounting to £4,908,950 in 1930 and to £2,479,833 in 1949 — had always been promptly serviced, however.

What of the future of British investments in Chile? Conditions in 1950 indicated the probability of contraction rather than expansion. But the investment did not appear to be on the verge of liquidation. No tendency toward a rapid amortization of the some £20 million in government bonds outstanding at the end of 1949 was apparent. The railway investment, with a nominal capital of over £16.2 million in 1949, would soon be reduced to half that sum, for only the Antofagasta and Bolivia Railway Company seemed destined to survive. The miscellaneous investment, somewhat more than £8.8 million at the end of 1949, probably would be restricted to branch plants engaged in manufacturing and merchandizing and to minority holdings in a few big and not entirely unprofitable consolidations engaged in the exploitation of nitrates and iodine.

⇋ XII ⇌

SURPRISINGLY PROFITABLE VENTURES IN URUGUAY

For more than seventy years after winning its independence in 1828 Uruguay was one of the most turbulent republics of Latin America, and its politicians displayed a decided tendency toward state socialism after it finally achieved stability. But in spite of political disorders and socialistic tendencies, Uruguay became a comparatively important and profitable field for investment by capitalists of the British Isles.[1]

Growth and Decline of the Investment; Average Yields

Beginning in the 1860's, this investment had a par value of some £7.6 million by the end of 1880, expanded by more than £27.7 by the end of the next decade, stood at slightly above £35.8 million at the close of 1900, and rose to its peak in 1923, when it reached £46,186,893. The contraction that followed was gradual at first, but more rapid during the 1940's. The aggregate British investment in Uruguay was approximately £39.2 million at the close of 1939 and somewhere between £20 and £26.6 million at the end of 1949.

The major part of the investment from the beginning had been in government securities. As observed in Chapter II, the first sterling loan, £1 million, was made to the City of Montevideo in 1864, and the second, £3,500,000, was a loan to the national government in 1871. In spite of three years of default in the late 1870's, the British investment in Uruguayan government bonds increased to over £16.1 million, figured at par, by the end of 1890. By the close of the year 1900 it was more than £22.4 million, and it rose to its highest point in 1910, when it exceeded £26.5 million. It then declined to approximately £18.5 million by the end of 1939 and to a little less than £16.2 million a decade later.

Next largest was the English investment in railroads, which amounted

Profitable Ventures in Uruguay

to approximately £2.4 million in 1880, £9 million in 1890, £11 million in 1900, and £15.3 million in 1913. The nominal investment was some £14.5 million at the close of 1947, and early the next year the British-owned railways were all sold to the Uruguayan government.[2]

Other fields of investment included public utilities, real estate, and manufacturing, especially utilities. From time to time Englishmen also placed small sums in mining and other enterprises. Their investment in commercial banking was in branch establishments the value of which has not been ascertained.

British capitalists had occasional difficulties with both the national government of Uruguay and the municipal government of Montevideo, especially with reference to subsidy contracts, railway and public-utility rates, and official labor and welfare policies. During the first two decades of the twentieth century, in particular, they complained of socialistic tendencies and rising tax rates. On the whole, however, relations were fairly harmonious, and Englishmen expressed their confidence in the honor and integrity of Uruguayan administrators and courts. Moreover, it is likely that their investment in Uruguay yielded as high returns over the years as their capital in almost any other Latin-American country, perhaps not even excepting Argentina and Chile. This was the impression of the *South American Journal*, which seems to be supported by the company records published in the *Stock Exchange Year-Book*. Among the favorable references to Uruguay published by the *Journal*, two may appropriately be quoted at this point. In its issue for August 22, 1931, the *Journal* remarked: "From time to time one hears complaints as to the alleged antagonistic attitude of the Government of Uruguay towards foreign capital, and the excessive costs of social services and taxation, especially the absentee landlord tax on British enterprises. On the other hand there are many investors who speak with enthusiasm of their Uruguayan financial experience and, moreover, the statistics show steady and consistent results not always observable in studying the affairs of other Latin-American countries."[3] In its issue dated August 1, 1936, the *Journal* made this positive statement: "Compared with the average return which British investors have received on their money placed in the Latin-American countries, their experience in Uruguay is fortunate. . . . The return is, and practically always has been, relatively greater than in any other country of Latin America."[4]

Country-by-Country Inspection

For more than half a century (until 1931) the nominal rate of return on the aggregate British investment in Uruguay rarely fell below 4.5 per cent. It was 4.5 per cent in 1910 and 4.6 per cent in 1913. It was 5.1 per cent in both 1928 and 1929, and it reached its peak in 1930 with a yield of 5.2 per cent. It dropped to its lowest point, 2.6 per cent, in 1936, and it was 4.9 per cent in 1948 and 4.7 in 1949.

After the late 1870's there was no default on Uruguayan government bonds except for the single year 1891, and this default was quickly remedied by the emission of bonds refunding the overdue interest. In connection with this settlement, however, the interest rate on all the Uruguayan sterling issues was reduced, so that the nominal return on this segment of the British investment never rose above 4 per cent again. In fact, with the exception of the period from 1923 through 1930, when 4 per cent was paid each year, the annual yield ranged from 3.5 to 3.9 per cent.

The railway investment, much of it guaranteed by the Uruguayan government, paid reasonably good returns until the crisis of the 1890's, when the government guaranty was reduced from 7 to 3.5 per cent. For a decade thereafter the annual nominal return on the railroad capital seldom rose above 4 per cent. It was 4.3 per cent in 1910 and 4.5 in 1913. It did not reach 5 per cent until 1926. It was 5 per cent again in 1927 and it rose to 5.1 in 1928. Then it began a decline from which it never recovered, dropping from 5 per cent in 1929 to 2 per cent in 1932. From that date until the railways were finally sold to the Uruguayan government early in 1948 for £7,150,000, less than half the total of their nominal capital, the annual average return never reached 2 per cent again; in fact, it was usually less than 1 per cent.

Returns on the British investment in other economic enterprises, described by the *South American Journal* as miscellaneous investments, were much higher. They were 7.5 per cent, for example, in 1910 and 7.6 per cent in 1913, and for the twenty-seven years beginning in 1923 and ending in 1949 the average annual nominal yield was approximately 7 per cent. The highest return for the period after 1900 was 11.2 per cent in 1930, which, as already observed, was the year when the nominal rate reached its peak of 5.2 per cent on the entire British investment in Uruguay. With the exception of the capital in the United Tramways of Montevideo, Limited, and the futile mining investment, practically all of the British enterprises in this miscellaneous

Profitable Ventures in Uruguay

group were profitable, some of them among the most profitable investments residents of the British Isles ever had anywhere in Latin America. The dividend records of the most important of them will be discussed in the section that follows.[5]

Survey of Companies Conspicuous for High Yields

The Pranges Estancia Company, Limited (name changed to La Concordia Estancia Company in 1916), founded in 1867 to raise sheep and cattle, began to pay dividends of 8 per cent annually on its £116,000 of ordinary shares in 1884. For the decade beginning with that year the average nominal rate of return, however, was only a little more than 5.3 per cent, owing to the depression of the early 1890's. For the decade beginning with 1894 the average annual nominal yield was 8.2 per cent and for the following decade it rose to 16.1 per cent. For the ten years beginning with 1914 the nominal average annual return was nearly 21.2 per cent, the dividend being 28 per cent during three years of the period. The ordinary share capital (there was never any other) had been raised to a par of £120,000 in 1916. The dividend was 12 per cent in 1924, 16.5 per cent in 1925, and 18 per cent in 1926. Then plans for liquidation began. Between 1927 and the end of 1929 a total of 122.25 per cent was returned to the stockholders and the company was dissolved in 1930. For a period of forty-five years there was not a single failure to pay a dividend.

Uruguay United Estancias, Limited, organized in 1905 likewise to enter the sheep and cattle business, was by no means as profitable as the Pranges ranch, but it returned some fairly high dividends, the highest being 20 per cent for the year 1920. From the time the enterprise was fully established in 1909 until it was finally liquidated in 1937–1938 with a return of £7.5 for each £5 share, its ordinary capital was £65,000. For the ten years from 1909 through 1918 the average annual nominal return was 9.5 per cent. For the next decade the average annual nominal yield dropped to 7.7 per cent, no dividend being paid in 1921 or 1923. For the next eight years the total dividend, including the 50 per cent profit returned at the time the company was dissolved, was 65 per cent, or a nominal annual average of a little over 8 per cent.

From the year after its organization in 1872 until the end of the year 1949 the Montevideo Gas Company, Limited (title changed to

Country-by-Country Inspection

Montevideo Gas and Dry Dock Company in 1919), failed only twice to return an annual dividend. Its ordinary shares ranged from £500,000 to £675,000. For the decade beginning with the year 1873 the annual average nominal return was 6.1 per cent. For the next decade it was 5.9 per cent. For the ten years beginning in 1893 it was 4.9 per cent and for the next ten it dropped to an annual nominal average of 3.55. It then rose to 4.1 for the period from 1913 through 1922 and to 5.1 for the next decade. The nominal annual average was approximately 4 per cent for the decade beginning in 1933 and the same annual average continued through 1949. This was a genuine investment; there was only one stock bonus, 12.5 per cent in 1929. Debentures, never more than £100,000 and usually much less, paid from 5 to 6 per cent.

The Montevideo Waterworks Company, Limited, organized in 1879, was not very profitable during the first decade of its existence, paying no dividend until 1883 and recording an annual nominal average of only 2.15 per cent for the ten-year period. For the next ten years, however, the annual average was 5 per cent and for the decade ending in 1908 it was 6.3. For the twenty years extending from 1909 through 1928 the annual average rose to 8 per cent and for the next twenty years it was 6.5 per cent. There were also two share bonuses, the first, in 1918, being 12.5 per cent and the second, in 1937, being 25 per cent. The ordinary share capital, a par of £350,200 when the company began to pay dividends in the early 1880's, was gradually increased until it reached £1,625,000 at the end of 1937, and outstanding debentures with 5 per cent coupons ranged from £252,500 in the 1880's to £500,000 in the 1940's. Capitalized at £2,125,000 in 1947, the company sold its assets to the Uruguayan government late in 1948 for the sum of £3,182,471. Holders of the ordinary stock were paid a dividend of 8 per cent in 1949, and in 1950 they received 50 per cent above par for every ordinary share they held, £1.5 for each £1 share (face value).

Profits from these two utilities were offset by the comparatively low returns from two others: Montevideo Telephone Company, Limited, organized in 1888, and United Electric Tramways of Montevideo, Limited, established in 1905. Control of the tramways company was acquired early in 1927 by the Atlas Light and Power Company, Limited (name soon changed to Atlas Electric and General Trust), and after more than forty years of rather unprofitable operation it was sold to the Municipality of Montevideo late in 1947 for the sum of 11,700,000

Profitable Ventures in Uruguay

Uruguayan pesos, the equivalent of £1,540,000, its owners suffering a capital loss of probably as much as £4,000,000.[6]

For the first decade of its existence United Electric Tramways paid fairly good dividends on its ordinary shares — £250,000 at the outset, £400,000 by 1910, and £500,000 from 1913 to 1927. It paid an annual average of 5.5 per cent for the decade. During the next ten years, however, only two dividends were returned, 4 per cent in 1915 and 4 per cent in 1921. No dividends were paid in 1922, 1923, or 1924, and only 3 per cent in 1925 and 1926. Atlas Electric and General Trust, the holding company, paid dividends of 5 per cent on its ordinary shares each year from 1927 through 1930. Then the return dropped to 3 per cent in 1931 and 1 per cent in 1932. Thereafter, until it sold its Montevideo tramway enterprise in 1947, no ordinary dividends were paid. Assuming that Atlas and General Electric Trust's main investment was in this tramway system, which seems to have been the case after it sold its Argentine properties in 1928, this was a very meager dividend record for the ordinary shares. But the total investment in the Montevideo tramways included much larger sums in preference shares and debentures. The interest rate on the preference shares, which usually involved the same, or a little more, capital than the ordinary shares, ranged from 6 to 7 per cent, cumulative, and this rate was promptly paid, as a rule. Debentures amounting to from £500,000 to £950,000 (Atlas Electric's stood at £750,000 between 1929 and 1947) paid 5 per cent regularly. The truth is that the United Electric Tramways were overcapitalized from the outset, and especially after 1929 when the total capitalization of Atlas Electric and General Trust was fixed at £6,750,000 (£3 million ordinary, £3 million in 7 per cent preference, and £750,000 in 5 per cent debentures).

Montevideo Telephone Company, Limited, was an unprofitable enterprise during the decade following its organization. Capitalized at the beginning at £215,000, of which £75,000 were ordinary shares and the rest preference, it paid only one ordinary dividend during its first decade — 2.5 per cent in 1889 — and its 6 per cent preference shares fell into arrears. The company was reorganized in 1898, perhaps with some actual losses to the shareholders. The ordinary share capital was reduced to £72,680 and the 6 per cent preference to £86,492, but both were later increased by the issuance of stock bonuses, and the issued capital stood at approximately £220,000 in 1929, all ordinary shares of £1 each. No dividend was paid on the ordinary in 1898 and only 2.5 per cent per annum was paid during the next four years. For 1903 and 1904 the return was only 3 per cent each year, but for 1905 it was 4 and for 1906 it was 5, and for the thirteen years extending from 1907 through 1919 the return was 6 per cent annually. During the three years ending in 1922 the dividend was 8 per cent annually; it was 5 per cent in 1923 and 1924 and 7 per cent in 1926. The next year the British shareholders sold their securities to the International Telephone and Telegraph Corporation at twice their face value, receiving £2 in cash for each £1 share. Thus there were seventeen lean years (1888–1904) for the Montevideo Telephone Company and twenty-three fairly fat ones (1905–1927).

The most profitable enterprise ever owned by Englishmen in Uruguay, Liebig's Extract of Meat Company, Limited, founded in 1865 to engage in both the raising of cattle and the processing of beef, remains to be described. Its first packing plant was built at Fray Bentos, Uruguay, but later it constructed plants in both Argentina and Africa, and it eventually invested in stock ranches in Argentina and Paraguay as well as Uruguay, so that its total capital was by no means confined to Uruguay. Nevertheless, it was from Uruguay that it drew its main profits for many years, even if not down to the middle of the twentieth century. Until 1900 its capital consisted entirely of ordinary shares, increased from a par of £250,000 at the outset to £600,000 in 1907, £1,200,000 in 1921, and £2,000,000 shortly afterward. For the decade beginning in 1874 the average nominal return on this part of the capital was slightly above 10 per cent. For the twenty years from 1884 through 1903 it was a little over 19 per cent. For the next decade it was 23 per cent, and for the next it was 22.5. Then there was a marked decline, but the returns were still high: an annual nominal average rate of 13.7 during 1924–1933 and a per-annum average of 9.8 for the decade of 1934–1943. For the years 1944 and 1945 the yield was 8 per cent each year and for 1946 through 1949 the annual return was 9 per cent. In addition, the shareholders were paid a bonus of £125,000 in 5 per cent preference shares in 1900, and by 1949 this preference capital, most of it sold to the ordinary stockholders at par, had been increased to £2 million.

The Liebig company, then capitalized at £4 million, and the company in possession of the gasworks and the dock at Montevideo, capi-

Profitable Ventures in Uruguay

talized at £682,045, were the most important economic enterprises owned by British investors in Uruguay at the end of the year 1949. The *South American Journal*'s estimate for miscellaneous investments in Uruguay at this time was £10,432,045, but the *Journal* seems to have included the nominal capital of Atlas Electric and General Trust in its estimate and it is not likely that the total investment of this trust, or even the major part of it, was still in Uruguay after the sale of its Montevideo tramway interests in 1947. It is possible, however, that Sphere Investment Trust, Limited, with a nominal capitalization of £1,800,000 in 1949, had some investments in Uruguay. Including £16,192,153 for Uruguayan government bonds, the *Journal*'s figure for the total British investment at the end of 1949 was £26,624,198. Its estimate was probably £5 million or £6 million too high.*

* In this contemporary era of investment trusts, holding companies, branch plants, and corporate subsidiaries, investments are difficult to trace and even more difficult to appraise. The Bank of London and South America, Dunlop Rubber Company, and some of the English oil, chemical, pharmaceutical, and electric companies have branches and subsidiaries in Uruguay; but their capitalization (and often even their names) fails to appear in the investment manuals.

⇋ XIII ⇌

BRAZIL: LARGE LATIN-AMERICAN RECIPIENT OF BRITISH CAPITAL

During the sixty years following 1824 Englishmen preferred Brazil as a field of investment to any other Latin-American country, largely for the reason that Brazil was politically more stable. By 1890, however, they had a bigger stake in Argentina, and their Argentine investment continued to exceed their Brazilian investment until 1948, when Brazil forged ahead again. Ranked according to the amount of British capital invested, Brazil occupied first place among the Latin-American nations for six decades, dropped to second place for another six, and then moved back into first place, a position which at mid-century she seemed likely to hold for some time to come.[1]

Size of the Investment and Profits Therefrom

Residents of the United Kingdom made their first important investments in independent Brazil in 1824 and 1825, purchasing two issues of government bonds with a par value of £3.2 million and organizing two mining associations with a nominal paid-in capital amounting to £220,000. The face value of their investment expanded to approximately £38.8 million by the end of 1880. It grew to no less than £68.6 million by the close of the next decade and to slightly more than £90.6 million by the end of 1900. Increasing more rapidly thereafter, it exceeded £151.4 million by the last days of 1910, rose to £223.8 million during the next three years, and reached £287.3 million by the end of 1930. Then a shrinkage set in. The nominal aggregate was only £260.7 million at the close of the year 1939 and not more than £170.5 million at the end of 1949 (the date set for the termination of this volume), with perhaps some further reduction in prospect, although no tendency to accelerate the redemption of the sterling debt was apparent

Brazil: Large Recipient of Capital

and the investment in public utilities seemed likely to expand rather than contract.*

More than half of the investment, at times almost three fifths of it, was in government bonds. The total in government securities was approximately £23 million by the end of 1880, £37 million a decade later, and £45.4 million by the close of the century. The total exceeded £100.4 million in 1910 and £117.3 million in 1913, and it rose to its peak of £168.7 million in 1930. The decline that followed was not so much the result of amortization as of default settlements which involved a reduction of the principal (20 to 50 per cent) as well as the interest rate, and the aggregate nominal British capital invested in Brazilian government bonds was still approximately £93.6 million at the end of 1949.

Next in size — until after 1900, when government ownership of railroads began to encroach seriously upon private ownership — was the English investment in railway enterprises. The nominal total in this category was more than £11.6 million by the end of 1880 and in excess of £26 million a decade later. It reached £33.6 million by the close of the century and rose somewhat higher by 1913, although probably not as high as the some £52.3 million estimated by the *South American Journal* for that year. Thereafter a contraction began. According to the *Journal*, the aggregate nominal British investment in Brazilian railways was £37.4 million in the final days of 1939 and £25.2 million at the end of 1949. Whatever the total, it would soon be liquidated; sales negotiations were well under way with the Brazilian government.†

Other investments, classified under the heading miscellaneous by the *South American Journal*, had long been of considerable importance. Amounting to over £4.2 million (par value) as early as 1880, capital under this classification increased to more than £5.6 million by the end of 1890, rose to over £11 million by the end of the century,

---

* The statistics in this paragraph do not include transatlantic shipping lines or banks. The operations of the shipping lines were, of course, not confined to Brazil, and the same was true of the commercial banks active in the country after the 1890's; it is almost impossible to allocate the capital under these two classifications to particular countries.

† All the British-owned lines were sold to the Brazilian government during the years 1946–1950. The *Journal's* estimates for 1913 and subsequent years are too high because large sums of securities of the late Farquhar enterprises were not held by English investors.

Country-by-Country Inspection

and, according to the *South American Journal*, mounted to £26.1 million by the close of 1910 and leaped up to £54.1 million by the last days of 1913. Nor, if one accepts the *Journal's* figures, was the peak reached until 1933, when the nominal total exceeded £73.7 million. Shrinking during the years that followed, although not as rapidly as the railway capital, the nominal total investment was still in excess of £51.6 million, according to the *Journal's* liberal estimate, at the end of 1949.*

Less diversified than the British miscellaneous investments in Argentina, the major part of this capital, almost from the outset, was concentrated in public utilities. While some of it was in mining, financial organizations, shipping and port works, rural and urban real estate, and manufacturing, none of these types of investment was ever as significant as the investment in public utilities, which amounted to over £2.9 million by the end of 1880, to well above £6.8 million by the close of the nineteenth century, and to around £40 million at its peak in the late 1920's. British capital invested in Brazilian real estate probably never amounted to much over £5 million, nor did the nominal English capital in mining ever reach £3 million, or British capital in manufacturing or shipping and port facilities ever rise far above £3 million.

For approximately a century British capital invested in Brazil brought good returns. The average annual nominal yield seldom dropped below 4 per cent until after 1931. It was 4.8 in both 1910 and 1913, and it was probably above 6 per cent in the 1880's and the late 1890's, if not also during the early years of the present century. The rate declined to 3.9 during the short recession of the early 1920's; but it rose to 5 per cent in 1929 and to 5.3 in 1930, and after sagging to a nominal annual average of 1.88 per cent during the depression decade of 1931–1940, it moved back up to an annual average of slightly better than 3 per cent for the nine years beginning with 1941, the rate of return being 3.2 in 1949. (None of these figures, however, makes any allowance for heavy capital losses.)

Although some of the Brazilian states and municipalities failed to fulfill their obligations, few countries had a better record than Brazil's for servicing their sterling government bonds until that record was

* Considerable blocks of Brazilian public-utility securities quoted on the London Stock Exchange were owned by Canadians.

Brazil: Large Recipient of Capital

marred, perhaps mainly because of the world depression, during the decade starting in 1932. But by virtue of this excellent record the national government of Brazil had been able to obtain sterling loans at comparatively low interest rates, so that British income from Brazilian government securities rarely rose above a nominal yield of 4.5 per cent. It was exactly 4.5 almost every year from 1910 through 1924. Then it gradually rose to 5.2 (in 1930) before it began to sag again. It dropped no lower than 4.3 in 1931, but during the next decade the annual average nominal yield was only 1.6, the low being reached in 1939, with every sterling issue in complete default. During the next eight years, however, the average annual nominal rate was slightly above 2.3, ignoring losses of principal.

The average yield of the nominal British capital invested in Brazilian railways seems to have remained steadily above 5 per cent annually for almost half a century, possibly excepting a few years during the depression of the 1890's.[2] The nominal rate of return was 5.7 in 1910, and it was even higher in not a few years preceding. Between 1910 and 1913, however, Englishmen imprudently invested in some of the pyramided Percival Farquhar railroad enterprises, so that the average annual nominal yield on their capital soon began to fall off. The nominal rate of return was only 4.7 in 1913, and it dropped to 2.5 by 1923. The rate was rising again, however, when the world depression arrived in Brazil, and in spite of the depression the annual average nominal yield was better than 1.5 for the years following 1931, until the San Paulo, the most profitable of the British railways in Brazil, was sold in 1946.

The rate of return on the miscellaneous investment was usually higher than the rate on either government bonds or railways. In fact, it was often several points higher, more likely to be above than below an average of 5 per cent in almost any year prior to 1933. The nominal yield was 5.3 in 1910 and 5.7 in 1913, and during the decade starting with 1923 the annual average was 5.28, the highest returns being paid in 1931 and 1932, 6.4 per cent each year. The annual nominal average fell to a little below 2 per cent during the next decade, but recovery began in 1943. The average nominal yield for 1943 was 5.6 per cent; for 1944 it mounted to 7.4, and the annual average for the seven-year period starting in 1943 and ending in 1949 was 6.6.

Such in broad outlines is the story of British investments in Brazil.

Country-by-Country Inspection

Income from this big republic amounted to as much as £7.3 million in 1910, reached a peak of £15.1 million in 1930, and although it shrank to hardly more than a million in the late 1930's, it soon expanded again until it approached £9 million in 1944, and it was still £5.6 million in 1949. The second part of this chapter will present a summary of the dividend records of a number of the most remunerative business enterprises owned by Englishmen in Brazil.

A Rapid Glance at the Most Profitable Companies

The most profitable British railway enterprise in Brazil or anywhere else in Latin America was the San Paulo Railway Company, Limited organized in 1858 to construct and operate a line from the city of São Paulo down the mountainside to the coffee port of Santos. For a period of fifty-five years starting with 1876 and ending in 1930 the average annual dividend rate on the par value of its ordinary shares — £2 million at the outset and £3 million after 1900 — was approximately 11.9 per cent. During the depression decade, however, dividends declined averaging only 3.1 annually from 1931 through 1940, and never recovered. For the six years beginning in 1941 the annual average was only 2.75. Exchange difficulties and a heavy load of loan capital — in addition to £3 million in ordinary and £1 million in preference share (5 per cents), there were nearly £2.5 million in 4 and 5 per cent debentures — were mainly responsible for these low dividends. But the management succeeded in selling its property to the Brazilian national government late in 1946 for the sum of £6,638,803, more than sufficient to redeem at par its outstanding securities, which amounted to £6,414,677.[3]

A few of the English-owned financial organizations operating in Brazil were almost as remunerative as this remarkably profitable railroad. This was especially true of two commercial banks whose activities were confined mainly to Brazil until the early 1890's. The London and Brazilian Bank, organized in 1862 with a paid-up capital of £450,000, soon raised to £500,000 and then to £750,000, yielded an annual average of slightly more than 9 per cent on the par value of its capitalization for a period of twenty years starting from 1873. The English Bank of Rio de Janeiro, established in 1863 with a nominal paid-in capital of £500,000, returned an annual average dividend of nearly 9.5 per cent on the face value of its securities for the 18 years beginning with 1874

Brazil: Large Recipient of Capital

Other British financial enterprises active in Brazil were less profitable. At least two of these, however, deserve attention. The Brazilian Warrant Company, Limited, which soon changed its title to Brazilian Warrant Agency and Finance Company, was founded in 1909 to conduct a warehouse business and finance the coffee trade. Its paid-in capital had a par value of £600,000, all in ordinary shares, in 1912 and £1,625,000, of which £500,000 was 7 per cent preference and the rest ordinary, by 1925. Somewhat overcapitalized, this firm confronted the oscillations of coffee prices, so that it frequently failed to pay dividends on its ordinary shares. The average nominal annual return on these securities was only some 3.2 per cent for the twenty-five years starting with 1912. But with rising prices for coffee in the 1940's it became a very profitable company. During the eight-year period beginning with 1942 its average annual nominal dividend was well above 18 per cent, the dividend for the year 1949 being 30 per cent. The Rio Claro Investment Trust, created under a slightly different name in 1912, had a more diversified investment and yielded steadier, though often smaller, returns. Without passing a single dividend, this financial firm paid an average rate of more than 7.1 per cent annually for the thirty-eight-year period starting in 1913, the dividend in 1950 being 10 per cent. The par value of its ordinary shares was £1,971,875 until they were reduced to £788,750 in the early 1920's by transforming £1,183,125 of them into 5 per cent cumulative preference. Outstanding debentures, with coupons ranging from 3.5 to 6 per cent, rose from £600,000 in 1913 to £998,912 in 1950.

Such was the record of four of the most profitable enterprises operating in the field of finance. Equally remunerative, if not more so, especially during the earlier decades of their existence, were some of the public-utility enterprises, particularly the gas companies. Besides a stock bonus of 50 per cent in the 1870's, the Rio de Janeiro Gas Company, Limited, paid a nominal 10 per cent annually, without a single failure, from 1865, the year in which it was created, through 1886. The company was then sold, perhaps at a handsome profit, to a Belgian syndicate. The San Paulo Gas Company, Limited, founded in 1869, paid an average dividend of nearly 9 per cent annually for the thirty-one years beginning in 1882 and ending in 1912, failing to make payment for only one year, 1892, and then sold its £10 ordinary shares — £275,000 in 1912, but only £80,000 in 1880 — for £14 each to another British company. (San Paulo Gas seems to have issued no other securities during the period.) The Bahía Gas Company, Limited, established in 1860, paid an annual nominal average of well above 8 per cent on its £100,000 in ordinary shares from 1880 until it was liquidated in 1894–1895. In addition, it managed to service regularly £20,000 in 10 per cent first preference shares and £30,000 in 7.5 per cent second preference. The Ceará Gas Company, Limited, organized in 1866, did almost as well until it encountered ill fortune during the decades following 1914, fell into receivership, and finally (1934) lost its concession. During the thirty-two years starting with 1883 and ending with 1914 this enterprise averaged more than 7 per cent annually on the par value of its £30,000 in ordinary shares, paid 10 per cent on from £8,225 to £14,710 of preference shares, and serviced regularly its 6 per cent debentures, which had increased to £25,000 by 1913. No other British-owned public utilities operating in Brazil matched the record of these four, but it was mainly the utilities that kept up the level of returns on the broad miscellaneous investment.

Unlike Argentina, Brazil did not prove to be a profitable field for British stock-raising, agriculture, and speculation in land. English investors lost money in their effort to develop plantation rubber in this part of the world during the first decade of the twentieth century. Nor did they garner any large profits from other agricultural activities or real-estate speculation, so far as I have been able to discover. Cambuhy Coffee and Cotton Estates, Limited, organized in 1925, one of the most profitable enterprises in this category, failed to pay any dividend on its ordinary shares — £500,000 paid up — and even fell behind in the payment of dividends on its £350,000 in 8 per cent cumulative preference shares during the first decade of its existence. After reorganization, however, perhaps accompanied by some loss of capital, the company's record improved. With only £420,000 in ordinary shares and no other securities issued, it paid an annual nominal average of nearly 11 per cent for the thirteen-year period beginning with 1936, skipping only two dividends; and soaring coffee prices promised much greater profits in the 1950's.

Deeply interested in Brazil's mineral wealth since the early 1820's, residents of the British Isles seem to have discovered only two bonanzas there, and one of these quickly played out. The Santa Bárbara Gold Mining Company, Limited, established in 1868, soon began t

Brazil: Large Recipient of Capital

pay handsome dividends on its £30,000 in ordinary shares. Dividends ranged from 10 to 35 per cent for several years, and the annual average rate, figured at par, was nearly 14 per cent for the period 1876–1886, while at the same time the company paid 10 per cent annually on preference shares amounting to £10,000.

Far more remarkable was the St. John del Rey Mining Company, Limited, organized in 1830 to work gold mines in Minas Geraes. This enterprise began with a paid-up capital of some £200,000, par value, all in ordinary shares; but this was expanded to £546,265 by the end of the first decade of the twentieth century, and an approximately equal amount of preferred shares and debentures, paying a steady rate of 10 per cent annually, was added. For the first four decades of the company's existence the average nominal ordinary dividend was in excess of 20 per cent per annum, and for the eight years beginning in 1876 the annual average climbed to 27.5. For the next fifteen years, however, there were no returns on the ordinary shares. The walls of the mine caved in and the company was reorganized. Ordinary dividends were finally resumed in 1897 with a payment of 2.5, raised to 5 in 1898 and to 11.25 in 1899; and the nominal annual average for the fifty years beginning in 1900 and ending in 1949 was a little better than 9 per cent.[4]

Among the manufacturing enterprises in which Britishers ventured their capital only one turned out to be very profitable. This was Rio de Janeiro Flour Mills and Granaries, Limited, which also operated a textile mill after 1910. Organized in 1886, this firm did not begin to pay dividends until 1893, but returns were remarkably high thereafter. Besides stock bonuses amounting to a total of 183 per cent issued during the two decades following 1902 — bonuses accounting mainly for the expansion of the firm's ordinary shares from a face value of £158,760 in 1890 to a face value of £1,364,838 by 1926 — cash returns were excellent. Ordinary dividends — no preference shares were issued and the amount of loan capital was insignificant — rose from an annual nominal average of 10.9 per cent for the decade 1893–1902 to a nominal per-annum average of 19.85 during the next ten-year period. The annual average then dropped to around 9 per cent for the decade of 1933–1942 and to 8 per cent for the next seven years, but the dividend was 10 per cent in 1950.

Such were the earnings of some of the most profitable enterprises

Country-by-Country Inspection

ever owned by Englishmen in Brazil. There were few others like them; and in order to avoid a distorted view, it will be well to point out that British capitalists had investments at one time or another in at least six times as many economic enterprises in Brazil and to recall that the average yield on such enterprises rarely amounted to more than a nominal 6 or 7 per cent annually.*

* It should also be remembered that no account has been taken of capital losses, which were quite substantial, especially in the investment in rubber plantations, the various Farquhar enterprises, and government bonds (because of reduction of principal in connection with resumption of service in the early 1940's).

⇌ XIV ⇌

ARGENTINA: LATE MAJOR FIELD OF BRITISH OVERSEAS INVESTMENT

For more than fifty years Argentina was an important field of operations for British capitalists. At almost any time between 1890 and 1946, approximately a tenth of the capital owned by inhabitants of the British Isles in lands overseas was invested in Argentina. If nearly a third of the English overseas investment during this period was in Latin America, the big Río de la Plata republic at times accounted for a third of that third.[1]

Chronology of the Investment and Summary of Profits

For several decades after the Argentinos won their independence from Spain, English capital trickled in but slowly. The total nominal British investment at the end of the year 1880, after Argentina had solved the problem of political stability (at least for a season), was only slightly more than £20 million. During the next decade, however, the flow was rapid. The nominal total rose to nearly £157 million by the end of 1890; and despite the adversities of the depression years that followed, the investment was approaching £207 million at the close of the century. The early years of the new century witnessed a marked acceleration. The nominal total rose to £290.6 million by the end of 1910 and to £357.7 million by the close of 1913. The peak was not reached until the end of 1934, when the nominal total stood at more than £453 million. It was still approximately £428.5 million in 1939; but the ravages of war and growing Argentine prosperity and nationalism reduced it to £68.5 million or less by the end of 1949, and considerable further shrinkage appeared clearly in the offing.

Although Englishmen purchased their first Argentine government bonds in 1824, an issue of £1,000,000 floated by the Province of Buenos Aires, they were not much attracted by this type of investment until

Country-by-Country Inspection

forty years later. The face value of Argentine government and government-guaranteed securities held by British capitalists at the end of 1880 was only a little more than £20.3 million. By 1900, however, the nominal aggregate was approximately £79 million. The peak was reached in 1918, when the total stood at £82.7 million. The nominal aggregate was still above £64 million at the end of 1939, but by the close of 1949 it was only a little more than £5.6 million.

The British investment in Argentine railways, destined eventually to become large and significant, lagged behind the investment in government securities until after 1890. Only some £7.6 million at the end of 1880 and only a little more than £64.6 million at the close of 1890, nominal British capital in Argentine railways mounted to £93.6 million in 1900, to above £174.4 million in 1910, to £215 million at the end of 1913, and to £277.1 million at the close of 1937. The nominal railway capital then began to shrink somewhat, but it was still reckoned at more than £252 million in 1946, when all the British-owned railways in the republic were sold to the Argentine national government for £150 million, a sum probably less than the actual investment, although the railroad capitalization included a liberal portion of water.

Other investments, listed by the *South American Journal* under the broad miscellaneous category, amounted to less than £1.5 million in 1880, but expanded to £35 million by 1910, to more than £61.1 million by the end of 1913, and to more than £111.2 million by the close of 1929. Then a shrinkage began, but the nominal aggregate was still above £63.7 million, according to the *South American Journal*, at the end of the year 1949. These miscellaneous investments were quite diversified, including at one time or another almost every conceivable economic enterprise. The major concentrations, however, were in public utilities, real estate, and financial organizations such as mortgage, loan, and trust companies and branches of giant commercial banks whose capital cannot easily be ascertained because they were operating in many other countries besides Argentina. British capital engaged in manufacturing was comparatively insignificant, except in the processing of meat, although small sums were invested in the brewery business, in the refining of sugar, and in the manufacture of metal, chemical, pharmaceutical, and a few other products. Englishmen also owned a large and famous department store in Buenos Aires.

Because the British investment in Argentine public utilities soon be-

Argentina: Late Major Field of Investment

came involved in holding companies — both British and international with British participation — its exact magnitude is difficult to determine. The following figures are offered as approximates: £9.5 million at the end of the year 1890, £39.6 million in 1913, and some £43 million in 1915, when this category of investment reached its maximum. As in the case of the railway companies, capitalization of public-utility enterprises was inflated. The aggregate nominal investment in Argentine public utilities may have been in the neighborhood of £25 million or £30 million at the close of the year 1949; but, whatever the total at that time, it would shortly be sold to the Argentine government or otherwise liquidated.

Real estate, especially immense livestock ranches and great stretches of timber lands, was a favorite type of English investment in Argentina. At their maximum in the second decade of the present century, British holdings probably amounted to around nine million acres. The nominal capital invested in Argentine real estate by residents of the British Isles was hardly more than £2.8 million at the end of the year 1890, but in excess of £13 million at the close of 1913; and the total was still in the neighborhood of £11 million in 1949.[2]

Englishmen derived a comparatively large income from their Argentine investments, particularly during the first three decades of the twentieth century.[3] Income from this overseas source was only a little short of £14 million by 1910 and more than £17.6 million in 1913. It reached a peak of some £24.4 million in 1929, perhaps not less than 2 per cent of the income received by Englishmen from all of their overseas investments at that time. But British income drawn from Argentina diminished rapidly after 1930, until it amounted to only some £2.3 million in 1949.

Few Latin-American countries yielded Englishmen a better rate of return on their nominal investment. The highest rates (possibly excepting two or three years in the middle 1880's, when the investment was not yet large) were returned in the late 1920's. The yield was 5.2 per cent on the aggregate nominal capital invested in Argentina in 1926. It was 5.3 per cent in 1927 and 5.6 per cent in both 1928 and 1929. It had been 4.8 per cent in 1910 and 4.9 per cent in both 1913 and 1924; and in spite of the onslaught of the world depression, the rate of return from Argentina was 5 per cent in 1930 and 3.6 per cent in 1931. Between 1932 and 1949, however, the annual nominal yield

Country-by-Country Inspection

never reached 3 per cent; the average for this period, depressed by the withholding of railroad income in 1947, was only 2.6 per annum.

The low rate of return that began in 1932 may be attributed largely to the slump in the yield of the railroad capital, which averaged only 1.74 per cent annually on the nominal investment during the fifteen years following 1931. It should be remembered, however, that the railway companies were greatly overcapitalized; that their profits were sometimes siphoned out by subsidiaries; and that, except for two or three years in the early 1890's, the nominal yield of British capital invested in Argentine railroads had never fallen below 3 per cent. It was 3 per cent in 1918 and 3 per cent again in 1930; but it had been 4.8 per cent in both 1910 and 1913. It rose from 4.9 per cent in 1925 to 5.3 per cent in 1926; it was 5.5 per cent in 1927, 1928, and 1929; and it was 4.7 per cent in 1930.

Argentine government bonds yielded moderate but steady returns for a period of over eighty years. Except for 1890 and 1891, there were no defaults on national issues, and provincial and municipal issues in default never amounted to as much as 5 per cent of the total face value of the British investment in Argentine government securities. The average annual nominal yield from 1910 through 1949 was approximately 4.3 per cent. The maximum income from this source was paid in 1918, £3,697,110, the nominal rate for that year being 4.4 per cent.

In spite of the low rate of return on many of the English-owned Argentine public utilities from 1932 through 1949, the broad miscellaneous group of British investments was more profitable than either the railway capital or the capital in government securities. The average nominal rate of return from miscellaneous companies never fell below 3.1 per cent at any time between 1910 and 1949, and this low rate was for the year 1935. The average nominal yield for the eighteen years beginning with 1932 was 3.6 per cent. The maximum rate of return and the maximum income were recorded in 1929, the income for that year being more than £7.4 million from the all-time peak miscellaneous investment of slightly above £111.2 million, and the nominal yield being 6.6. The nominal rate of return had been 5.7 per cent in 1910 and 6.1 per cent in 1913, and it was 6.5 in 1928 and 6.2 in 1925. These comparatively high averages can be attributed in the main profitable investments in ranch, farm, and timber lands and in mor

Argentina: Late Major Field of Investment

...ge, loan, and trust companies which dealt largely in real estate and ...al-estate mortgages. Argentine bonanzas were found in land and timber rather than in mines and oil wells.

The Argentine Bonanzas

Between 1870, the year when the Argentine Central Land Company, Limited, was established, and the end of the year 1912, when the last of the large British land companies founded to operate in Argentina came into being, British promoters organized some thirty big real-estate enterprises concerned exclusively with Argentina and three or four others for the purpose of operating in Argentina along with one or two of the adjacent countries. Most of them were intended primarily to engage in raising livestock, mainly sheep and cattle, and there were two periods of enthusiastic investment, the 1880's and the twelve years following 1900. Some of the land enterprises were purely speculative ventures, however, created with the view of profiting from anticipated rise in prices, and some mixed colonization and speculation with the livestock business. A few were ephemeral and a few went through a number of reorganizations and permutations; but the majority continued under the same name for decade after decade, and a third of the companies were still in existence as late as 1949.

The *South American Journal* kept a record of eight of these land companies for a period of twenty-one years and a record of seven of the eight that continued to exist (after one had been liquidated in 1935) for another eleven years.[4] For the period beginning in 1914 and ending in 1934 the average nominal rate of return per annum, including income from debentures as well as from shares, was slightly more than 7 per cent, and for the first eighteen of these twenty-one years was almost 8, the highest yields, 11 per cent, 13.9, and 15.8, being for the years 1916, 1917, and 1920. For the eleven years starting with 1935 the average nominal yield was 7.2 per cent. And only four of the most profitable land companies owned by Englishmen in Argentina were included in the *Journal*'s list! A different selection would have pushed the average up. Four of the big British enterprises engaged in ranching would have raised the annual average by 40 or 50 per cent if they had been substituted for four of the less profitable companies included in the *Journal*'s calculations.

Associated Estancias,[5] organized in 1900 with a paid-in capital of

£40,070 in ordinary shares, with no preference stock, and with never more than £20,000 in debentures, returned an annual average dividend of 23 per cent on its nominal ordinary capital during the fifteen years beginning in 1905 and an average of 12.25 during the first twenty years of its existence. The rate of return declined following 1919, after the company had inflated its ordinary share capital to a total of £400,800 without any apparent expansion of its holdings. During the decade starting in 1920 the average annual nominal yield was only 4.35, and the rate of return continued to decline until the company sold its two ranches in 1947 for a sum amounting to 40 per cent of its inflated capital.

Estancias and Properties, Limited, created in 1899 with a paid-up capital of £110,000, all in ordinary shares, yielded an annual nominal average of 14.45 per cent during the decade beginning in 1912, an annual nominal average of 7.15 during the next ten years, and an annual average of nearly 6 per cent for the fifteen-year period starting in 193. For some reason, perhaps because of liquidation, the *Stock Exchange Official Year-Book* ceased to list this enterprise after 1947.

Espartillar Estancia, organized in 1886, with a paid-in capital of £120,000 in ordinary shares and with never more than £30,000 in debentures (bearing 5 per cent), returned an annual nominal average ordinary dividend of 7 per cent for the forty-five-year period beginning in 1901. No year passed without a dividend on its ordinary shares, and the company sold its ranch in 1946 at a profit which brought the shareholders a capital return of nearly £25 for every £1 share they owned.

Las Cabezas Estancia Company, founded in 1876, recorded an average annual yield of 11.28 per cent during a sixty-eight-year period (1882–1949), never skipping a dividend or paying one of less than 4.5 per cent (in 1906). For many years the par value of its paid-up capital, all ordinary shares, was £80,000, but this was doubled in 19 by issuing a stock dividend of 100 per cent. The decades of highest returns for the shareholders, leaving the big stock dividend out of the reckoning, were those beginning in 1882 and 1922, the first returning a total of 125.25 per cent and the second an aggregate of 16. Starting out with a single ranch in the Province of Entre Ríos, the company eventually increased its holdings to three ranches by plowing back a part of its profits.

Argentina: Late Major Field of Investment

Even more profitable than some of the land companies were the mortgage, loan, and trust companies, particularly the four oldest and most important of the group. The first of the four, River Plate Trust, Loan and Agency Company, Limited, was founded in 1881. The other three were all established in 1888. They made their profits by selling debentures bearing 4.5 per cent interest or less in the British market and lending the proceeds at high rates to Argentinos accustomed to paying dearly for their loans, particularly to those engaged in farming and stock-raising or in the real-estate business.

River Plate Trust, Loan and Agency had two classes of ordinary shares, one yielding only moderate, if regular, annual returns of from 5 to 8 per cent and the other paying very handsome dividends. After 1913, there were also £1,500,000 in 5 per cent preference shares. Amounting to only £100,000 in the beginning, the more profitable class of ordinary shares was soon increased to £375,000 and then to £500,000. The capital in the less profitable ordinary shares began at £250,000 and eventually totaled £1,000,000. These two classes were described as "A" shares and "B" shares. During the first half-century of the company's operation, the "A" shares received a nominal average annual dividend of 17.38 per cent and the "B" shares 5.16 per cent, and for the twenty-nine years beginning with 1931 and ending in 1949 the average annual nominal yield was slightly above 14 per cent for the first class and a little over 4 per cent for the second. In addition, the owners of "A" shares were paid two stock bonuses, one in 1919 and the other in 1928, amounting to a total of £300,000, figured at par, and holders of these shares were given the exclusive privilege of purchasing the preference shares, while owners of "B" shares received £180,000, par value, in the stock bonuses mentioned.

The share capital, paid up, of the River Plate and General Investment Trust Company was £500,000 at the outset, but it was increased in 1919 to £550,000, and was always equally divided between ordinary and preference shares. Permanent debentures with coupons of 4 per cent were sold in 1907–1908. Preference shares yielded 4.5 per cent cumulative. Ordinary dividends were low for the first two decades (1888–1907), averaging a little less than 4 per cent on the nominal paid-in capital. Thereafter the returns mounted, however, averaging nearly 12 per cent per annum during the forty years beginning in 1908 and ending in 1947 and 13 per cent annually for the next three years.

Country-by-Country Inspection

For more than six decades there was not a single failure to pay a dividend.

The Mortgage Company of the River Plate rewarded its stockholders handsomely from the beginning, returning an annual average of 9.2 per cent on its nominal paid-up ordinary shares during the first decade, paying a per-annum average of 12.45 per cent for the first six decades of its operation (1888–1947), returning 10 per cent each year in 1948, 1949, and 1950, and never passing a dividend. In addition, a total of £150,000, reckoned at par, was paid in stock bonuses. The paid-up ordinary shares amounted to £200,000 soon after the company was launched, but this sum was increased to £300,000 by the issue of a 50 per cent stock bonus in 1919. Preference shares — £250,000 floated shortly after 1900, but raised to £300,000 in 1928 by the payment of a stock bonus of £50,000 to the ordinary shareholders — yielded a cumulative 5 per cent.

The New Zealand and River Plate Land Mortgage Company, which soon disposed of its New Zealand business and centered its operation in Argentina, did not prosper during the depression of the 1890's. It returned an average nominal annual dividend of only 4.1 per cent on its ordinary shares for the decade beginning in 1888, failed to make any payments during three of the ten years, and perhaps suffered a small loss of capital. Reduced from £200,000 at the outset to £178,16. in 1895, the ordinary shares of this company were gradually increased to £350,000 and then doubled in 1920 by the payment of a stock dividend of 100 per cent. For the half-century starting in 1898 the average nominal return on the ordinary shares was 7 per cent per annum. From 1920 through 1949, with half of this capital probably consisting of water, the average annual yield was a nominal 5.2 per cent. There were no preferred shares.

Such were the dividends of the most profitable companies owned by English investors in Argentina. In order to avoid a false impression it would be well to recall that the annual yield of the total nominal British investment in Argentina, making no allowance for capital losses, probably never exceeded 5.6 per cent and that the annual nominal average from 1932 through 1949 was only 2.6 per cent. Failure to describe these remunerative land and finance companies would be to leave an interesting part of this story untold, but failure to point out that these were only a fraction of the some eighty or ninety British

Argentina: Late Major Field of Investment

sh-owned enterprises active in Argentina at one time or another would result in serious distortion. Such animosity as the Argentinos expressed over the years in respect to the economic activities of Englishmen in their country usually referred to railroads and public utilties rather than to these far more profitable ranching, farming, speculating, and money-lending organizations.*

The future of British investments in this land once so important as center of English economic activities and as a source of income from overseas seemed obscure at the beginning of the second half of the twentieth century, clouded by ardent nationalism in Argentina and by the fog of political and economic anxieties in the United Kingdom. No expansion seemed likely during the years immediately ahead, save possibly in the capital devoted to local manufacturing and to the disribution of goods made in England.

* The most profitable railroad enterprise ever owned by Englishmen in Argentina was the Buenos Ayres Great Southern Railway Company. Its most prosperous decade began in 1882; for that decade the average return on its ordinary shares — a nominal £3 million at the beginning of the period and £5 million in 1891 — was 9.4 per cent. Ordinary shares with a par value of £32 million paid no dividend, however, between 1932 and 1946, and the company's property was sold in 1946 at a price that would repay the shareholders only about 20 per cent of the face value of their securities. Rosario Waterworks Company was the only British-financed public utility in Argentina that ever paid an average nominal ordinary dividend of as much as 8 per cent for as long as twenty years in succession.

PART THREE

The Crux of the Matter in Global Setting

⇋ XV ⇌

A COMPARATIVE SAMPLE OF BRITISH OVERSEAS COMPANIES

What Groups Profit Most from Foreign Investments? Writing in the early 1940's of more than a century of international investments, E. H. Carr declared that in the end such investments had proved disappointing to those who ventured their capital. "The system seemed profitable to all," he said, only "because those who benefited from it succeeded in unloading the loss on posterity." Carr did not specify the groups that benefited or indicate specifically whether he thought that the recipients of the capital were among them; but he at least put forth the suggestion that foreign investments served the creditor countries as a whole by keeping the engines of production running at higher and more regular speeds, and he concluded with this statement: "It is not certain that the same confidence trick can be played again. If it cannot, it seems probable that those who occupy the most privileged position within any international financial system will be obliged from time to time to make deliberate sacrifices in order to make the system work."[1] John Maynard Keynes grew pessimistic about the home benefits of British foreign investments as early as the 1920's,[2] and Samuel Flagg Bemis once wrote that foreign investors had not exploited Latin Americans but rather Latin Americans had exploited foreign investors,[3] although Bemis admitted later that he was referring mainly to investors in Latin-American government securities and remarked that the truth regarding direct investments in economic enterprises in Latin America could be ascertained only by examining the history of each foreign company operating in the region.[4]

Bemis's suggestion of the necessity for company histories is so obviously sound that he was not the first to think of it; but it lays out for the economic historian a tremendous task, on which I have been engaged for years without arriving at any firm conclusion regarding the difference between development and exploitation. In the first place, no precise definition of exploitation seems possible. The word cannot be defined precisely with reference to profits, for these naturally vary with time and circumstance and there is no general agreement on the meaning of "fair return." The subject of wages and working conditions is involved, as likewise the question of taxation by the governments of the recipient countries. These topics alone call for extensive research, for which the sources are not readily available; and there is the further problem of the advisability or inadvisability of a rapid increase in wages above the customary level in underdeveloped regions, as well as the hard choice between the relative merits for the retarded countries of higher wages for the workers and higher taxes for the government. For such economic problems as profits, wages, working conditions, prices, and taxes there seems to be no solution except balanced negotiations that result in reasonably satisfactory arrangements for all concerned. Legal and moral codes are inadequate and no entirely reliable automatic adjuster exists.

For the present, we can be sure of only a few facts. One of these is that imperialism of whatever variety has come to have an unpleasant connotation in both the well-developed and the retarded regions. A second fact is that hostility to imperialism includes a feeling on the part of the peoples of the underdeveloped areas, whether colonial or semi-colonial, that they have been "exploited" by foreign capitalists with the backing of the governments of the capitalist nations. A third fact is that a good many individuals in the capitalist countries have agreed with this point of view. And perhaps it is also a fact that resentment against exploitation, real or imaginary, has arisen from acquaintance with the actual record of large profits "siphoned out" by some foreign companies. If resentment may be traced largely to this source, it is only fair to point out that such resentment is often founded upon incomplete or incorrect impressions of what really occurred. Limiting himself to British investments in Latin America, for example, the investigator will be compelled to conclude that for every highly profitable investment there were many others which yielded only moderate profits and not a few that resulted in losses. Moreover, if it be conceded that exploitation has sometimes taken place, it should also be observed that many inhabitants of more fully developed coun-

A Sample of British Overseas Companies

ries have been exploited along with the peoples of Latin America and other such regions. Inhabitants of capitalist nations have suffered disadvantage from foreign investment in two ways: (1) as consumers, they sometimes have had to pay higher prices for commodities because increased exports and raw material monopolies have tended to sustain or increase prices, and (2) as investors, they have been cheated by poor investments that have been palmed off on them. In short, profits have been siphoned off from the people of the nations engaged in foreign investment as well as from the people of the recipient countries.

Students of economic history might profit by approaching the subject of foreign investments from the viewpoint of group interests. Adopting this approach, one might arrive at the conclusion, although the evidence is difficult to obtain in some cases, that four groups are most likely to benefit from such investments: (1) bond-selling bankers and speculators; (2) shipping companies; (3) officials and agents of recipient countries; (4) manufacturers, managers, and other technicians of the investing nations. The bankers, of course, usually reap profits from the sale of securities, good or bad, although the exact size of the harvest is customarily not revealed, unless and until disclosed by a parliamentary investigation; and speculators profit by buying up securities from discouraged or hard-driven investors and gambling on a rise in price, which may result from the pressure they are able to exert upon the parties involved, from market manipulations, or from some other cause. Shippers benefit from the increased international trade that foreign investments stimulate. Officials and agents (or attorneys) of debtor countries sometimes share in the sales commissions or profit as open or concealed partners in foreign enterprises — although, here again, the evidence is hard to ferret out — or prolong their political control by virtue of foreign loans. Manufacturers and managers and other technicians of the investing countries, by and large, probably benefit most of all. Manufacturers are not only provided with increased export outlets to prevent the sagging of prices; they are also supplied with additional raw materials and food for factory workers. Information on salaries and other remunerations of managers and technicians engaged in operating economic enterprises in foreign countries is not readily available to the historian, but one may reasonably conclude that the compensation is higher as a rule than

The Crux of the Matter

the same persons could command at home or else they would not venture out to distant lands. On the basis of rational expectations, investment bankers, steamship companies, and manufacturers producing for export, along with managers and technicians,* should be, and probably are, the most enthusiastic advocates of foreign investments

The foregoing comments are offered as a friendly gesture to philosophers and moralizers. The main purpose of this chapter is to deal with a set of facts, to present an analysis of the profits derived from enterprises owned (or partly owned) by British investors in Latin America and in other overseas countries, twenty-three of these enterprises in Latin America. In order to guard against a false impression let it be clearly noted that British capitalists controlled at one time or another nearly a thousand economic enterprises in Latin America and that the average annual income from the entire investment in such enterprises, taking no account of capital losses, rarely exceeded 5 or 6 per cent of the par value of the investment, although, of course the average ran higher in some countries than in others; and let it be remembered also that a major part of the investment was in government bonds, which, as a rule, averaged a slightly lower income. According to the statistics presented by the *South American Journal*, for illustration, the nominal average return on the aggregate British investment in Latin America, including government bonds as well as economic enterprises, for the prosperous year 1913 was only 4.7 per cent; and for the prosperous eight years beginning with 1923 the annual nominal average was only 4.2 per cent, while for the depression decade starting with 1931 the annual nominal average return hardly exceeded 2 per cent. These were not exploitative profits, even if it be assumed that there were no capital losses and that half of the capitalization was water.

An Examination of the Most Profitable British Companies in Latin America

A list of the Latin-American enterprises to be examined here is presented in Table 30.[5] Englishmen held only minority interests in two of the twenty-three companies under inspection, namely, Havana

---

* There are convincing indications that the technicians of the United Nations and those selected to carry out the foreign economic programs of the United States during the postwar period have been well paid and will continue to be handsomely remunerated.

Table 30. A Sample of Profitable British Enterprises Operating in Latin America

Company	Year Begun	No. of Years Calculated	Initial Year	Nominal Annual Average Return	Highest 5 Years	Nominal Annual Average Return	Nominal Capital in Ordinary Shares	
							At Beginning of Dividend Period	At End of Dividend Period
San Paulo Railway Company	1858	55	1876	11.2%	1896–1900	13.2%	£2,000,000	£3,000,000
London and Brazilian Bank	1862	51	1873	12.8	1910–14	19.2	500,000	1,500,000
London and River Plate Bank	1862	48	1876	14.7	1908–12	20.7	600,000	2,040,000
River Plate Trust, Loan and Agency	1881	69	1881	16.5	1926–30	24.0	350,000	1,500,000
Butters Salvador Mines	1899	14	1903	55.1	1912–16	66.4	150,000	150,000
Cie. Aramayo de Mines en Bolivie	1906	40	1910	15.5	1922–26	33.2	494,090	1,000,000
Esperanza (Mexico)	1903	10	1904	50.7	1905–09	88.5	455,000	455,000
Mexico Mines of El Oro	1904	19	1909	69.1	1917–21	83.0	180,000	210,000
Pato Mines (Colombia)	1909	14	1919	90.0	1923–27	118.0	100,000	100,000
St. John del Rey Mining Company (Brazil)	1830	75	1875	9.2	1875–79	36.0	223,000	546,265
Lobitos Oilfields (Peru)	1908	38	1912	18.2	1921–25	52.0	360,000	1,000,000
Venezuelan Oil Concessions	1913	23	1926	27.4	1926–30	62.2	1,000,000	7,100,000
Alianza Nitrate	1895	26	1903	20.4	1920–24	47.0	500,000	500,000
Liverpool Nitrate	1883	40	1885	56.3	1917–21	128.0	44,000	350,000
London Nitrate	1887	38	1888	35.2	1888–92	178.5	50,000	200,000
Salar del Carmen Nitrate Syndicate	1896	28	1898	19.7	1904–08	34.0	109,500	220,000
Forestal Land, Timber and Railways (Argentina and Paraguay)	1906	44	1906	10.0	1915–19	21.7	500,000	3,708,837
Las Cabezas Estancia (Argentina)	1876	68	1882	11.3	1926–30	19.2	60,400	160,000
Pranges Estancia (Uruguay)	1867	43	1884	12.9	1916–20	25.6	48,000	120,000
Havana Cigar and Tobacco Factories	1898	40	1911	24.0	1925–29	49.0	250,000	250,000
Henry Clay and Bock and Company	1889	32	1919	26.6	1926–30	59.0	159,900	159,900
Liebig's Extract of Meat (Uruguay)	1865	77	1874	16.1	1904–09	23.5	357,200	2,000,000
Rio de Janeiro Flour Mills and Granaries	1886	58	1893	13.5	1923–27	20.0	158,760	1,364,838

The Crux of the Matter

Cigar and Tobacco Factories and Henry Clay and Bock and Company, and may not have held a controlling interest at all times in two others: the Aramayo mining properties in Bolivia and Mexico Mines of El Oro. In all cases, the rates of return stated in the following discussion have been based upon the nominal value of the investment and without taking stock dividends, which were rather numerous, into account.

Railroads, on the whole, were not among the most profitable English investments in Latin America. The San Paulo Railway Company, the most profitable British railroad enterprise in the region, managed, however, to pay a nominal annual average of 11.2 per cent on its ordinary shares for a period of fifty-five years (1876–1930).

Among the British financial organizations were three which paid rather high dividends for several decades. The River Plate Trust, Loan and Agency Company returned an average annual nominal dividend of 16.5 per cent on its preferred ordinary shares and 4.7 per cent on its deferred ordinary shares, the latter representing mainly stock bonuses, for sixty-nine consecutive years (1881–1950) without passing a single dividend. The London and Brazilian Bank paid an average nominal dividend of 12.8 per cent per annum for a period of fifty-one years beginning with the year 1873, and the annual average nominal yield of the London and River Plate Bank for the forty-eight years starting with 1876 was 14.7 per cent.

Of the many mining companies owned by Englishmen in Latin America, hardly more than fifteen were conspicuous for high dividends for more than a decade and only six or eight of these were remarkably profitable. Butters Salvador Mines yielded a nominal annual average of 55.1 per cent for the fourteen years beginning with 1903; Compagnie Aramayo de Mines en Bolivie (called Aramayo, Francke and Company at first) returned a nominal annual average of 15.5 per cent during a period of forty years starting with 1910; Esperanza (Mexico) yielded an annual nominal average of 50.7 per cent for the decade starting in 1904; Mexico Mines of El Oro, with considerable French capital, returned an annual nominal dividend of 69.1 per cent for the nineteen years beginning with 1909; Pato Mines (Colombia) yielded a yearly nominal average of 90 per cent for the fourteen years starting with 1919; and St. John del Rey (Brazil) recorded a nominal average yield of 9.2 per cent per annum for three quarters of a century

A Sample of British Overseas Companies

beginning with the year 1875, after yielding an average nominal of 23 per cent during the three decades preceding 1875.

At least three British petroleum companies operating in Latin America yielded high returns. Mexican Eagle Oil Company, organized in 1908 by the Lord Cowdray interests, was among the three, but the complex and inflated capital structure of this organization makes its dividend record almost meaningless. Lobitos Oilfields (Peru) returned an annual nominal average of 18.2 per cent for the thirty-eight years beginning with 1912 and Venezuelan Oil Concessions paid an average nominal dividend of 27.4 per cent annually for the twenty-three years starting in 1926.

Many of the some thirty-five or forty British nitrate companies which operated in Chile at one time or another were profitable, and some were conspicuous for their bountiful yields. Alianza paid an annual nominal average dividend of 20.4 per cent on its ordinary shares for a period of twenty-six years starting with 1903; Liverpool Nitrate yielded a nominal annual average of 56.3 per cent for the forty years beginning with 1885; London Nitrate paid an average nominal of 35.2 per cent per annum for thirty-eight years beginning with 1888; and Salar del Carmen returned an average nominal dividend of 19.7 annually for the twenty-eight years starting with 1898.

Two British companies engaged in ranching and one engaged mainly in the exploitation of forest products (especially quebracho) were rather profitable. Las Cabezas Estancia Company (Argentina) paid an average nominal dividend of 11.3 per cent for a period of sixty-eight years (1882–1949) and Pranges Estancia Company (Uruguay) yielded an annual nominal average of 12.9 per cent for forty-three years (1884–1926). Forestal Land, Timber and Railways Company (Argentina and Paraguay) returned a nominal annual average of 10 per cent for the forty-four years beginning with 1906.

Four manufacturing enterprises, two of them controlled by United States capital (American Tobacco Company) with English minority holdings and two owned by British investors, yielded high returns. Havana Cigar and Tobacco Factories paid an average nominal dividend of 24 per cent per annum for forty years starting in 1911 and Henry Clay and Bock (Cuba) yielded an average annual return of 26.6 per cent for the thirteen-year period of 1919–1950. Liebig's Extract of Meat Company, operating largely in Uruguay, yielded an

The Crux of the Matter

average nominal return of 16.1 per cent per annum for a stretch of seventy-seven years beginning with 1874 and Rio de Janeiro Flour Mills and Granaries returned an average nominal dividend of 13.5 per cent yearly for the forty-eight years starting with 1893.

Such was the dividend record — or a good part of the record — of twenty-three of the most profitable British (or partly British) economic organizations in Latin America. Table 30 recapitulates the data and gives the average annual nominal return for the most prosperous five-year period of each company, from which it can be seen that only three of the twenty-three failed to recoup their entire capital in half a decade and that an equal number more than recovered it in a single year (taking no account of stock dividends). (The reader should observe that ordinary share capital is the only capital considered in this analysis. Several of the companies listed had outstanding at one time or another either preference shares or debentures, but these yielded much lower returns.)

Summary of the Most Profitable Companies in Other Regions

Profitable as these companies may seem to be, it has not been difficult to discover four times as many English economic enterprises even more profitable operating in Malaya, India, Burma, Iran, Siam (Thailand), and Africa. The dividend records of twenty-three of these will not be summarized for comparison. They are listed in Table 31. Capitalization, as in Table 30, is for the years for which the dividend record will be examined.

Among the enterprises listed in Table 31 are five engaged in the production of rubber in Malaya, five mining tin in the Federated Malay States and Siam, five engaged in mining in Africa, two producing and refining petroleum extracted from Burma and Iran, and six operating tea plantations in India and Ceylon. Readers familiar with mining in South Africa may miss two of the famous companies — Consolidated Gold Fields of South Africa and De Beers Consolidated Mines — from which Cecil Rhodes drew his great fortune. The dividend records of these two large enterprises are somewhat less remarkable than those of the mining enterprises included in Table 31. The nominal annual returns of the twenty-three companies there tabulated are so impressive that comment seems unnecessary. The dividends

Table 31. Some Profitable British Enterprises Operating in the Orient and Africa

Company	Year Begun	No. of Years Calculated	Initial Year	Nominal Annual Average Return	Highest 5 Years	Nominal Annual Average Return	Nominal Capital in Ordinary Shares	
							Beginning of Dividend Period	End of Dividend Period
Batu Caves Rubber	1904	12	1908	144.2%	1912–16	187.0%	£26,750	£216,000
Bukit Rajah Rubber	1903	12	1909	90.0	1909–13	126.0	66,700	333,500
Linggi Plantations	1905	13	1906	107.4	1909–13	162.0	90,000	560,000
Pataling Rubber Estates Syndicate	1903	13	1907	196.5	1912–16	225.0	22,500	222,500
Vallambrosa Rubber	1904	12	1909	107.1	1909–13	147.0	50,600	50,600
Kampong Kamunting Tin Dredging	1916	28	1923	72.4	1946–50	280.0	140,000	7,000
Kinta Tin Mines	1900	41	1910	19.1	1946–50	30.5	60,000	120,000
Kramat Pulai	1907	39	1912	39.4	1934–38	97.7	100,000	5,000
Malayan Tin Dredging	1911	37	1914	28.9	1936–40	60.5	110,000	200,000
Siamese Tin Syndicate	1906	38	1913	27.2	1923–27	49.0	120,000	150,000
Crown Mines	1892	48	1908	99.0	1936–40	189.0	300,000	943,062
Globe and Phoenix Gold Mining	1895	51	1900	54.7	1910–14	132.0	200,000	200,000
New Modderfontein Gold Mining	1895	45	1906	56.8	1927–31	132.5	1,200,000	840,000
Premier (Transvaal) Diamond Mining	1902	23	1905	367.8	1916–20	520.0	40,000	40,000
Rand Mines	1893	47	1904	138.4	1909–13	246.0	448,989	537,749
Burmah Oil	1902	44	1906	24.0	1921–25	38.0	1,100,000	13,736,513
Anglo-Iranian Oil	1909	30	1920	17.1	1945–49	28.0	7,500,000	20,137,500
Allynugger Tea	1892	35	1915	26.6	1924–28	47.0	70,000	90,000
Assam Estates	1910	34	1917	36.9	1922–26	60.0	15,000	30,000
Borbheel Tea	1908	35	1915	37.2	1922–26	83.0	14,800	22,200
Hope Tea	1907	44	1907	26.8	1923–27	50.0	84,000	168,000
New Dimbula		52	1899	27.4	1923–27	53.0	78,954	259,390
Rajmai Tea	1890	61	1890	27.9	1924–28	75.0	30,000	56,000

The Crux of the Matter

distributed by the managers of these enterprises during their most prosperous five-year periods are truly amazing.[6] Nor should it be assumed that the day of big profits has passed, even in the case of plantation rubber. Rubber profits will depend upon conditions in the Orient and upon competition, or lack of it, between the plantation and the synthetic producers. The five rubber companies listed in Table 31 paid the following dividends on the par value of their ordinary shares in 1950: Batu Caves, 20 per cent; Bukit Rajah, 5; Linggi Plantations, 25; Pataling, 50; Vallambrosa, 25.*

British companies growing tea in India and Ceylon have been more prosperous over the years than British companies cultivating rubber in Malaya. The dividend records of twenty-two tea plantations are presented in Table 32.† Numerous profitable British enterprises may also be found among those mining tin in Malaya, Nigeria, and Thailand (Siam). Table 33 exhibits the record of twenty of the most prosperous.‡ Most profitable of all have been the British mining companies operating in Africa. Table 34 sets forth the dividend record of twenty-four of the most remunerative.§

British economic enterprises operating in the Commonwealth and Empire during the fifty years beginning with 1900, and probably also for the preceding three or four decades, were far more prosperous on the whole than British enterprises operating in most of the Latin-American countries during these years. Returns from capital invested in government securities, railways, and public utilities were probably no larger in the Commonwealth and Empire than in Latin America during the most profitable periods, but the income was steadier and more dependable.

British investments in the Commonwealth and Empire yielded higher returns than British capital in Latin America for various rea-

* More than half of the British rubber companies listed in the *Stock Exchange Official Year-Book* for 1951 paid nominal dividends of 10 per cent and above on their ordinary shares in 1950; twenty-five of them returned from 30 to 80 per cent.

† Three fourths of the more than 200 British companies growing tea returned nominal dividends of above 10 per cent in 1950 and 49 enterprises paid from 25 to 50 per cent.

‡ Two thirds of the more than 70 British tin companies yielded a nominal return of more than 10 per cent in 1950 and 29 paid from 30 to 900 per cent!

§ The decade beginning in 1942 was one of the most profitable in the history of mining in British Africa. Of the approximately 180 companies (excluding those engaged in tin-mining in Nigeria) listed in the *Stock Exchange Official Year-Book*, at least half paid an annual average nominal dividend of above 10 per cent during this ten-year period and 17 returned annual averages ranging from 69.6 to more than 200 per cent.

Table 32. Some Profitable British Investments in Tea Plantations in India and Ceylon

Company	Year Begun	No. of Years Calculated	Initial Year	Annual Average Return*	Highest 5 Years	Annual Average Return*	Nominal Capital in Ordinary Shares	
							Beginning of Dividend Period	End of Dividend Period
Allynugger Tea	1892	59	1892	18.4%	1924-28	47.0%	£70,000	£90,000
Assam	1839	72	1879	12.3	1919-23	26.0	187,000	1,000,000
Assam-Dooars Tea	1895	49	1902	23.9	1924-28	46.5	100,000	200,000
Assam Estates	1910	34	1917	26.9	1946-50	60.0	15,000	30,000
Bagracote Tea	1923	28	1923	15.8	1923-27	50.0	65,000	78,000
Balmoral Estates	1898	47	1904	24.2	1924-28	51.0	52,035	52,035
Bamgaon Tea	1903	47	1904	16.2	1921-25	38.0	10,000	50,000
Battalgalla Estate	1889	45	1906	22.6	1924-28	74.0	15,000	45,000
Borbheel Tea	1908	43	1908	31.7	1922-26	83.0	14,800	22,200
Borelli Tea	1874	72	1879	14.5	1923-27	50.0	78,170	78,170
Buxa Dooars Tea	1895	47	1904	19.2	1923-27	39.0	50,000	100,000
Doom Dooma Tea	1877	71	1880	15.1	1923-27	42.0	116,100	265,000
Eastern Assam	1864	55	1896	16.3	1922-26	42.0	61,120	197,240
Hope Tea	1907	44	1907	26.8	1923-27	50.0	84,000	168,000
Isa Bheel Tea	1904	40	1911	18.7	1923-27	39.0	21,000	42,000
Kukicherra Tea	1914	37	1914	16.6	1924-28	48.5	25,000	50,000
Lankapara Tea	1895	50	1901	17.5	1911-15	26.0	50,000	100,000
Leesh River Tea	1877	68	1883	14.0	1924-28	38.0	15,000	40,000
Moran Tea	1893	58	1893	19.7	1924-28	51.0	25,500	172,000
New Dimbula Tea	1890	52	1899	27.4	1923-27	53.0	78,954	259,390
Rajmai Tea	1890	61	1890	27.9	1924-28	75.0	30,000	56,000
Travancore Tea Estates	1897	43	1908	21.4	1923-27	42.0	33,500	106,500

* Share bonuses are not included in the figures for rates of return; only cash dividends have been considered.

Table 33. Some Profitable British Investments in the Tin Mines of Malaya, Nigeria, and Siam

Company	Year Begun	No. of Years Calculated	Initial Year	Annual Average Return*	Highest 5 Years	Annual Average Return*	Nominal Capital in Ordinary Shares	
							Beginning of Dividend Period	End of Dividend Period
Ayer Hitim Tin Dredging	1926	21	1930	20.4%	1937–41	41.0%	£180,000	£180,000
Gopeng Consolidated	1912	38	1913	12.5	1923–27	20.0	329,750	395,768
Kampong Kamunting Tin Dredging	1916	34	1917	72.4	1946–50	280.0	140,000	7,000
Kamunting Tin Dredging	1913	36	1915	12.5	1924–28	28.5	130,000	668,750
Kinta Tin Mines	1900	48	1903	18.5	1946–50	30.5	60,000	120,000
Kramat Tin Dredging	1926	20	1931	21.1	1946–50	28.0	165,000	165,000
Kramat Pulai	1907	39	1912	39.4	1934–38	97.7	100,000	5,000
Malayan Tin Dredging	1911	37	1914	28.9	1936–40	60.5	110,000	200,000
Pahang Consolidated	1906	38	1913	13.5	1934–38	28.0	286,907	375,000
Renong Tin Dredging	1913	35	1916	12.9	1925–29	23.5	76,767	175,000
Southern Kinta Consolidated	1934	16	1935	14.1	1937–41	23.0	874,269	962,000
Southern Malayan Tin Dredging	1926	23	1928	25.3	1946–50	41.0	328,584	432,500
Southern Tronoh Tin Dredging	1927	21	1930	17.9	1946–50	47.0	200,000	200,000
Sungei Besi Mines	1909	35	1916	18.9	1936–40	48.0	111,407	163,580
Tronoh Mines	1901	49	1902	26.3	1946–50	55.0	160,000	300,000
Ex-Lands, Nigeria	1912	36	1915	12.7	1946–50	34.0	134,901	200,000
Jantar Nigeria	1912	38	1913	15.2	1940–44	34.0	60,000	135,000
Kaduna Prospectors	1913	32	1919	15.1	1939–43	30.4	10,750	18,000
Kaduna Syndicate	1910	39	1912	43.0	1946–50	70.0	10,000	38,000
Siamese Tin Syndicate	1906	38	1913	27.2	1923–27	49.0	120,000	150,000

* Share bonuses are not included in the figures for rates of return; only cash dividends have been considered.

Table 34. Some Profitable British Investments in African Gold and Diamond Mines

Company	Year Begun	No. of Years Calculated	Initial Year	Annual Average Return*	Highest 5 Years	Annual Average Return*	Nominal Capital in Ordinary Shares	
							Beginning of Dividend Period	End of Dividend Period
Ashanti Goldfields Corporation	1897	51	1900	58.5%	1930–34	96.0%	£130,000	£1,248,557
Brakpan Mines	1903	39	1912	40.3	1936–40	62.0	750,000	1,150,000
Consolidated African Selection Trust	1924	25	1926	45.7	1946–50	65.0	249,778	1,516,554
Consolidated Gold Fields of South Africa	1892	58	1893	18.9	1893–97	65.0	1,250,000	4,200,000
Crown Mines	1892	53	1898	91.2	1936–40	189.0	300,000	943,062
Daggafontein Mines	1916	18	1933	55.3	1946–50	76.5	1,750,000	1,750,000
De Beers Consolidated Mines	1888	62	1889	34.3	1946–50	82.0	3,948,955	4,375,000
East Geduld Mines	1927	19	1932	54.2	1946–50	71.5	1,560,000	1,800,000
East Rand Proprietary Mines	1893	48	1903	19.5	1907–11	39.5	994,500	1,980,000
Ferreira Deep	1898	25	1903	28.0	1910–14	53.5	900,000	980,000
Ferreira Estate	1929	15	1936	278.3	1936–40	505.0	57,829	9,638
Ferreira Gold Mining	1887	21	1891	200.7	1906–10	383.0	44,000	95,000
Geduld Proprietary Mines	1899	37	1914	42.6	1936–40	85.7	875,000	1,460,857
Gledenhuis Deep	1893	54	1897	25.0	1946–50	70.0	300,000	28,333
Globe and Phoenix Gold Mining	1895	50	1901	55.8	1910–14	132.0	200,000	200,000
Government Gold Mining Areas (Modderfontein)	1910	34	1917	65.8	1932–36	113.0	1,400,000	1,400,000
Modderfontein B Gold Mines	1908	39	1912	58.7	1920–24	96.5	700,000	560,000
Modderfontein Deep Levels	1899	20	1915	99.2	1920–24	141.0	500,000	500,000
Modderfontein East	1917	24	1927	27.5	1939–43	37.0	465,445	930,805
New Modderfontein Gold Mining	1895	45	1906	56.9	1927–31	132.5	1,200,000	840,000
Premier (Transvaal) Diamond Mining	1902	23	1905	367.8	1916–20	520.0	40,000	40,000
Rand Mines	1893	53	1898	127.5	1909–13	246.0	448,989	537,749
Sub Nigel	1895	39	1912	68.6	1935–39	159.0	431,580	885,937
Union Corporation	1918	32	1919	47.0	1934–38	65.6	875,000	1,162,500

* Share bonuses are not included in the figures for rates of return; only cash dividends have been considered.

The Crux of the Matter

sons, most of them rather obvious. In the first place, there was greater stability within the Commonwealth and Empire and greater capacity to determine the investment climate. Second, labor was probably cheaper. Third, investors had more effective control over prices and output of such products as tea, rubber, and diamonds, market domination of Latin-American products being restricted mainly to natural nitrates (until around 1920), quebracho, and the small output of diamonds. Fourth, fewer difficulties were occasioned by oscillations in currency values and rates of exchange.

But let it be reiterated, with apologies if necessary, that only the most profitable British overseas investments have been dealt with in this chapter. Many others ventured in the Commonwealth and Empire yielded low returns or resulted in losses, although the relative number of such investments was smaller than in Latin America. Chapter XVI will attempt a more realistic perspective, at least for the years 1939–1948.

⇋ XVI ⇌

A RECENT DECADE OF INCOME FROM BRITISH OVERSEAS INVESTMENT

Excepting such global data as C. K. Hobson furnished in his *Export of Capital*, readily available statistics on income derived from British overseas investments have been scanty until quite recently. Among the compilations that have appeared since the termination of World War II, the most comprehensive was published in 1950 by the Bank of England under the title of *United Kingdom Overseas Investments, 1938 to 1948*.[1] Although this compilation does not include rates of return, it presents data from which such rates can be ascertained by means of patient and persistent calculation. A summary, based upon these data, of British overseas investments during the decade starting with 1939 and ending with 1948, emphasizing average yields for this ten-year period, may have some significance for the postwar programs intended to speed the economic growth of the underdeveloped (or hitherto improperly developed) countries of the world. At any rate, such a summary should help to place the British experience in Latin America in its global setting.

A few comments on the nature of the statistics dealt with seem necessary before beginning the analysis. The figures for capital investment represent par values and not market values and are incomplete (including only some three fourths of the total), insurance companies, maritime shipping companies, some private firms, and several other enterprises, most of them of minor importance, being omitted. Moreover, aggregates for both capital and income are given in round numbers, and my statistics for rates of return, calculated on the basis of par values, take no account of share bonuses, additions to reserves, or capital losses, but consider merely the income actually received in the United Kingdom, whether by investors or by the Commissioners of Inland Revenue. Capital losses, however, were by no means as great

The Crux of the Matter

as the contraction of the investment over the decade might suggest, for the capital was reduced mainly by the sale of assets. Capital statistics refer to the end of the years specified.

The overseas investment of residents of the British Isles — or that part of it identified by the Bank of England — shrank from £3,490 million in 1939 to £1,960 million in 1948, and income actually received declined from £143.8 million to £116.4 million. The average nominal rate of return for the decade was approximately 4.4 per cent annually, but was close to 6 per cent in 1948.

Income from the Commonwealth and Empire

Capital invested by residents of the United Kingdom in the countries of the Commonwealth and Empire stood at £1,978 million, more than half of the total, in 1939 and at £1,111 million, nearly 60 per cent of the aggregate, in 1948. Income received from this portion of the investment declined from £102.1 million in 1939 to £71.7 million in 1948, the average annual nominal yield being 5.4 per cent and the rate for 1948 being approximately 6.5. The average annual nominal rate on the share capital invested in these countries, capital which contracted from £545.3 million in 1939 to £469 million in 1948, was 7.7 per cent for the decade and 10 per cent for 1948.

The most profitable segment of this part of the investment was in Africa. The nominal average annual rate of return from British Africa — excluding the Anglo-Egyptian Sudan, from which the income was at the annual average rate of 7 per cent on £11 million to £14 million — was 8.7 per cent on a total capital that shrank from £356 million to £268 million during the period; but the average yearly nominal rate on share capital, running from £169.9 million in 1939 to £179 million in 1948, was 11.3 per cent. The largest profits were drawn from the Union of South Africa, a nominal per-annum median of 10.4 per cent on a total investment ranging from £110 million to £206 million, with more than half of the total, the investment in share capital, paying at the average nominal rate of 14 per cent annually. For other sections of Africa, the median annual nominal yields of share capital during the decade were as follows: Central Africa (the two Rhodesias and Nyasaland), 9.5 per cent; West Africa (Nigeria, Gold Coast, Gambia, and Sierra Leone), 8 per cent; East Africa (Kenya, Uganda, Tanganyika, and Zanzibar), 4.6 per cent.

A Recent Decade of British Investment

Only a little less profitable than the investment in British Africa was the capital in India (including Pakistan) and Ceylon. The average annual return from India and Pakistan for the decade was 7.7 per cent on a par capital that contracted from £379 million to £69 million. From the investment in share capital the annual average received was 10.9 per cent on a nominal principal ranging from £74.6 million to £51 million. The nominal rate of return from Ceylon averaged 7.8 per cent annually on £25 million to £27 million, the yearly return on approximately £21 million, par value, in share capital averaging 8.4.

Income from British Malaya probably would not have been startling even if the Japanese invasion had not occurred. Because of that catastrophe, almost no income was received during the last seven years of the decade under inspection. But the average annual rate was 6.9 per cent on an investment with a par value of £64 million to £67 million for the four years starting with 1938, and the nominal annual average was approximately 19 per cent for the same period on the approximately £20 million in the share capital of economic enterprises.

Burma, likewise harried by the second global war, sent English investors almost no income between 1942 and 1948. For the four years beginning with 1938, however, the average annual return on a nominal £20 million was no less than 10.6 per cent, while the yearly average for this quadrennium on the slightly more than £10 million invested in share capital was 11.8.

Income from Australia, New Zealand, and Canada was at a rather low rate during the decade, less than 4.5 per cent on the par value of the aggregate investment in all three countries. The par value of the capital invested in Australia shrank from £522 million in 1939 to £397 million in 1948 and the annual rate of return averaged less than 4.3 per cent; the investment in share capital, contracting from £47.4 million to £40.7 million, averaged 6.5 per annum. A nominal investment shrinking from £144 million to £66 million in New Zealand returned an annual average of slightly more than 4.4 per cent, with the share-capital segment, £6.8 million to £8.2 million, paying a yearly average of 5.8. Canada, with an aggregate nominal investment contracting from £395 million in 1939 to £162 million in 1948, yielded a yearly average of only 4.3 per cent, while share capital made returns at the average rate of only 4.4 per cent per annum, the nominal capital in this category slumping from £114.5 million to £84 million.

Table 35. Income from British Investments in Commonwealth and Empire Countries, 1939–1948

Country	Nominal Capital (In Millions)		Average Rate of Return, 1939–1948
	1939	1948	
All countries *			
Total capital	£1,978.0	£1,111.0	5.4%
Share capital	545.3	469.0	7.7
British Africa			
Total capital	356.0	268.0	8.7
Share capital	169.9	179.0	11.3
South Africa			
Total capital	206.0	127.0	10.4
Share capital	89.6	102.2	14.0
Central Africa			
Total capital	72.0	79.0	6.6
Share capital	37.2	33.3	9.5
West Africa			
Total capital	54.0	47.0	6.3
Share capital	35.1	35.2	8.0
East Africa			
Total capital	24.0	15.0	4.8
Share capital	8.0	8.3	4.6
India and Pakistan			
Total capital	379.0	69.0	7.7
Share capital	74.6	51.0	10.9
Ceylon			
Total capital	27.0	26.0	7.8
Share capital	21.0	21.8	8.4
Australia			
Total capital	522.0	397.0	4.3
Share capital	47.4	40.7	6.5
New Zealand			
Total capital	144.0	66.0	4.4
Share capital	8.2	6.8	5.8
Canada			
Total capital	395.0	162.0	4.3
Share capital	114.5	84.0	4.4
Other British America			
Total capital	22.0	21.0	5.9
Share capital	11.2	10.4	8.6

* A. R. Conan, in his *The Sterling Area* (London, 1952), Chapter IV, using par values for government securities and market values for other investments, arrives at a total of £2,450,000,000 for British funds invested in the Commonwealth and Empire countries in 1938 and at the same total for 1950! He includes India, Pakistan, and Burma in both estimates.

A Recent Decade of British Investment

The remainder of British America, principally Guiana, Trinidad, and small island possessions, sent higher returns than did Canada to investors in the United Kingdom. On a nominal total of £18 million to £22 million the average yearly return for the decade was 5.9 per cent. On an investment in shares ranging from £9.3 million to £11.5 million the average yield for the period was 8.6 per cent, the rate probably being pushed up mainly by the handsome returns on the capital in Trinidad petroleum.

Table 35 summarizes the story for the major divisions of the Commonwealth and Empire. British Malaya and Burma are omitted because of the abnormalities of the war period.

Income from Foreign Countries

On the whole, residents of the United Kingdom derived very modest income from their investments in foreign countries during the decade under consideration. World War II was largely responsible for the meager returns from Europe and the Orient. Income from Latin America was pared down by economic nationalism, defaults on government bonds, exchange controls, and inflation of the currency.

The par value of the British investment considered by the Bank of England in foreign countries contracted from £1,417 million in 1939 to £749 million in 1948. Although total income did not decline so sharply, dropping from £37.3 million to £28.8 million, the average nominal rate of return for the ten-year period was only slightly above 3 per cent annually and was only 4.8 in 1948.

Profits from Egypt and Iran, however, were excellent, and returns from the United States were fairly high. On an investment of from £7 million to £11 million in Egypt the average annual nominal yield was 15.8 per cent. The yearly average derived from a nominal of £34 million in Iran was 14.6 per cent. The British investment in the United States, shrinking from a nominal £250 million in 1939 to £75 million in 1948, returned an average of 6.2 per annum, and the rate for share capital in economic enterprises, which dropped from a par of £188.8 million in 1939 to £63.8 million in 1948, averaged a little above 7 per cent annually.

But British capital in Egypt, Iran, and the United States, according to the Bank's figures, represented less than a fourth of the aggregate of British assets in foreign countries. The nominal rate of return for

The Crux of the Matter

war-torn Europe declined from 3.4 per cent in 1938 and 3.2 in 1939 to around 1 per cent in 1944 and rose to a mere 2.1 per cent in 1948, while the par value of the investment shrank during these years from £217 million to £167 million. Returns from the uninvaded countries, mainly Spain and Portugal, were only a little higher than the general European average; namely, an annual median of a little less than 3 per cent for the decade beginning with 1939 on a nominal capital ranging from £44 million to £67 million.

British income from the Netherlands East Indies, invaded by Japan late in 1941 and disturbed by revolution after the Japanese withdrawal, amounted to an annual average of only 4.4 per cent for the four years beginning with 1938 on a nominal capital of between £23 million and £24 million and practically ceased during the next seven years.

The Bank of England's statistics for Latin America are very incomplete. Income from the British investment in South America, capital which shrank from £665 million in 1939 to £260 million in 1948, according to the incomplete data of the Bank, averaged a bit less than 1.3 per cent per annum during the decade, and the nominal rate of return for the share capital, £294.2 million at the beginning and £127.4 million at the end of the decade, averaged hardly more than 1.9 per cent annually! The average annual nominal rates for some of the major countries during the period were Argentina, on a nominal capital declining from £355 million in 1939 to £51 million in 1948, a mere 3.2 per cent, with share capital averaging only 1.4 per cent; Brazil, on a nominal aggregate shrinking from £163 million to £82 million, a meager 2.5 per cent, with share capital, which slumped from £48.7 million to £37.9 million, paying no more than a nominal yearly average of 3.2 per cent; Chile, on a nominal total dropping from £62 million to £47 million, approximately 1.6 per cent, while from £4.4 to £7.1 million in shares of business enterprises paid a nominal yearly average of 3.6 per cent; Peru, on capital ranging from £22 million to £25 million, an average of a bit less than 1.7 per cent annually, with share capital amounting to some £15 million yielding an average of barely 1 per cent; Uruguay, on a total of £22 million to £23 million, a yearly average of a little more than 2 per cent, and a per-annum average of around 1.4 per cent on an investment of between £9 million and £10 million in share capital.

Table 36. Income from British Investments in Foreign Countries, 1939-1948

Country	Nominal Capital (In Millions)		Average Rate of Return, 1939-1948
	1939	1948	
All foreign countries *			
Total capital	£1,417.0	£749.0	3.0%
Egypt			
Total capital	11.0	7.0	15.8
Iran			
Total capital	34.0	34.0	14.6
United States			
Total capital	250.0	75.0	6.2
Share capital	188.8	63.8	7.0
South America			
Total capital	665.0	260.0	1.3
Share capital	294.2	127.4	1.9
Argentina			
Total capital	355.0	51.0	3.2
Share capital	182.5	29.2	1.4
Brazil			
Total capital	163.0	82.0	2.5
Share capital	48.7	37.9	3.2
Chile			
Total capital	62.0	47.0	1.6
Share capital	7.1	4.4	3.6
Uruguay			
Total capital	23.0	22.0	2.0
Share capital	10.0	9.5	1.4
Peru			
Total capital	25.0	22.0	1.7
Other South America			
Total capital	37.0	33.0	5.7
Share capital	21.8	20.2	7.7
Cuba			
Total capital	28.0	24.0	0.5
Mexico			
Total capital	65.0	30.0	1.3
Share capital	23.6	7.9	3.2

* Reckoning government securities at par and other investments at the market, A. R. Conan in *The Sterling Area* arrives at an aggregate of slightly more than £2 billion for British investments in foreign countries in 1938 and a total of £1.75 billion in 1950, excluding India, Pakistan, and Burma. Adding these sums to his figures for the Commonwealth and Empire countries, the aggregate British investment would be £4.5 billion for 1938 and £4.2 billion for 1950. These various totals seem too high. But the Bank of England's figures are admittedly incomplete.

The Crux of the Matter

Income from the other five South American countries, lumped together by the Bank of England, was considerably higher, the average rate having been increased by the returns from Venezuelan petroleum, Bolivian tin, and Colombian gold. On a nominal aggregate ranging from £33 million to £37 million invested in Colombia, Venezuela, Ecuador, Bolivia, and Paraguay, the average nominal annual rate for the decade was 6.7 per cent, and the approximately £20 million in share capital of business firms in these five republics yielded an annual nominal average of 7.7.

Returns from Cuba during the decade were amazingly low, the nominal rate of return on a total of from £24 million to £28 million being scarcely more than an average of 0.5 per cent annually. The Bank of England's statistics for Central America are too skimpy to permit any generalization regarding profits except that they were very small; and the Bank furnishes no data at all for Haiti and the Dominican Republic. The nominal rate on from £30 million to £65 million invested in Mexico averaged only 1.3 per cent annually for the decade, with shares of business enterprises paying an annual median of 3.2 per cent, the yield of this type of capital being sharply reduced by Mexico's seizure of British oil properties early in 1938.

Table 36 presents the most significant statistics of British investments in foreign countries, omitting devastated Europe and the smaller nations of Latin America for which the Bank of England's data are inadequate or lacking.* The figures for capital invested in most of the Latin-American countries are somewhat too low.

The Most Profitable Types of Investment

What types of British overseas investments were most profitable during this decade? The Bank of England furnishes data from which the answer to this question can be found. In descending order of nominal rates of return, investments paying an annual average of more than 6 per cent during the period were in petroleum, breweries, tea and coffee (mainly tea) plantations, mining, banking, manufactur-

* Japan and China are also omitted because of the immense abnormalities created by prolonged war. The investment in Japan ranged from £46 million to £50 million, mostly in government bonds; the average annual rate of return was 5.1 per cent for 1938-1941 and almost nothing for 1942-1948. The investment in China, the major part of it also in government securities, was between £36 million and £37 million; the average yearly rate of yield was 2.1 per cent for 1938-1941, and practically nothing during the next seven years.

A Recent Decade of British Investment

...g and trading, and electric light and power. It may seem surprising ...hat rubber plantations, which once rewarded British investors so ...andsomely, are not in the list. But returns from these were depressed ...oth by the Japanese invasion and by the growing competition of ...ynthetic rubber.

Share capital of British overseas petroleum organizations yielded a ...ominal average of 11.6 per cent yearly on an aggregate of from £108.5 ...illion to £114.4 million. Very little loan capital was invested in oil.

The British overseas investment in breweries yielded income at the ...ominal average rate of 11.3 per cent annually during the decade. This ...cludes share capital only; but most of the investment was in that ...rm, and the total remained fairly constant, £6.6 million in 1939 and ...3 million in 1948.

The rate of return from coffee and tea plantations averaged 9.1 per ...nt annually on shares with a par value running from £38.5 million ...£39.9 million. This capital, as already suggested, was more profitable ...ring this decade than the investment in mining. A total of £37 mil...n to £44 million ventured in shares of companies mining gold re-...rned a nominal average of only 7.6 per cent per annum. Income from ...are capital in mines other than those producing gold was somewhat ...gher, an average of 8.1 per cent annually on an aggregate capital of ...tween £61.7 million and £66.5 million, copper, tin, diamonds, and ...anganese yielding better returns than gold. Nearly all of the British ...erseas capital invested in mining enterprises was in the form of ...dinary and preference shares.

Income from capital invested in banks operating overseas — all ...are capital — averaged 7.5 per cent annually during the decade and ... per cent in 1948. The investment in these banking organizations ...d a par value of somewhat more than £45 million.

Overseas commercial and manufacturing enterprises paid annual ...erage dividends of 7.1 per cent on their share capital. The par value ... this capital, which included the major part of the investment, was ...22.1 million in 1939 and £119.8 million in 1948.

Returns on the shares of companies producing electric light and ...wer averaged 6.5 per cent per annum. But the total capital thus ...vested contracted from a nominal £33.5 million in 1939 to a nominal ...2.1 million in 1948.

The less profitable types of British overseas investments in economic

The Crux of the Matter

Table 37. Rates of Return from the Most Profitable British Overseas Investments for the Decade 1939–1948

Type	Nominal Share Capital (In Millions) 1939	1948	Average Rate 1939–1948
Petroleum	£108.5	£114.4	11.6%
Breweries	6.6	6.3	11.3
Tea and coffee (mostly tea)	39.9	38.5	9.1
Mining, other than gold	66.6	61.7	8.1
Gold mining	44.0	37.0	7.6
Banking	45.0	45.9	7.5
Trading and manufacturing	122.1	119.8	7.1
Electric light and power	33.5	22.1	6.5

enterprises were these: tramways, cables and telegraph lines, tel phones, gas plants, waterworks, railways, docks and canals, ranchir and farming, urban real estate. Table 37 lists the share capital ar average rates of return from the most profitable types of investmen Neither those mentioned in this paragraph nor investments in go ernment bonds are entitled to be included among them.

What Are the Practical Conclusions?

From these data a few conclusions seem evident. With minor e ceptions, British investments within the Commonwealth and Empi were more profitable during the decade than foreign investments. F investors of the United Kingdom, the most profitable segments of t Commonwealth and Empire were South Africa, British Central Afri (the Rhodesias and Nyasaland), India and Pakistan, and Ceylo Australia, New Zealand, and Canada were among the least profitab The most remunerative British foreign investments were the inve. ments in Egypt and Iran, the most profitable of all British overse investments during this particular period. Also fairly profitable w British capital operating in the United States, Venezuela, and Boliv Except for investments in the United States, which seem to dep from the norm, the obvious conclusion appears to be that rates of turn tend to be highest from countries where the masses are poore

But this generalization is affected by another important fact namely, the type of activity in which the capital is engaged. If t capital is in breweries, or in banking or trading companies, or in t manufacture of tobacco, chemicals, medicines, or cosmetics, it is lik

A Recent Decade of British Investment

to be profitable almost anywhere. If it is in tea plantations, it is apt to be profitable in Ceylon, India, Pakistan, and certain parts of British East Africa where tea grows best. If it is in petroleum, it will probably be most profitable in regions where the richest deposits of petroleum exist: in Iran, Burma, Saudi Arabia, Trinidad, Peru, and Venezuela, for example. If it is in mining, it is likely to bring high returns from British Malaya and certain parts of Africa, India, and Latin America where tin, diamonds, gold, copper, and manganese are plentiful. And the masses are poor in all the countries and regions mentioned.

Aside from organizations engaged in the production of electric power and light (and perhaps some enterprises operating wireless systems), public services — broadly defined so as to include railways, docks, canals, and possibly irrigation systems, along with telephones, gas plants, public health and sanitation, education, and the like — returned meager profits to the British overseas investor. But such public services will have to be included in any effective program intended to raise levels of living in the retarded countries.

Granted that the recent British experience is typical, this poses a major problem, one of the most serious economic problems that a development program is likely to encounter. Must these public services be subsidized by cheap loans and gifts from the governments of the more prosperous nations until the peoples of the underdeveloped regions attain sufficient prosperity to pay for them? If the burden of providing such services must be carried by the taxpayers of the wealthier nations, should the governments of these nations attempt to set limits on the profits of private investors who engage in the more remunerative activities in the underdeveloped regions? Will private capital continue to migrate to such regions if public officials place rigid limits on private profits? To what extent are higher profits made at the expense of native labor and to what extent are they extracted from consumers in the more intensively developed countries? Should such consumers be compelled to increase their contribution in order to stimulate the flow of capital, paying higher prices as well as heavier taxes? If private enterprise, in possession of the freedom of action it has generally enjoyed during most of the past century, has not succeeded in abolishing poverty on a good part of the earth, what has been lacking, efficiency, or moderation and generosity? Or is it mainly

The Crux of the Matter

time that is lacking? And if the key requirement is more time, how much more time will be needed? Will a program that requires a long period to become effective succeed in preventing the spread of Communism? Are there barriers and imponderables in the retarded region as well as in the more highly developed countries? Is the program necessary in order to prevent depression in the industrialized economies? Will the attempt to carry out the program enrich the poor or impoverish the rich and the well-to-do? Will it promote free enterprise or state socialism?

⇆ XVII ⇌

SOME BRITISH VIEWS ON FOREIGN INVESTMENTS

Regarding the advantages of foreign investment, opinion has seldom been uniform or stable in either the countries exporting capital or in those receiving it. Opinion has tended to swing from one extreme to the other — from approval to disapproval, from cordiality to hostility — lenders and borrowers alike considering the process from the standpoint of their own interest and rarely from that of mutual advantage.

The nations exporting capital, by and large, have taken the initiative. The role of the recipient countries, although sometimes quite active, has been mainly passive. Back of the great epoch of capital export, which did not begin to reach its maximum significance until near the end of the nineteenth century, was a long period of colonial enterprise, accompanied by some overseas investment, during which non-European peoples were subjected to external control without their consent. It may be that the welfare of such peoples was never wholly ignored, but their welfare was not given primary consideration. Other objectives were paramount.

The Main Motivation

Without ignoring the influence of love of power, prestige, and adventure, or denying the existence of religious and other benevolent motives, one may still insist, with sound justification, that the major objectives of the long era of colonialism that began with the Age of Discovery were economic. It was not merely that Europeans, and eventually not a few people in the United States, were moved by a strong desire for new commodities and bigger profits. Colonialism, in its later stages at least, was perhaps largely a by-product of the economic systems of the new nation-states, which suffered more and more severely from business cycles and sought to prolong the periods of prosperity and avoid depressions by exporting actual or alleged surpluses and

The Crux of the Matter

importing food and raw materials from distant and less developed lands. In the course of the nineteenth century in particular, colonies began to be viewed by ruling groups as a major remedy for a chronic disease of the more highly developed national economies.

But colonies were not looked upon as the sole outlets for surpluses or as the only foreign sources of foods and crude materials. When no formidable barriers were raised, underdeveloped independent countries might, and often did, serve equally well in both capacities. Trade, capital, and people moved in large streams back and forth across the boundaries of sovereign states and apparently mitigated the economic ills of the more intensively developed nations.

At some period following the Age of Discovery — the exact date is not important here — the word imperialism, Roman in origin, not only became a synonym for colonialism but was expanded so as to include the promotion and protection of capital investment in underdeveloped but presumably independent countries. Sometimes it was even said that such new or retarded countries came to occupy approximately the status of colonies; but on this there was disagreement. Many who concerned themselves with the subject refused to accept such an extreme view. Others talked of two types of imperialism, applying to colonialism the single word imperialism and employing the term "economic imperialism" to describe official promotion and protection of international trade and investment; but eventually they found themselves almost in agreement with those who contended that there was little difference between the two types, either in their motivations or their ultimate effects. The fundamental motives of both were essentially the same: (1) the desire for vents for "surplus" commodities — especially manufactured products, "surplus" capital, "surplus" population, and "surplus" skills in technology and business management; (2) the desire for more abundant raw materials for factories and food for factory workers; and (3) now and then a benevolent impulse to uplift colonials and other economically retarded peoples. Both political imperialism and alleged economic imperialism, in short, were impelled largely by the profit motive and both represented a search for relief from an economic malady — or fear of it — that worsened with the growth of manufacturing enterprises. And for the peoples of the retarded independent nations and the inhabitants of the colonial areas, the impact often turned out to be similar because large investments in the

British Views on Foreign Investments

theoretically independent but economically underdeveloped nations resulted in the injection of considerable political influence.

Whatever one may think of these contentions, it is a fact that the welfare of the recipients of exported capital was for many years ignored by the investing nations or else the investors tacitly assumed that what was supposed to be good for the lender would also be good for the borrower. And when the advantages of foreign investment were questioned in the nations presumed to have surplus capital, doubts did not arise from any tender consideration for the welfare of the recipient countries. It was mainly a question of profits or losses for the nations exporting capital. Not until around 1900, perhaps, was any serious attention given to the mutuality of advantage or disadvantage.

Shifts in the British Attitude

Writing in 1851 of progress in the United Kingdom, G. R. Porter dismissed the subject of overseas investments with this brief statement: "It is evidently impossible to form a correct estimate of the profit and loss . . . ; the general impression is that hitherto the losses have much exceeded the gains."[1] And with respect to one type of investment, investment in the bonds of foreign governments, the official impression was the same as the general impression. A circular sent out early in 1848 by the Foreign Office to British diplomats in foreign countries declared:

It has hitherto been thought by the successive Governments of Great Britain undesirable that British subjects should invest their capital in loans to foreign Governments instead of employing it in profitable undertakings at home; and with a view to discourage hazardous loans to foreign Governments . . . the British Government has hitherto thought it the best policy to abstain from taking up . . . the complaints made by British subjects against foreign Governments which have failed to make good their engagements in regard to such pecuniary transactions. For the British Government has considered that the losses of imprudent men who have placed mistaken confidence in the good faith of foreign Governments would prove a salutary warning to others. . . .[2]

Already, however, the British Foreign Office had begun to doubt the wisdom of continuing its hands-off policy, for it remarked that "the loss occasioned to British subjects by the non-payment of interest upon loans made to foreign Governments might become so great that

The Crux of the Matter

it would be too high a price for the nation to pay for such a warning as to the future." If that should turn out to be the case, "it might become the duty of the British Government to make these matters the subject of diplomatic negotiations." Viscount Palmerston, who sponsored this circular letter, had no doubt that the British government had the right to use its influence in behalf of such investors. It was simply a question of discretion whether it should or should not support imprudent Englishmen in their efforts to induce foreign governments to honor their contractual obligations; and the "decision of that question of discretion" would turn "entirely upon British and domestic questions." [3]

The forebodings of the Foreign Office were well founded. Englishmen continued to make imprudent investments abroad. In 1880, however, on the eve of another period of brisk movement of British capital into distant lands, Robert Lucas Nash published a booklet in which he contended that overseas investment — with the exception of investment in mining — had been profitable for Great Britain and supported his contention by marshaling a decade of dividend records of English companies operating in the British colonies and in foreign countries and by pointing to an upward trend in the price of government and other securities.[4] The pendulum of English opinion was swinging from pessimism to optimism. Nash's book sold rapidly; a second edition was published in 1881. But after depression had begun to put an end to the overseas investment boom of the 1880's, the London *Economist* remarked: "South American investments have for half a century been a thorn in the flesh of the British investors, and it is, perhaps, because we have become so accustomed to the infliction that the country has, time after time, shown its readiness to increase the sore." [5] So far, there was little or no consideration for the recipients of the capital.

John A. Hobson, in a work published in 1902, protested against the exploitation of the colonial peoples but was also much concerned with the metropolitan costs of imperialism and the injuries he supposed it inflicted upon the masses in the British Isles. He insisted that the "economic tap root" of imperialism and international investment was the same: "mal-distribution of consuming power which prevents the absorption of commodities and capital within the country." By the acquisition of colonies and the promotion and protection of foreign

British Views on Foreign Investments

investments the British government was providing a "vast system of outdoor relief for the upper classes." "Where the distribution of income is such as to enable all classes of the nation to convert their felt wants into an effective demand for commodities, there can be no overproduction, no under-consumption of capital and labour, and no necessity to fight for foreign markets," Hobson declared. "The struggle for markets, the greater eagerness of producers to sell than of consumers to buy, is the crowning proof of a false economy of distribution. Imperialism is the fruit of this false economy; 'social reform' is its remedy." [6]

C. K. Hobson, an outstanding British student of the export of capital, was compelled in 1914 to mention the hostility toward foreign investment that had developed in England in recent years. "Foreign investment," he said, "was regarded as a . . . portentous phenomenon . . . a running sore, sapping the life blood of British industry and adding fresh strength to our most formidable rivals and competitors. The matter was discussed in Parliament." Proposals were made to restrict the investment of funds outside of the United Kingdom and the Empire.[7]

Unlike the other Hobson, C. K. favored the export of capital. Although admitting that English workers benefited last and least from the process, he felt that the gains for the nation as a whole greatly outweighed the losses. "The income and wealth of the United Kingdom are clearly . . . increased by the high returns obtained on foreign investments, and by the cheapening of goods to consumers through the increased production. One of the principal effects of British foreign investments has been to increase the supplies of food and raw materials, without which the life of our growing population could not have been sustained." He noted that the export of capital had probably raised the interest rate, but failed to observe that it may also have supported or even raised the price of manufactured goods by stimulating exports. As for the recipients of the capital and the rest of the world, he maintained that all had benefited by increased production. Nevertheless, he felt compelled to make some qualifications: "If the capital is employed with the object of securing a development of the borrowing country's resources, it will clearly tend to increase the income of the country, to enlarge the demand for labour, and to improve the economic condition of the working classes. But

The Crux of the Matter

history shows that capital may be used for purposes of exploitation in the worst sense of the word. . . . Cases of the misapplication of capital have been excessively common. . . . The self-interest of individual investors is but an unreliable guide to the interest of nations and of the human race." He was rather reluctant, however, to admit the need of government intervention for constructive and benevolent purposes, fearing that neither might be achieved by government action, and he concluded this part of his discussion on a cheerful and humanitarian note and with an exhortation: "But happily the resources of European States have been exported predominantly for purposes of genuine development, for constructing railways and public works, and for providing the fixed capital of industry. . . . The task of . . . investors should be not to provide or withhold capital from the world at their own whim and fancy, but to guide and direct the flow for the common benefit of humanity."

At one point in his introductory remarks C. K. Hobson aroused but disappointed the expectations of the reader. "The phenomenon is not merely economic in nature," he said; "it has a profound moral and ethical significance." "Seeds of material civilization of Western Europe are being scattered more and more thickly over the most distant parts of the world, particles of energy which are destined to exert an influence of increasing potence upon human life and thought. It is from this aspect that the subject requires perhaps the most careful examination, for the whole future of society is concerned, and endless vistas of speculation and enquiry are opened up." But he quickly dropped this phase of the subject with the remark that he would attempt no such ambitious task.[8]

Approaching the phenomenon in 1924 entirely from the viewpoint of national advantage, John Maynard Keynes was pessimistic about the domestic benefits of most British foreign investments. He believed that the "hazarding of capital resources in foreign parts for trading, mining, and exploitation" had generally proved very beneficial, but disapproved of investments in foreign government bonds and public services, pointing out that there was no effective remedy for defaults on government loans and that foreign governments were subjecting railway and public-utility rates to control and refusing to accord fair treatment to the foreign investor. With a few brief sentences, Keynes attempted to refute the two main arguments for wholesale capital

British Views on Foreign Investments

export: "It is often said to be a primary and sufficient justification of such investment that it stimulates our exports. That is quite true. But I see no especial virtue in exports for their own sake, which are not required to pay for imports. . . . Investment abroad stimulates employment by expanding exports. Certainly. But it does not stimulate employment a scrap more than investment at home." Contending that too much capital was being exported from the United Kingdom, Keynes urged the British government to restrict this export and ration overseas borrowers.[9]

Theodore E. Gregory, another noted English economist, was friendly toward foreign investment, but he did not fail to point out that opinion in the United Kingdom was sharply divided on the subject in the 1920's. The orthodox free traders and the imperialists strongly favored the export of capital, and the imperialists would even have the government promote and direct the movement. A third group, however, the economic nationalists, wished to confine foreign investment to agricultural and extractive enterprises and retain a greater share of British savings for investment at home. Gregory illustrated the attitude of this third group by two quotations, one from the London *Times* and the other from the London *Nation*. The *Times* remarked regarding a Dutch loan floated in 1924: "We cannot afford the luxury of financing municipal building programmes in Amsterdam or any foreign capital." The *Nation* expressed the following sentiment the next year: "What is wanted is systematic discouragement of the issue of large foreign, including colonial, loans and systematic useful public works at home." With respect to government interference with the free market in capital, Professor Gregory remarked: "If one starts by rejecting the assumption that pecuniary standards . . . are to be the deciding factor in settling where capital is to flow, then the problem of excessive investment abroad is only a special case of the general problem of redistribution of wealth. . . . Administrative action, if it is to follow this road, has nothing but a vague presumption of rightness to guide it."[10]

Such were some of the shifts in the opinions of Englishmen regarding overseas investments before the economic catastrophe of the 1930's. The sharp decline in income from abroad that accompanied this severe global depression caused further doubts regarding the advantages of capital exports for the investing nations. Englishmen began

The Crux of the Matter

to complain that a good part of their recent commodity exports had been a total loss to the nation because of the defaults of foreigners on British loans and to call for the protection of home and imperial industries. A letter published in the *Economist* on April 15, 1933, pointed out, however, the dilemma which protection would create for a nation that expected to receive income from its foreign investments. Such a nation must either receive payment in the form of goods or services from its creditors or give its goods away. If an "unfavorable balance of trade" should cause unemployment in the United Kingdom, must the dilemma be solved by the "distribution of doles to the people of the debtor nations?"[11]

Propagandists for the groups favoring foreign investments, such as the editors of the *South American Journal* so often mentioned in these pages, argued in vain that the unhampered export of capital had been a major factor in creating the prosperity of the United Kingdom before 1914 and might create prosperity again. The British Treasury, which had been controlling capital exports since the beginning of World War I, refused to permit the free flow of funds to foreign countries. The alleged reason for its policy, the protection of gold reserves, was perhaps not the main reason. An important motive was probably the desire to induce the investment of savings in the United Kingdom and the Commonwealth and Empire, a desire based mainly upon the conviction that investments in foreign lands were no longer profitable.

During the Second World War, however, prominent Englishmen began to contend — probably in part because they hoped to obtain from the United States gifts or cheap loans for their own country — that large-scale international investment must continue. Lord Keynes, with a group of experts, went to the United States to argue its universal advantage. International investment was necessary, they declared, to keep the world economic system running on an even keel. It would be difficult to find a more blunt statement of this view than that by the Englishman E. H. Carr:

> The international financial system which flourished until 1914 is often spoken of as if it had operated to the profit and advantage of everyone concerned. This system, in fact, involved a continuous flow of loans from Great Britain and certain other countries (especially France) the repayment of which was provided when the time came for further loans; and when this cumulative process came to an end, de-

British Views on Foreign Investments

fault was the inevitable result. The advantages of the international system were paid for in the end by the British and French investors who lost their millions. . . . The system seemed profitable to all because those who benefitted from it succeeded in unloading the loss on posterity.

This was not a full statement of the case. Carr failed to note that unwary investors as well as posterity were losers, minimized the recent investment role and losses of citizens of the United States, and failed to specify the beneficiaries or to indicate whether he numbered the recipient nations among them. But what he had in mind becomes clear in the following passage:

It is not certain whether the same confidence trick can be played again. If it cannot, it seems probable that those who occupy the most privileged position within any international financial system will be obliged from time to time to make deliberate sacrifices in order to make the system work.[12]

It is evident that Carr was referring to the United States, and probably to its government agencies. Since private foreign investments had apparently become more risky and less profitable, especially investments in railroads, highways, dams, irrigation systems, sanitation, and various public utilities, let the United States Treasury assume the burden and let the United States government compel the people of this country to make heavy contributions to promote global prosperity, leaving, however, the more profitable undertakings in foreign lands to private enterprise in the United States and other investing nations.

This is essentially the policy that the United States government, frightened by the possibility of another terrible economic depression and later confronted by the Soviet peril, began to adopt shortly before the termination of World War II, a policy that includes the subsidizing of exports as well as the production of raw materials both at home and abroad. No patriotic citizen will be likely to complain about the objectives but some of the results could be almost catastrophic. Such a policy, accompanied by a prolonged war economy, seems destined to bring about fundamental economic and social changes in the United States. The mass-producing industries will expand and prosper, increasing the concentration of big industrial plants in the North and Northeast if not in the Far West. High-ranking bureaucrats of gov-

The Crux of the Matter

ernment and business will increase and prosper. Attorneys, commission men, and salesmen of the products of the big industries will increase and prosper. Unionized labor working in the colossal mass-producing plants will expand and prosper. But farmers and industrialists producing solely or mainly for the domestic market probably will receive a smaller and still smaller share of the national income, and the tax burden will eventually become heavier than any nation has ever had to bear. The salaried and fixed-income groups, other than public employees of some types and corporation managers and technicians, seem bound to suffer a sharp decline in their levels of living. Those accustomed to devote themselves to the "higher culture" — clergymen, teachers, writers (except those engaged in propaganda), artists, philosophers, librarians, in short, all those who neither produce nor sell material goods but must consume such goods if they are to survive and must surrender a part of their meager incomes to the tax collectors — probably will suffer most of all, since they will be compelled to pay both heavy taxes and high prices without a compensating increase in real income. Cultural progress will almost certainly be impeded; indeed, cultural decline and increasing materialism are most likely to occur. They can be avoided only by a full realization of the dangers ahead, by an appropriate shifting of the tax burden, and by an enlightened generosity toward the more unfortunate groups on the part of both the government and those who reap most of the economic benefits flowing from the current foreign economic policy of the nation. I suggest an amendment to the income-tax law in favor of those in the lower income brackets, a special earned-income exemption of some 25 per cent for all net incomes up to $6,000 annually. In the long run this would cost less than federal aid to education or federal relief for low-income groups, and would be less inflationary than the system of linking industrial wages and farm prices to rising living costs.

Finally, it should be observed that this tremendous expansion of our manufacturing industries requires an immense consumption of raw materials, depleting our own and increasing our dependence upon foreign sources of supply. This growing dependence may well turn out to be troublesome in time of peace. In periods of war it could become a grave peril. I doubt the wisdom of the slogan "trade instead of aid." A drastic adoption of such a slogan by wholesale removal of tariffs and quotas might slaughter the little manufacturers producing mainly for

British Views on Foreign Investments

domestic consumers and either deprive many farmers of a decent living or double the cost of maintaining parity for farm prices. Such a policy would also lead to further concentration of the mass-producing industries in the North and Northeast by compelling those connected with the ruined little manufacturing plants to migrate to the new centers, and exaggerate the dependence of the national economy upon foreign outlets for mass-produced commodities, a development that could become both painful and dangerous because, in these circumstances, depression or war might prove far more devastating than ever before.

⇋ XVIII ⇌

VIEWS OF THE LATIN-AMERICAN RECIPIENTS

In Latin America as in the United Kingdom opinion regarding the advantages of foreign investment has been neither uniform nor stable. Attitudes have tended to swing from one extreme to another. By and large, however, Latin Americans have viewed the presence of foreign capital and foreign investors in their midst with suspicion and, in recent years, with near hostility, or at least with the conviction that foreign private enterprise would not promote the development of their countries unless it could be subjected to the guidance and control of Latin-American governments.

The Trends of Sentiment

Until shortly after 1900, and later in some countries, the outstanding leaders of Latin America — whether noted or notorious — were usually cordial to the foreign investor. This was true of Porfirio Díaz of Mexico, Justo Rufino Barrios of Guatemala, Marco Aurelio Soto and Luís Bográn of Honduras, the Zamorros of Nicaragua, Tomás Guardia of Costa Rica, Antonio Guzmán Blanco of Venezuela, Rafael Núñez and Rafael Reyes of Colombia, Gabriel García Moreno and Eloy Alfaro of Ecuador, Ramón Castilla and José Balta of Peru, Manuel Montt and Aníbal Pinto of Chile, Juan B. Alberdi, Domingo F. Sarmiento, and Bartolomé Mitre of Argentina, and Emperor Pedro II of Brazil. Likewise cordial to foreign capitalists were several of the later chief executives — some more and some less despotic — such as Anastasio Somoza of Nicaragua, Jorge Ubico of Guatemala, Mario García Menocal and Gerardo Machado of Cuba, Juan V. Gómez of Venezuela, Augusto B. Leguía of Peru, Carlos Ibáñez of Chile (at least during his first administration), Hipólito Irigoyen of Argentina, and most of the earlier presidents of Brazil.

This long list of friendly names does not mean, however, that there

Views of the Latin-American Recipients

were no fears, no warnings, and no opposition. Suspicion of foreigners and their activities was a heritage of the Hispanic colonial régimes. The loudest, if not the earliest voices of alarm and protest were raised by the publicists Carlos Calvo of Argentina and Rafael Seijas of Venezuela, the first in the late 1860's and the second in the early 1880's.[1] What they objected to, and what they feared, was the use of force by foreign governments to protect the alien immigrant, the foreign trader, and the foreign investor and to exact indemnities for injuries which they suffered at the hands of Latin-American governments or insurgents. Nor were their apprehensions and resentments without foundation. England, France, and Spain had employed force or menace repeatedly for these purposes during the half-century following Latin America's achievement of independence, and Argentina and Venezuela as well as Peru, Colombia, Mexico, and several other countries of the region were the victims. One cause of the war of 1846–1848 between the United States and Mexico was the unredressed grievances of American citizens, and the alleged maltreatment of citizens of the United States by the Paraguayan government provoked the James Buchanan administration into sending a good part of the American navy to the Río de la Plata in 1859.

Calvo, Seijas, and other writers of their generation might be quoted at length; but this would be pointless. They did not deny the benefits brought by the immigrant, the foreign merchant, and the foreign investor; they merely complained that the vigorous support of them by foreign governments raised them to a privileged position and warned against the danger of foreign domination. Meantime most of the autocrats and dictators of the nineteenth century welcomed foreign investments. They welcomed them for personal or patriotic reasons, or both. Foreign capital could mean the sinews of political power, the accumulation of private fortunes, or the means of accelerating the development of national resources and public services and of acquiring more of the amenities and conveniences of civilized life.

Later complaints might be quoted at even greater length; but it will be sufficient for the moment to mention the three objections which Latin Americans added to the earlier objection that national sovereignties might be imperiled and citizens reduced to an inferior status. First, they contended that government bonds sold abroad led to extravagance and corrupt enrichment of politicians. Second, they argued that foreign

The Crux of the Matter

investors charged too much for their services, siphoning out large sums in profits, and exploiting rather than developing the resources of the recipient countries. Third, they complained that foreign investments tended to produce lopsided economies by too great emphasis upon the export industries, neglecting production for the home market. The second and third objections were not often mentioned until after 1930.[2]

Complaints and criticisms were sometimes followed by official pronouncements and policies. Calvo's contention, first put forward in 1868, that foreign governments should never employ menace or force in Latin America to redress the grievances of their nationals frequently resulted in the insertion into alien contracts of "Calvo clauses" which attempted to deprive concessionaires of the privilege of ignoring local judicial and administrative authorities and appealing to their home governments to protect them in the assertion of their rights, real or alleged. The Argentine government, through its minister of foreign relations, Luís Drago, proclaimed in 1902 the doctrine that force should never be employed to collect payments on public debts; and the second conference at The Hague, seeking a compromise between the debtor and the creditor nations, agreed, with some reservations, to the Porter Doctrine, which declared:

The contracting powers agree not to have recourse to armed force for the recovery of contract debts claimed from the Government of another country as being due to its nationals.

This undertaking is, however, not applicable when the debtor State refuses or neglects to reply to an offer of arbitration, or, after having accepted the offer, prevents any *compromis* from being agreed on, or, after the arbitration, fails to submit to the award.[3]

But these official policies and attitudes did not signify any widespread doubt in Latin America in respect to the economic benefits of foreign capital. The public authorities of the region were merely seeking to obtain the capital they needed without jeopardizing or curtailing national sovereignties in the process, a danger which armed intervention in the Caribbean was even then making more manifest, but which was soon mitigated by the intensification of Europe's strife, the abandonment by the United States of its Caribbean protectorates, and the signing of Pan American nonintervention pacts. The first restrictions on the fields of foreign investment were seldom expressions of

Views of the Latin-American Recipients

hostility toward foreign economic enterprises as such. The national governments took over most of the telegraph systems soon after they were installed, for example, mainly with the hope of suppressing political disorders; and the earliest movements of national governments into the field of railway ownership and operation, with some exceptions, were designed to hasten the completion of transportation networks, the governments taking action because private capital was reluctant to do so or wished to dispose of unprofitable lines.

One of the first high officials to question the benefits of foreign investments was José Balmaceda of Chile, who made himself unpopular with English investors by talking of nationalizing the nitrate deposits. But Balmaceda merely talked; the Chilean government did not take control of the nitrate business until the 1930's. José Batlle and his party associates in Uruguay not only talked but acted, launching a policy of mild state socialism shortly after 1910;[4] and the revolt starting the same year in Mexico against the rule of Díaz was largely a protest against alleged exploitation by foreign investors which finally led to a decided curtailment of their opportunities for enrichment. Aside from Argentina under Juan D. Perón and Bolivia under two of its dictators, no other Latin American country took such drastic action, although nearly all of them, especially after 1930, revealed a strong tendency to control, regulate, and restrict the operation of foreign enterprises.

Possible Influence of Opinions Expressed Abroad

Doubts regarding the benefits of foreign capital were not entirely the result of spontaneous generation within Latin America itself. Foreign ideas as well as alien investments flowed into the region and played their part in shaping attitudes: the utterances of critics of corporate capitalism and high finance, of Marxists and other extremists, and of those who had no set economic theories but merely protested against alleged flagrant maldistribution of wealth and income and felt deep sympathy for the poor. Such writings, pronouncements, and denunciations were read and heard by Latin Americans at home and abroad, whether in the United States or in Europe. To mention them in detail would belabor the point. It will be sufficient to refer to the well-known views of William Jennings Bryan and "Fighting Bob" La Follette and quote Woodrow Wilson, Franklin D. Roosevelt, and

The Crux of the Matter

a few other politicians of the United States, none of whom could be described as unfailingly friendly to speculators, big bankers, and other forms of corporate capital.

Note, for instance, the assertions and implications of Wilson's Mobile address of October 27, 1913:

You hear of "concessions" to foreign capitalists in Latin America. . . . States that are obliged . . . to grant concessions are in this condition, that foreign interests are apt to dominate their domestic affairs, a condition . . . always dangerous and apt to become intolerable. . . . They have had harder bargains driven with them in the matter of loans than any other people in the world. Interest has been exacted of them that was not exacted of anybody else, because the risk was said to be greater; and then securities have been taken that destroyed the risk. . . . The United States . . . must regard it as one of the duties of friendship to see that from no quarter are material interests made superior to human liberty and national opportunity.[5]

Examine also this passage from an interview with Wilson published in the *Ladies' Home Journal* of October 1916:

The system by which Mexico has been financially assisted has in the past generally bound her hand and foot and left her in effect without a free government. It has in almost every instance deprived her people of the part they were entitled to play in the determination of their own destiny and development.[6]

Similar sentiments were often expressed by Bryan, who actually proposed that the United States adopt a policy of making cheap government loans available to some of the smaller Latin-American governments in order to shield them from the exactions of bankers. Moreover, when Wilson rejected this proposal, Bryan sometimes used his influence as Secretary of State to moderate the terms of bank loans.

Robert Lansing, in memoranda written in 1914 and 1915 but not published until 1940, included the following critical statements:

Eager investors . . . lend their money readily in exchange for special privileges, concessions, and large rates of interest. . . . As a result some of the smaller American republics, ruled by military dictators and oligarchies, who have enriched themselves at the expense of their countries, have become hopelessly bankrupt. . . .

A revolutionary leader finds little difficulty in financing his venture among foreign speculators in exchange for concessions and other privileges. . . . As a result the people of these countries are the victims of constant strife between rival leaders, and their condition is little improved by the governments, which . . . are used to enrich their rulers and those who have financed them.[7]

Such assertions, true or not, were sometimes used as arguments for the establishment by the United States of quasi-protectorates in the Caribbean; and in any case they were probably typical of the views held by Wilson and Roosevelt Democrats. Franklin D. Roosevelt referred approvingly to Wilson's Mobile address on more than one occasion. In an article published in *Foreign Affairs* for July 1928,[8] for instance, he berated the Republicans for their alliance with American bankers: " 'Dollar Diplomacy' as adopted by President Taft and Secretary Knox placed money leadership above moral leadership. . . . This policy was extended to Honduras and Nicaragua. . . ." Woodrow Wilson "threw 'Dollar Diplomacy' out of the window" in 1913, Roosevelt continued, and made a "notable declaration" of principles in Mobile. Then FDR quoted with emphatic endorsement these two sentences from Wilson's speech: "The United States will never again seek one additional foot of territory by conquest. She must regard it as one of the duties of friendship to see that from no quarter are material interests made superior to human liberty and national opportunity." In an address at Monterrey, Mexico, on April 20, 1943, FDR declared: "We know that the day of the exploitation of the resources and people of one country for the benefit of any group in another country is definitely over."[9] And a few weeks later he made apologies to President Enrique Peñaranda of Bolivia regarding the bond flotations of American investment bankers in the 1920's. "I apologized on behalf of my fellow citizens," Roosevelt told a press conference on May 7, "and I told him that if I had anything to do with it . . . we would never lend money to anybody on that basis again." He was referring especially to Bolivian government bond issues.[10]

The implications of such statements are obvious. And utterances of a still more emphatic character were made. They can be illustrated by the remarks of two members of the Senate Committee on Foreign Relations as recently as May of 1955. Referring likewise to Bolivia, Senator George D. Aiken asserted: "Up until the time they nationalized the tin mines, the people of Bolivia were given nothing at all out of that tin. . . . A few people living outside the country got everything." Surely this was an extreme view; but it was no less extreme than the declaration made by Senator Hubert Humphrey on the same occasion. Alluding to the owners of the mining properties expropriated by the Bolivian government in 1952, Humphrey remarked with vehemence: "I hope they have not got a nickel back. . . . Our Government ought to take some kind of action. . . . I think these people ought to be in jail. . . . When we consider aid to Latin American countries, where there have always been prime examples of capital exploitation and human exploitation, we ought to know a little bit about these characters who get these countries into a mess that necessitates . . . bailing them out." [11]

Whatever the influence of such statements in Latin America, public policy in several countries of the region after 1930, and earlier in some instances, seemed designed to limit the scope of foreign enterprise rather than to foster it on a broad front, to regulate and direct rather than to invite and stimulate. Sometimes the governments expressed eagerness for foreign capital, but it usually turned out that they hoped to subject it to their own terms and channel it into carefully selected activities.

The Drift toward State Control and State Enterprise

In general, Latin Americans have preferred portfolio to direct investments and, in recent years, loans and credits from foreign governments rather than capital supplied by alien private investors. They both recognized and proclaimed their great need for transportation and communication systems, sewers and sanitation, education, irrigation works, hydroelectric plants, and manufacturing establishments, but they expected to finance most of these by means of cheap loans and even grants to their governments from the public treasuries of foreign countries. In view of their long and almost universal defaults on government bonds sold abroad during the 1920's, they knew that the time was not ripe to tap private sources of revenue again in this fashion.

One of the few fields into which private investors were invited to enter was the field of manufacturing, but there was some opposition on the part of national industrialists even in this sector of their economy. Public services — not merely telegraph and telephone systems but electric utilities, railways, truck and omnibus lines, and fluvial and coastwise shipping — were staked out, as a rule, for ownership and operation by the state or by native private enterprise, or were hampered

Views of the Latin-American Recipients

by close regulation and impending threats of expropriation; and the same was true of mining and petroleum activities in several countries and of banking and insurance in a few. New investments by aliens in agriculture or in commercial organizations were often viewed with misgivings or jealousy. Investments in all fields were handicapped far more than in earlier days by labor laws and labor unions, mounting taxes, state planning and state competition, inflationary trends and unstable currencies, and restrictions on remission of profits or withdrawal of capital, to mention only a few.[12]

A persistent trend toward state socialism was evident in many Latin-American countries. It seemed to be the result of their colonial heritage, of political and economic theories, of the waxing influence of bureaucratic and labor groups, and of a sentimental factor usually described as "economic nationalism." Railways owned and operated by the state were now the rule rather than the exception. Those still in private hands were unprofitable to the shareholders in the main, and often yielded very small returns to the holders of bonds and debentures. Telegraphs, as already pointed out, had long been owned and operated by the governments. Telephones, electric utilities, radio, and river and coastwise shipping were being taken over by the state. Merchant marines, where they existed, were usually owned and operated by the governments, which were likely also to own the local airways or have controlling investments in them. State-owned enterprises were crowding out the foreign oil companies or giving them strong competition, and were likewise competing in the processing of meat, in the manufacture of cement and steel, and in several other activities. State marketing agencies had set up monopolies not only in marketing but also in some minor phases of production, such as salt, matches, and alcoholic liquors, or had established production quotas along with their marketing activities. State credit institutions had rapidly expanded.

Many investment fields in which profits had been attractive in the past were thus occupied either by government corporations or by the branches and subsidiaries of large foreign corporations. New private foreign investments were confined mainly to such corporate branches, subsidiaries, and affiliates. There appeared to be little opportunity for the small alien investor unless he planned to plant himself as well as his savings in Latin America; and, even then, he would be likely to see his business captured by the state, or officially transferred to nationals, if his success should make him conspicuous.

In short, prospects for the rapid development of Latin America by a flood of foreign private capital were not bright at the middle of the twentieth century. The private investor must confront numerous irritations and handicaps: tax collectors, economic planners, labor bosses backed by potent politicians, bureaucrats hankering for government posts, many varieties of pressure groups, widespread exchange controls, economic nationalism, and often the suspended sword of expropriation — if not without prior or prompt compensation, as required by most Latin-American constitutions, at best with the terms of compensation determined largely by the agents of the Latin-American governments themselves.[13] Public policy and public attitudes were not precisely the same from decade to decade and from country to country. They were somewhat more favorable in Cuba under Fulgencio Batista and in Peru under Manuel Prado for instance, than they were in Mexico under Lázaro Cárdenas or Argentina under Juan D. Perón; more favorable perhaps in Nicaragua, Venezuela, and Uruguay than in some of the other countries. But the general situation was not greatly changed by these distinctions, which might easily become invidious. Although a few other pacts dealing with the subject were signed in 1955, five years of previous negotiations by the United States had resulted in only one satisfactory investment treaty, an agreement with Uruguay, hitherto supposed to be the most socialistic of all these republics!

Optimism in respect to the feasibility of pumping large sums of private capital speedily into Latin America (or almost any other economically retarded region), perhaps excepting the capital of a few giant corporations which are usually able and sometimes not unwilling to risk "other people's money," seemed not to have a very sound basis The bureaucrats in such regions were expanding like green bay trees The small moneyed groups were eager to reserve the profits for themselves. The working classes were growing more articulate and assertive and exerting stronger influence in the formulation of public policy. The emotions of all groups were easily stirred by any politician who sought to arouse them by evoking memories of past "exploitation." The conviction that most foreigners were avaricious or the covert agents of "economic imperialism" was not far beneath the surface.

Views of the Latin-American Recipients

The underdeveloped regions of the New World and the Old would probably accept all the technical aid they could obtain at half price or less. Most of them would accept gifts, and long-term government loans at low interest rates when sufficient gifts to satisfy them were not available. And some private investors might be willing to send their money abroad on terms fixed mainly by the recipients and under guaranties by the governments of the creditor countries covering every hazard save bad judgment and bad management. But, in spite of this, the "bold new program," otherwise known as Point Four, or described as an economic development plan, seemed likely to turn out to be a project to stimulate economic progress in the retarded countries at the expense of the taxpayers of the United States and some other highly developed nations, and as much for the economic benefit of exporters, importers, shippers, and bureaucratic technicians as for the welfare of recipients abroad.

Illustrative Statements of 1954

The attitude of prominent Latin Americans was illustrated in two Pan American conferences held in 1954.* Speaking at the Caracas conference of March 1954, the Brazilian minister of foreign relations remarked:

I am well aware that private initiative and private capital, both domestic and foreign, were and still are great pioneers of progress and deserve protection and respect, when . . . they . . . cooperate towards development.

But . . . there are economic activities that must necessarily be carried out or controlled by the state, particularly in countries in the process of development, and these are activities that are the basis of the economic organization of a country.

Commercial activities and industrial practices for profit are one thing, and another, quite different, is the basic organization of the economy that should be carried out at a higher level of economic policy, through investments made available in a spirit of cooperation under favorable conditions as to time and rate of interest, and in accordance with the possibilities of each nation, with an eye on the future and not on the immediate present.[14]

The Bolivian foreign minister declared:

We are aware of the fact that when capital is risked abroad, it ex-

---

* A third conference, convened in Rio de Janeiro later in the year, seems to have given occasion for Latin Americans further to insist upon cheap government loans.

The Crux of the Matter

pects to obtain considerable profit. . . . As one can note, it is neither pertinent nor exact to say that private investment is going to meet our capital requirements in Bolivia, except perhaps in the fields of mining and the petroleum industries, which have a great appeal to all investors.

. . . There is no doubt that more capital has been exported from Latin America in the form of profit than has been brought to it. . . Foreign private investments that have to take their income to their country of origin and amortize their capital rapidly in order to satisfy the investors are . . . a constant drain on the country.

. . . There does not seem to be any other solution than the granting of loans for development, under favorable conditions and terms, on the part of institutions whose essential aim is not to make unlimited profits. . . .[15]

Both high officials were almost demanding cheap government loans And the Chilean foreign minister had the same idea in mind when he observed: "It is necessary that we should know if we are or are not to expect cooperation in order to complement our national efforts, if on the difficult road ahead we are alone or accompanied, if the well-being of our people is a national problem or one of continental concern." [16] It would not be easy for private investors to attract customers who had in plain view two government windows, one bearing the label "cheap loans" and the other labeled "grants."

Two addresses before a Pan American conference at Columbia University in October 1954, one by the late Claude Bowers and the other by Eduardo Santos, ex-president of the republic of Colombia, called for a Marshall Plan for Latin America and received acclaim from some of the delegates.[17] A third address, which was not applauded by at least a few members of the United States delegation, denounced foreign investments and investors in a fashion reminiscent of earlier times. The speaker was Fernando Díez de Medina of Bolivia, who complained of "fifty years of economic penetration of colonial type on the part of . . . investors who have often taken advantage, and continue to do so, of the low living standards of the . . . worker," of "economic organizations more powerful than the state, for which financial resources take priority over human resources," of "powerful financial groups interested in keeping the workers uneducated in order to exploit them more easily." Moreover, Díez de Medina asserted that the Latin Americans were "incensed . . . against that form of capitalism which treats free people like colonies," and that they were "demanding economic

Views of the Latin-American Recipients

liberation and social justice" because they were "tired of being the helpless victims of financial rapaciousness." Surely, these were intemperate statements with which the majority of Latin Americans would not have agreed.[18]

The governments of Latin America and possibly of other economically retarded countries may not need to rely so emphatically as they seemed to assume on imports of capital, either government or private. They might resort instead to heavy taxes on strategic and critical materials, price squeezes on such materials and certain foods and beverages (coffee, tea), and compulsory investment by their own and other affluent groups in their midst. Those who operate in the underdeveloped regions would not like the increased tax load and the forced investment, nor would foreign consumers relish the high prices; but this horn of the dilemma would probably be no more painful to either foreign consumers or foreign investors than the other; namely, the heavy taxes required to pay the cost of government grants and cheap loans. That the governments of the underdeveloped countries will employ these devices at the same time that they continue to demand cheap foreign capital does not seem improbable. In fact, it appeared likely at mid-century that they would pursue both policies rather than decidedly improve the climate for investment of private capital.

Technical aid, if accompanied by birth control and economic reforms looking toward greater efficiency in production and a more equitable distribution of the benefits of economic enterprise, should eventually raise the levels of living among the masses in Latin America and other economically retarded regions. So likewise should the investment of private capital, native or foreign, if not too severely hampered by bureaucratic costs and restrictions, and if infused with a benevolence not hitherto characteristic of the capitalistic system *per se*, or accompanied by liberal distribution abroad of personal fortunes after they have been accumulated (Kellogg, Rockefeller, Ford). What seems to be needed in the United States and other economically advanced countries is a missionary spirit on the part of both capitalists and technical experts, a willingness to work for modest material rewards in order to attain humanitarian goals. Government experts and technicians were demanding and receiving salaries that were too high; businessmen still seemed to be too eager for profits. Austerity appropriate to these critical times, and so frequently recommended by government officials,

The Crux of the Matter

appears not to have extended beyond the taxpayers who produced nothing for export, held no government posts, and suffered severely from the postwar price inflation. Let readers who have any doubts regarding the upward trend of bureaucratic salaries of the United States take note of this amazing statement read into the *Congressional Record* on July 27, 1956, by Thomas Murray of Tennessee, chairman of the House Committee on the Post Office and Civil Service, and let them remember that salaries of the United Nations bureaucracy were keeping pace with those paid to government employees in the United States:

Today's employee has security in his job. He has had salary increases amounting to over 60 percent [since 1946?]. His retirement annuity has been directly increased by over 25 percent, with new and much more liberal provisions for his surviving widow and children. . . . If he dies his beneficiaries receive a year's salary. . . . He has opportunity for monetary awards up to $25,000 for outstanding service. . . . He has protection against reduction in his salary in cases where his position has been downgraded as a result of reclassification. Compensation for overtime, Sunday, and holiday work has been greatly increased. . . .

In my judgment, in no other employment . . . does the employee have as many benefits as he does in the Federal Government. These benefits are in the main the result of recommendations made by the executive branch and legislation approved by this committee over the past few years.[19]

Confronted by the suspicions, hostilities, and restrictions of nations and governments in need of capital, compelled to compete with cheap loans and benevolent government grants administered by managers and technicians who are the most highly paid "missionaries" that the world has ever seen, private investors in underdeveloped countries seemed to have a hard and treacherous road ahead.

Notes, Appendixes, and Index

NOTES

Chapter I. The Crisis and British Experience

[1] American Academy of Political and Social Science, *The Annals*, July 1950, p. 64.
[2] *Ibid.*, March 1950, pp. 58–59.
[3] *American Economic Review*, May 1951, pp. 336–337. This statement was made in December 1950.
[4] *The Annals*, March 1950, p. 59.
[5] *Ibid.*, July 1950, p. 53.
[6] See my *Latin America and the Industrial Age*, 2nd ed. (New York, 1947).
[7] I have summarized the experience of these three countries in articles published in the following journals: *Inter-American Economic Affairs*, Autumn 1948, pp. 52–71, and Winter 1948, pp. 3–16 (French); *Political Science Quarterly*, Dec. 1949, pp. 560–578 (French); *Journal of Business*, Oct. 1947, pp. 212–219, Jan. 1948, pp. 50–54, and Apr. 1948, pp. 63–73 (German); Jan. 1949, pp. 17–29, and Oct. 1950, pp. 238–247 (United States).

Chapter II. Early Imprudence and Vexation, 1822–1880

[1] The best sources for a study of the reckless investments of the period are three contemporary pamphlets by Henry English, who is described as a "stock and exchange broker": *General Guide to the Companies Formed for Working Foreign Mines* (London, 1825), *Information Relating to the Companies for Working British Mines* (London, 1826), *A Complete View of the Joint-Stock Companies Formed during the Years 1824 and 1825* (London, 1827). Satisfactory summaries are given by Leland Hamilton Jenks, *The Migration of British Capital to 1875* (New York, 1927), C. K. Hobson, *The Export of Capital* (London, 1914), and Paul H. Emden, *Money Powers of Europe in the Nineteenth and Twentieth Centuries* (London, 1937). R. A. Humphreys's *British Consular Reports on the Trade and Politics of Latin America, 1824–1826* (London, 1940) contains useful data. The consuls and diplomats, as well as several British travelers who acted in the role of Moses, spying out the Latin-American Promised Land, published books which deal with British activities; but most of these can be identified in Humphreys's bibliography and need not be mentioned in detail here.

Differing from some of the other European countries, the British Isles sent comparatively few emigrants to Latin America (no more than a few hundred annually, perhaps fewer than 160,000 during the period 1825–1950), mostly to Argentina, Uruguay, and Chile, and only a small fraction of these settled down permanently. The immigrant phase of British relations with Latin America will therefore be considered only incidentally in this book.

[2] Harriet Martineau, *History of the Peace: Being a History of England from 1816 to 1854*, 4 vols. (Boston, 1865), II, 406–407. These and subsequent pages give a good description of the boom and the panic.

[3] Brief histories of these bonds are included in the annual reports of the Council of

British Investments in Latin America

the Corporation of Foreign Bondholders (London) for 1873 and subsequent years and in the *Stock Exchange Year-Book* (London) for the years 1875 and following. The annual reports of the Council are numbered consecutively, the one for 1873 being entitled *First Annual Report*. Countries floating bonds in the British market are listed alphabetically in both manuals. Page citations therefore seem unnecessary.

[4] J. B. McCullock, *Dictionary of Commerce and Commercial Navigation*, 2 vols. (London, 1840–1843), II, 189–191.

[5] English, *A Complete View of the Joint-Stock Companies*, pp. 29–30, mentions more than 20 of these. Some were not fully organized before the panic set in; others went down in the crash or failed soon afterward.

[6] *Stock Exchange Year-Book* for 1876 lists 16 British mining companies for Latin America; only 3 of them were organized before 1860.

[7] C. K. Webster's *Britain and the Independence of Latin America*, 2 vols. (London, 1938) is the outstanding work on this subject. See especially his long introductory essay in Vol. I.

[8] Table 1 and the analysis presented in the preceding three paragraphs are based mainly on Hobson, *op. cit.*, p. 101, which gives the most reliable summary of the loans; but his figures have been carefully compared with those published by the editors of the *Stock Exchange Year-Book* and the reports of the Council of the Corporation of Foreign Bondholders.

Brazil's bonds were by far the best investment in the lot; after the defaults of 1827–1828, the Brazilian government resumed the service on its two flotations, issuing £400,000 in 5 per cent bonds at 54 (the bankers bought them at 52) in payment of arrears (J. F. Normano, *Brazil, A Study of Economic Types* (Chapel Hill, 1935), p. 54 and note 58). Yet Brazil's early flotations were less than half as large as those of either Mexico or Colombia.

[9] Jenks, *op. cit.*, pp. 46–49; Emden, *op. cit.*, pp. 37–50. Emden says that the young Benjamin Disraeli sold his pen to the loan sharks.

[10] Hobson, *op. cit.*, p. 101; Jenks, *op. cit.*, pp. 48–49.

[11] Jenks, *op. cit.*, pp. 46–49, 353, notes 41 and 42; *Colombia; A Geographical, Statistical, and Political Account*, 2 vols. (London, 1822), I, xcvii–xcviii, cx.

[12] C. A. True, "British Loans to the Mexican Government, 1822–1832," *Southwestern Social Science Quarterly*, XVII (March 1927), 353–362.

[13] Normano, *op. cit.*, p. 154. But Normano erroneously states that the face amount of the first Brazilian loan was only £1,000,000.

[14] A. B. Martínez and M. Lewandowski, *The Argentine in the Twentieth Century* (London, 1911), p. 314.

[15] See the works cited in note 11. In most instances the bonds were not marketed by investment bankers but by firms of merchants: Hullet Brothers; Frys and Chapman; Herring, Graham, and Powles; Barclay, Herring, and Richardson; B. A. Goldschmidt; J. and S. Ricardo; Thomas Wilson; A. L. Haldimand. Barclay, Herring, and Richardson and Goldschmidt went into bankruptcy with Mexican and Colombian funds on deposit. The Barings, however, handled the Province of Buenos Aires bonds and Nathan M. Rothchild managed the second Brazilian issue (Jenks, *op. cit.*, p. 48; Humphreys, *op cit.*, pp. 24, 99, 118, 230, 325 *passim*).

[16] True, *op. cit.*, pp. 353–355.

[17] Consult English, *A Complete View of the Joint-Stock Companies*; Martineau, *op. cit.*, II, 406–442; Michael G. Mulhall, *The English in South America* (London, 1878), pp. 445–452; and Humphreys, *op. cit.*, Introduction and Bibliography.

[18] English's *General Guide to the Companies Formed for Working Foreign Mines* summarizes the prospectuses.

[19] McCullock, *op. cit.*, II, 189–190.

[20] Their activities are revealed in part by English's pamphlets. See also Henry George Ward, *Mexico in 1827*, 2 vols. (London, 1828), I, 63–135; *A Sketch of the Society and Customs of Mexico* (London, 1828), pp. 239–242; J. C. Jefferson, *The Life of Robert*

Notes

tephenson, 2 vols., 2nd ed. (London, 1866), I, 66–115; H. W. Dickinson and Arthur 'itley, *Richard Trevithick* (London, 1934), pp. 159–215; and various English books of ravel listed in Humphreys's bibliography.

[21] Some of it was no doubt left to rust along the mountain trails and canyons, but ome reached its destination. The works cited in note 20 indicate that several steam ngines were introduced into the mining regions of Mexico during this period, and that ney reached the Peruvian Cerro de Pasco district in 1816 and the years immediately ollowing, thanks in part to the efforts of Richard Trevithick, the famous inventor of igh-pressure engines. It is not certain that Robert Stephenson, another British inventor f steam engines, managed to get one of his new machines into Colombia; but he surely ent several months in the employ of the Colombian Mining Association at Maraquita. Vard, *op. cit.*, I, 528–547, published an interesting letter written by Robert Phillips, ho probably introduced the first steam engine into the Mexican mines.

[22] Consult the *Stock Exchange Year-Book* for 1889 and subsequent years and the *Mining Manual* for the same period.

[23] Tables 4–7 and the remainder of this chapter are based primarily upon the following sources: *South American Journal* for the years 1880 and 1881; Council of the Corporation of Foreign Bondholders, *Annual Report* for the years 1877 through 1881; tock Exchange Year-Book for 1881 through 1887. All three of these are published in ondon. Government securities are described in alphabetical order in the second and iird and listed in the first. The *Journal* contains lists and descriptions of British enter-·ises. The *Year-Book* describes them in alphabetical order grouped under such classifi-tions as railways, banks, mining companies, tramways, and so on. For these reasons, id because both the *Journal* and the *Year-Book* have good indexes, specific citations pages have not seemed necessary. Scores of computations were required in compiling ie tables, and some errors may have crept in; but I hope the figures are approximately curate. For the loan scandals of 1867–1872 the reader may profit by consulting Great ritain, House of Commons, *Reports of Committees*, IX (1875): "Report of the Select ommittee on Loans to Foreign States." This is a document of 119 pages dealing with e flotations of Costa Rica, Honduras, the Dominican Republic, and Paraguay. Useful so are Jenks, *op. cit.*, and an article by H. S. Ferns on British investments in Argen-1a in *Inter-American Economic Affairs*, V (Autumn 1950), 67–89.

Chapter III. Brisk Investment and Depression

[1] The summary and analysis presented in this chapter are based mainly on three urces: Council of the Corporation of Foreign Bondholders, *Annual Report* for each of e years 1881 through 1891; *Stock Exchange Year-Book* for 1891 and 1892; *South merican Journal*, Vols. 28–31 (1890–1891). For reasons stated in Chapter II, note 23, ecific references seem unnecessary. Where the figures given in these sources have dif-·ed, I have usually followed the *Year-Book*. The reader will note, however, that I ve given further sources of information on the mining and nitrate investment.

[2] For estimates of investments in Mexico, Argentina, and Brazil, see the following ues of the *South American Journal*: Vol. 28, pp. 19, 169; Vol. 29, pp. 664, 793–95; ıl. 31, pp. 209, 449, 502.

British investors owned at least one oil company in 1890. It was the London and cific Petroleum Company, Limited, organized in 1889, although it did not appear in e *Stock Exchange Year-Book* until 1913 or 1914. Its capital was probably slightly ore than £250,000 and it was operating in northwestern Peru.

[3] This analysis of British mining investments in Latin America is based mainly upon careful scrutiny of the *Mining Manual* (London), 1891–1930, *Stock Exchange Year-ok*, 1882–1946, and *South American Journal*, 1882–1947. Except for occasional lists d descriptions of companies, information supplied by the *Journal* is rather fugitive. th the *Mining Manual* and the *Year-Book* describe British companies operating all er the world in alphabetical order, so that the discovering of companies operating in

Latin America was no easy task. It was also necessary to make many tedious computations; but I had the assistance of Miss Martha Bell Bowers with an adding machine and I am confident that no serious errors were made. Let the reader take note that the totals for both mining enterprises and aggregate capital are larger than those given in Table 7 because the data supplied by the *Mining Manual* are more complete.

⁴ But capitalists from the United States were already crowding British investors in Mexico and Honduras. United States capital invested in Mexican mines was estimated at $20,000,000 early in 1888 (*Consular Reports*, No. 89, Feb. 1888, pp. 339–340). I have found no satisfactory statistics for 1890. *Mining Directory and Reference Book* (Chicago, 1892) lists 31 companies, with an aggregate capital of $55,165,600, owned by citizens of the United States and operating in Mexico before this work went to press (late 1891 or early 1892). This figure probably represents authorized capital, but the list also includes (pp. 479–482) some 20 more American companies whose capital is not given. The Council of the Corporation of Foreign Bondholders, in its *Fourteenth Annual Report* (London, 1887), mentions (p. 81) 5 United States mining companies that were active in Honduras in 1886 and states that their combined capital was $9,276,000. Ce Charles, in her *Honduras: Land of Great Depths* (Chicago, 1890), lists (pp. 54–70) more than 20 American-controlled mining organizations which were operating in Honduras at the time her book went to press and describes each enterprise briefly, but presents little data on capitalization.

⁵ Among the best sources for such an investigation are *Mining Manual, Mining World, Stock Exchange Year-Book,* and *South American Journal*. The first began publication in 1887, the second in 1871, the third in 1875, and the fourth — under the title of *Brazil and River Plate Mail* — in 1863, so that, taken together, they provide an extensive coverage.

⁶ I have dealt more fully with the subject of British mining activities and the returns therefrom in *Inter-American Economic Affairs*, Winter 1953, pp. 65–72, and Autumn 1954, pp. 43–53.

⁷ United States Department of Commerce, Bureau of Foreign and Domestic Commerce, *Trade Information Bulletin No. 731* (Washington, D.C., 1931), pp. 18–19, and *Economic Series No. 20* (Washington, D.C., 1942), p. 13. These aggregates include British Honduras and European colonies in the West Indies and the Guianas, so that the totals are somewhat too high for Latin America alone. The figures for capitalization represent book values.

⁸ The most convenient sources of information regarding British participation in the Chilean nitrate industry are *South American Journal* for the years 1883 to 1950 and *Stock Exchange Year-Book* for 1889 and following years. Fuller details may be found in such English journals as *Financial News, Financial Times, Pall Mall Gazette,* and *Economist*. *Stock Exchange Year-Book*, which is fully indexed, lists and describes each company in alphabetical order in the section entitled "miscellaneous companies" included in each issue, so that page references seem unnecessary in the narrative that follows.

⁹ The statistics in this paragraph have been compiled from the *Stock Exchange Year-Book*, 1889, 1891, 1901, 1914, 1919, 1931, and 1946. I have not included British-owned railroads in northern Chile not primarily engaged in the transportation of nitrate. At least 3 British railway companies were operating in this region — Arica and Tacna, Taltal, and Antofagasta and Bolivia — and English capitalists also had minority investments in some of the Chilean companies.

¹⁰ Professor Osgood Hardy, in an intriguing article entitled "British Nitrates and the Balmaceda Revolution," *Pacific Historical Review*, Vol. 17 (Los Angeles, 1948), pp. 1–180, includes a brief sketch of North's life, citing Chilean sources. North's career as a promoter can be followed in detail in the publications mentioned above. *South American Journal*, Vol. 40 (Jan.–June 1896), pp. 510, 524, 549, gives a useful account of his career, his death, and his funeral. The Prince of Wales, the King of Belgium, and the Khedive of Egypt, along with several lords, knights, ladies, and many business associates, either sent flowers or attended the burial ceremonies at Eltham, Kent.

Notes

[11] Hardy suggests that North and other nitrate capitalists — English, Chilean, and European — financed and perhaps helped to foment this revolution, which resulted in the downfall and death of President José Balmaceda, who had nullified North's railway monopoly and advocated the nationalization of the nitrate industry. It is interesting to observe, in this connection, the attitude of the *South American Journal*. A careful examination of Vols. 30 and 31, which cover the year of the Congressional Revolt, discloses decided hostility toward the Chilean chief executive and the deepest sympathy for the nitrate capitalists, especially North, and the Chilean insurgents. An editorial in the number for September 5, 1891, entitled "Balmaceda Overthrown," contains this statement: "It is with great satisfaction that we have to record the realization, not only of our hopes, but of the expectations we have throughout ventured to express. . . ." The following number (Sept. 12, p. 295) speaks of "Colonel North's friendly relations with the new government." The *South American Journal* carefully recorded North's promotional activities and enthusiastically recommended his companies for almost a decade, giving special attention to his sensational voyage to the South American Pacific coast, the festivities preceding his departure, the elaborate banquets in Chile, and the welcome home (see almost any issue for the year 1889).

[12] Paul H. Emden, *Randlords* (London, 1935), has written an interesting volume on British millionaires who drew their wealth from South Africa. I am urging a volume on the Nitrate Knights and the Fertilizer Plutocrats. Among the nitrate directors who powered into knighthood were Sir A. Brocklebank, Sir T. Fry, Sir W. Greenwell, Sir Robert Harvey, and Sir Harry North. Members of Parliament were equally numerous; Colonel North almost won a seat in the House of Commons in 1895 (*South American Journal*, Vol. 40 (May 9, 1896), p. 524).

[13] *South American Journal*, Vol. 39 (July–Dec. 1895), pp. 491, 495, 529.

[14] *Ibid.*, Vol. 26 (Jan.–June 1889), pp. 193-194; *Stock Exchange Year-Book*, 1891, under "Nitrate Railways Company," gives the capitalization. See also William H. Russell, *A Visit to Chile and the Nitrate Fields of Tarapacá* (London, 1890), pp. 354-359.

[15] Hardy, *op. cit.*, pp. 173-174.

[16] Hardy, p. 177, says the price paid by North was £110,000; *South American Journal*, Vol. 41 (July–Dec. 1896), p. 127, places the figure at £210,000, including water supply and machinery, but also mentions the smaller sum on p. 503.

[17] See *Stock Exchange Year-Book* for 1887-1897.

[18] *South American Journal*, Vol. 25, pp. 193, 403, presents information that suggests copious watering of the stock of Tarapacá Waterworks Company; it acquired most of the assets from North, who had controlled the water supply of Iquique and Arica for several years.

[19] Statistics compiled from *Stock Exchange Year-Book* for 1915. The nominal British capital invested at the end of 1913 was around £23,000,000.

[20] Statistics obtained from *Stock Exchange Year-Book* for 1918 and 1919.

[21] For a quarter of a century following 1890 from 55 to 60 per cent of the Chilean nitrate business was in the hands of British capital; the rest was controlled by Chileans and foreigners residing in Chile or elsewhere (Hardy, *op. cit.*, p. 180; *South American Journal*, Vol. 29 (December 13, 1890), p. 711; Vol. 40 (January 16, 1896), p. 62 et passim).

[22] Between 1880 and 1930 these revenues averaged nearly 43 per cent of the ordinary revenues of the national government, reaching a maximum in 1894 of almost 68 per cent. Exports exceeded a million tons in 1890, rarely fell below that figure during the next years, and occasionally rose well above two million. The export tax ranged from $2.20 to $13.50 per ton, U.S. currency (United States Tariff Commission, *Chemical Nitrogen* (Report No. 114, second series, Washington, D.C., 1937), p. 109; Jack Pfeiffer, Development of Manufacturing Industry in Chile" (unpublished dissertation, University of Chicago, 1947), pp. 109-129).

[23] Nitrate wage earners numbered 2,848 in 1880, over 13,000 in 1890, nearly 20,000 in 1900, and approximately 44,000 in 1914 (Pfeiffer, *op. cit.*, p. 109). Different wage

scales for various types of work and oscillating rates of exchange make it almost impossible to present an accurate statement regarding wages. Nitrate workers suffered from the decline in the value of the Chilean paper peso until they demanded and obtained payment in silver in 1890 (*South American Journal*, Vol. 24, 1887, p. 673, and Vol. 29, 1890, pp. 580–81). The *Journal* remarked in 1887: "The wages of men employed in nitrate-producing are very good, but the truck system prevails there and at most of the mines, so that a good deal of the wages earned return to the employer as profits on sales of goods." The *Journal* was greatly disturbed by the strikes that occurred in 1890 and expressed the view that the Chilean government should either send in troops to suppress the workers or else compensate the nitrate *oficinas* (production plants) for the injuries suffered. As for the workers' exaction of pay in silver instead of paper pesos, the nitrate companies probably could recoup their losses by raising the price of "provisions and supplies at the stores which all of them have." (*Ibid.*, Vol. 29, pp. 35–36, 65, 77, 90, 581.) William H. Russell, in spite of the fact that he was a North propagandist, remarked in 1890 that the dwellings of the laborers were "patchwork." "Pieces of zinc corrugated iron, matting, and shreds of sacking do duty as walls to some of the shanties." (*Op. cit.*, p. 176.) An article by Professor Walter S. Tower, entitled "The Nitrate Fields of Chile," published in *Popular Science Monthly* for September 1913 (see especially pp. 224–227), gives the impression that wages and working conditions had not greatly changed since the days of the Nitrate King.

The Chilean chief executive who inaugurated drastic government regulation and interposition in the nitrate business, much in accord with the policy forecast by the ill-fated José Balmaceda, was Arturo Alessandri, widely and favorably known in Chile as the "Lion of Tarapacá." Big yields from nitrate investments in Chile ceased to be siphoned out by foreign investors in the late 1920's. Most of the figures were on the other side of the ledger in the 1930's, but the best horses escaped before the barn door was shut. Citizens of the United States, influenced by the promoters employed by the Guggenheims, made some poor investments in the Chilean nitrate business, receiving very small returns and losing considerable capital.

Chapter IV. Investments at the End of 1913

[1] This chapter is based mainly upon information supplied by the *South American Journal*, Vol. 76, pp. 110, 137, 168, 198, 226, 254, 284–285 *et passim*, and *Stock Exchange Year-Book* for the years 1913 and 1914. Since the latter describes government bonds in the alphabetical order of the issuing governments and English companies under various classifications in the alphabetical order of their names, citations to specific volumes and pages seem unnecessary. See Appendix A for details about British gas companies.

[2] Statistics for economic enterprises, over 600 in all, including railway organizations are based on the *Stock Exchange Year-Book* for 1913 and 1914. Rough calculations of the aggregate capitalization of this group of investments indicate that the aggregate somewhat larger than estimated by the *South American Journal*. The enterprises described in this brief analysis may not exactly correspond with those considered by the *Journal* in arriving at its estimates; the *Journal* does not specify the firms it included in its calculations. The editors state, however, that they take no account of any enterprise which does not trade its securities on the London Stock Exchange, and they publish (Vol. 76, Jan. 7, 1914, pp. 73–78) a "Latin-American Directory" which includes over 700 firms, although many of these are trading firms that may not have had investments in the region. In order to make my enumeration conform as nearly as possible with the *Journal*'s estimates of nominal capital, I have omitted enterprises which had no securities listed on the London Stock Exchange. (The *Mining Manual* and *Oil and Petroleum Manual*, for instance, describe a few companies not included in the *Stock Exchange Year-Book*.) I have also excluded, because adequate information was not available, investment banks, insurance companies, and motion-picture concerns which may have h

Notes

small investments in Latin America. In short, the actual total of British-financed enterprises may have been 650, or even more.

³ *South American Journal*'s figure of £15,363,230 for shipping probably does not include all of the 45 enterprises operating steamboat lines and port facilities. But please note that I have not included transatlantic shipping lines in my estimates of British investments in Latin America in 1880, 1890, and 1900.

⁴ Capitalists from the United States owned the cable connections of several of the countries. See my *Latin America and the Industrial Age* (New York, 1947), pp. 33–39, 250.

⁵ *Mining Manual* for 1914 lists several more, but does not include some of the companies listed by *Stock Exchange Year-Book* for the same year. I have assumed — correctly, I think — that the data in both manuals are for 1913.

⁶ *Oil and Petroleum Manual* (London) for 1914 lists some 30 companies that can be identified as operating in Latin America.

Chapter V. British Investments at Their Peak

¹ Data presented in this chapter have been compiled from the *Annual Report* of the Council of the Corporation of Foreign Bondholders for the year 1928, from *South American Journal* for the years 1929–1932, and from *Stock Exchange Year-Book* for 1929–1932. Page citations to these sources are not given for reasons already repeatedly stated. Information regarding the purchase of English enterprises by American corporations during the year 1928 and subsequently has been gleaned in part from Moody's manuals.

² The financial record of this and other companies discussed below can be found in *Stock Exchange Year-Book* for the years 1929–1931. Consult the indexes.

³ For the dividend record of Pato Mines, see *Mining Year Book* (London), 1931, pp. 437–438. The rates of return are based on paid-up nominal capital.

Chapter VI. A Decade of Rapid Contraction

¹ Vol. 147, p. 25. Data for this chapter have been obtained mainly from three frequently-mentioned sources: *South American Journal* for the years 1940 and 1950, especially the volume covering the first half of each year; *Stock Exchange Official Year-Book* the word "official" was added to the title early in the 1930's) for the years 1940, 1941, 1950, and 1951; and the Council of the Corporation of Foreign Bondholders, *Sixty-fifth Annual Report* and *Seventy-fifth Annual Report*, covering the years 1939 and 1949. For details regarding Latin-American sterling loans, the second and the third are more satisfactory than the first, and the *Year-Book* is an excellent manual for the capitalization and financial record of individual British companies operating in Latin-America and elsewhere, an accurate index of the companies it lists and describes being one of its outstanding merits. Any reader who desires to check the facts and figures which I present with reference to any specific company can easily do so by consulting the exhaustive indexes to the volumes for the years I have mentioned (or one or two volumes preceding or following them). Although I have found the *Journal*'s investment figures inaccurate in some respects and incomplete in others, I have accepted them, in general, as the most satisfactory statistics on the subject, perhaps more reliable than I could compile without a large staff, almost unlimited time, and full access to mountains of business records. In arriving at its annual estimates of British investments in Latin America, the *Journal* uses the par value, and not the market value, of the securities involved and, as a rule (though not invariably), includes only the securities quoted on the London Stock Exchange on, or near, the last day of the year under review. General estimates for the previous year are usually published toward the end of January; estimates for specific countries follow during the next three or four months. In some instances Englishmen do not own all the securities quoted.

² *Hearings*, 81 Congress, 1 sess., on the "Foreign-Aid Appropriation Bill," p. 446. The quoted phrase is from Paul Hoffman's testimony.

British Investments in Latin America

Chapter VII. Mexico: Bonanzas and Heartbreaks

¹ *South American Journal*, Vol. 147, p. 92, gives the following totals for the years 1910, 1924, and 1949, but they are wide of the mark because they are based upon the aggregates of securities relating to Mexico quoted on the London Stock Exchanges at the close of these three years: 1910, £144,345,199; 1924, £216,424,528; 1949, £140,048,494. It is certain that all the securities quoted were not by any means owned by Englishmen. My estimates for 1910, 1924, and 1949 are in some respects no better than approximations, but they are based upon a careful examination of data contained in *Stock Exchange Year-Book*, and I am confident that they are far more accurate than those presented by the editors of the *Journal*. Regarding the nominal capital for the years 1880, 1890, and 1900, I feel sure that the margin of error is insignificant.

Among the few who have dealt with British investments in Mexico there is wide disagreement. Consul Marion Letcher, in *U.S. Daily Consular Reports*, July 18, 1912, estimated the total British investment (including the property owned by Englishmen living in Mexico) at the equivalent of some £64.3 million. The Fall Committee contended that the English investment in 1912 was nearer £160 million (around $800 million) (*Senate Document* No. 285, 66 Congress, 2 sess., Serial 7666, p. 3322). Edgar Turlington, in his *Mexico and Her Foreign Creditors* (New York, 1930), pp. 319–323, places the total at approximately £90 million for 1929. Senator Fall's figure is clearly an exaggeration, but the estimates of Letcher and Turlington seem far too low. In all probability, none of the three consulted *Stock Exchange Year-Book*, which is the most reliable source of information on this subject. *Statist* (London), Supplement, Feb. 14, 1914, estimates the total English investment in Mexico in 1913 at £99 million.

² *Mining Manual* is the best source for data on British mining enterprises in Mexico and elsewhere.

³ For statistics on rates of return for 1910, 1913, and 1924–1949, consult *South American Journal*, Vol. 147, p. 92. I have compiled my own figures for earlier years by using data from *Stock Exchange Year-Book*, and on the basis of information supplied by the *Year-Book* I have rejected some of the figures given by the *Journal* for the later period.

⁴ On the dividend record of these banks, see, in addition to *Stock Exchange Year-Book*, the *Mexican Year Book* (Mexico City, 1908), pp. 275–276, and 1914, p. 37. Their capitalization was in Mexican pesos whose value in sterling gradually declined. The sterling equivalents given in the text are therefore only approximate.

⁵ These statistics on mining profits may be verified by tracing the companies mentioned through the indexes of the *Stock Exchange Year-Book* and the *Mining Manual*. Rates of return are based upon the par value of the capital paid up.

⁶ The terms of settlement are outlined in *Stock Exchange Official Year-Book*, 1951, pp. 1070–1073. Eagle Oil Transport Co., Limited, organized in 1912, paid an average return of more than 6 per cent annually on its nominal capital of £2,240,000 for at least two decades following 1913.

⁷ *Ibid.*, 1927, pp. 2935–2936.

⁸ *Stock Exchange Year-Book*, 1926, p. 3117, and 1936, p. 1704.

⁹ *Ibid.*, 1931, p. 1289.

¹⁰ J. A. Spender, *Weetman Pearson, First Viscount Cowdray, 1856–1927* (London 1930), sketches Cowdray's Mexican activities. A wealth of data may also be found in *Mexican Year Book* for 1908 and following years, especially 1908, pp. 94, 275–276, 372–375, 388–390, 497–498, 568–569, and 722–725. Lord Cowdray employed an able American geologist named C. W. Hayes, later head of the U.S. Bureau of Mines, to search for petroleum deposits in Mexico.

Chapter VIII. The Small Caribbean Countries

¹ In the preparation of this chapter, I have had to lean heavily upon the *Stock Exchange Year-Book*. The *Annual Reports* of the Council of the Corporation of Foreign

Notes

Bondholders have been helpful in supplying information on sterling government issues and default records, but their figures for government securities outstanding at the end of any particular year do not always agree with those given by the *Year-Book*, so that I have been compelled to make a choice, and I have as a rule accepted the *Year-Book*'s statistics. *South American Journal* is not entirely reliable when its editors deal with the minor countries of Latin America. In the first place, its record is rather skimpy in respect to the Central American countries and the Dominican Republic; and in the second place, its custom of accepting securities quoted on the London Stock Exchange as a measure of the British investment has resulted in exaggeration in the cases of Cuba and Guatemala, as I shall point out in the course of my narrative. Another not entirely reliable source of information, but a useful one nevertheless, is Frederic M. Halsey's *Investments in Latin America and the British West Indies* (Washington, D.C., 1918, Department of Commerce, Special Agents Series, No. 169). Halsey has been useful mainly in the discovery of the names of the companies active in Central America. Since all four of these sources are either well indexed or provided with a detailed table of contents, I have reduced note references to the minimum. My facts and figures on any of the companies mentioned may be tested without difficulty by following the *Year-Book* indexes. Data on government bonds may be verified both in this manner and by referring to the table of contents of almost any *Annual Report* of the Council of the Corporation of Foreign Bondholders. General summaries of British investments in these countries will be found especially in the following volumes of *South American Journal*: 76, 110, 125, and every odd-numbered volume thereafter through Vol. 147 (see the indexes under "Cuba" and the 5 countries of Central America; no information is given on the Dominican Republic).

[2] *South American Journal*, Vol. 76, pp. 254, 284; Vol. 147, p. 25; *Stock Exchange Official Year-Book*, index under the countries mentioned.

[3] See the references cited in note 2.

[4] The reader may remove his doubts by following this company through *Stock Exchange Year-Book* for the years 1917–1936, with the help of the indexes.

[5] Let the incredulous reader trace the record of Butters Salvador through the *Stock Exchange Year-Book* for the years 1906, 1917, and 1918. Apparently the company was liquidated in 1918. Some of its capital was probably owned by citizens of the United States.

[6] These are my own estimates, based for the most part on the *Stock Exchange Year-Book*. I have not accepted the higher figures presented by the *South American Journal*. Investors in Honduran government bonds lost considerable capital.

[7] Jacob Hollander's *Debt of Santo Domingo*, a confidential report made to President Theodore Roosevelt after a personal investigation in the republic and published as a confidential document (Executive Document No. 1, 59 Congress, 1 sess.) in 1905, contains a wealth of information on foreign investments and the vicissitudes of foreigners and their capital. For British complaints regarding the treatment they received at the hands of the United States government, see Council of the Corporation of Foreign Bondholders, *Annual Report*, 1910, p. 320.

[8] Again I refer to the *Stock Exchange Year-Book*, especially for the years 1906, 1917, 1927, 1931, 1939, 1946, and 1951 (see the indexes under "Henry Clay and Bock" and "Havana Cigar and Tobacco"). Rates of return are all based upon the par value of capital paid up.

Chapter IX. Northern South America

[1] This chapter is based primarily upon three bulky sources of information: Council of the Corporation of Foreign Bondholders *Annual Report* for the years 1876 to 1950; *Stock Exchange Year-Book* for the same period, but especially for the years 1881, 1891, 1901, and 1906 to 1950; and *South American Journal* for 1881–1950, particularly the volumes for 1881, 1891, 1901, 1914, and 1931–1950. The first source deals almost ex-

British Investments in Latin America

clusively with the sterling debts of foreign governments, arranging them alphabetically so that any particular government is easy to find. The second source has the same arrangement for sterling government issues; but, in addition and more important, it contains a descriptive list of thousands of British economic enterprises operating all over the world, listing these, however, not by country but by the kind of activity in which they are engaged. The major task has been to discover the companies operating in Ecuador, Colombia, and Venezuela; for once they have been discovered, their financial history can easily be traced by making use of the *Year-Book*'s exhaustive indexes. The discovery of the British enterprises active in these three countries is facilitated by the *Journal*, which is almost certain, sooner or later, to describe or mention the most important of them. Moreover, the editors of the *Journal* assemble from time to time statistics on the aggregate nominal investment of Englishmen in Latin America as a whole and in its major republics, the following pages being most useful for presenting a view of investment trends and rates of return: Vol. 76, pp. 254, 284–285; Vol. 110, pp. 255, 321; Vol. 147, pp. 114–140. Confident that the reader, by using the excellent indexes of these sources, will have no difficulty in checking my facts and figures, I have reduced specific citations to the minimum. The *Journal*'s estimates of total investments for a series of years starting with 1913 are based, I repeat, upon London Stock Exchange quotations at each year's end. If a security happens not to be quoted at that particular time, it is not included. This is a matter of little importance in countries where the investment is large; but in respect to countries like Ecuador, Colombia, and Venezuela, where the investment is comparatively small, it sometimes results in a false impression. I have therefore rejected the *Journal*'s figures when I have felt certain that they conveyed an erroneous view of investment trends or rates of return and have used data laboriously compiled from the *Year-Book* instead.

² *Stock Exchange Official Year-Book*, 1953, p. 335. Holders of ordinary shares received 120 per cent; other securities were repaid at par.

³ *Ibid.*, 1935, p. 439. The sale price was stipulated in U.S. currency: $1,644,816.

⁴ *Stock Exchange Year-Book*, 1928, p. 835.

⁵ *Ibid.*, 1931, p. 1352. Citizens of the United States acquired a controlling interest in this company in 1931.

⁶ *Ibid.*, 1927, p. 2190.

⁷ *Ibid.*, 1892, p. 507. See also P. L. Bell, *Venezuela: A Commercial and Industrial Handbook* (Washington, D.C., 1922), pp. 257–258.

⁸ Among the other profitable companies were Darién Gold Mining, Nechí Mines, and subsidiaries of Oroville Dredging Company and Placer Development, Limited. I have dealt more fully with British investments in Colombian mines in *Inter-American Economic Affairs*, Winter 1953, pp. 65–72.

⁹ *Stock Exchange Official Year-Book*, 1950, p. 985.

Chapter X. Paraguay, Bolivia, and Peru

¹ Statistics on the total nominal investments of Englishmen in Paraguay and Bolivia and the income from these investments as estimated by the *South American Journal* in its issues for the first semesters of 1914, 1940, and subsequent years, exaggerate both the amount of capital and the income produced because of the method employed; but the *Journal* is more dependable for Peru. The Council of the Corporation of Foreign Bondholders, *Annual Report* for the years 1877 through 1949, deals with the sterling issues of these three countries, especially Peru and Paraguay. In the various issues of the *Stock Exchange Year-Book* one may find not only the story of the sterling government bonds of these three countries but also, by diligent perusal, the financial history of the leading British companies active within their boundaries. Once the names of the economic enterprises are discovered, there is no difficulty, as a rule, in ascertaining their capitalization and their dividend records. The United States Department of Commerce has published a scholarly handbook on each of the republics dealt with

Notes

in this chapter: W. L. Schurz, *Paraguay: A Commercial Handbook* (1920); W. E. Dunn, *Peru: A Commercial and Industrial Handbook* (1925); W. L. Schurz, *Bolivia: A Commercial and Industrial Handbook* (1921), and these works contain data on English economic activities in these republics. Since these various sources of information have either extensive tables of contents or indexes, or both, and because I have desired to economize space, I have avoided elaborate specific citations.

[2] *Stock Exchange Year-Book*, 1892, p. 96; 1896, pp. 625–626; 1906, pp. 166–167 and 1251.

[3] *Ibid.* for the years 1910 and following, index under "Aramayo" and "Compagnie Aramayo."

[4] *Ibid.* for the years 1927 and following, index under "Patiño." Both this company and the Aramayo enterprise were "expropriated" by the Bolivian government in 1952.

[5] See *South American Journal*, Vols. 125 and every odd-numbered volume thereafter, index under "Bolivia, British investments." The *Journal* gives a distorted view of the shrinkage and expansion of the investment and rates of return from year to year because securities which happen not to have been quoted at the end of the year in question are omitted, and at times the magnitude of the capital is exaggerated for the reasons stated in the text.

[6] *Mining Manual*, already frequently mentioned, is the most useful source of information on English mining activities; but a thorough combing of its indexes is required to discover the names of the companies active in Peru and other Latin-American countries, since the listing is not by countries but merely alphabetical for British mining enterprises operating all over the world.

[7] *South American Journal*, Vol. 147, p. 150. The *Journal's* estimates are too high for some years and too low for others. They should be checked with the figures given by *Stock Exchange Year-Book* for the years 1910–1950.

[8] W. E. Dunn, in his *Peru: A Commercial and Industrial Handbook*, pp. 190–204, gives a satisfactory summary of the evolution of Peru's petroleum industry. International Petroleum's ordinary shares have no par; but since they rate equally with its preference shares for dividends, I have assigned them the same nominal value in computing the total capital and the annual dividends. The combined capitalization of Lobitos and London and Pacific amounted to only £1,158,090 in 1915, but I have made allowance for the not infrequent liberality of holding companies when they absorb operating companies.

[9] One of the English enterprises active in Peru, Peruvian Amazon Company, Limited, organized in 1907 and compelled by the British courts to begin liquidation in 1912, caused an international scandal by its excesses in the rubber forests, horribly abusing its Indian labor. Its English directors were not wholly to blame, since they formed only a minority influence; but they were shockingly indifferent or careless. One of them was a titled nobleman; two others had spent many years in business in Peru and Chile; one of the two was a director of the Peruvian Corporation and a British bank. The atrocities are exposed in United States Congress, *House Document* No. 1366, 62 Congress, 3 sess., Serial 6369: "Slavery in Peru," and in Great Britain, Parliament, House of Commons, *Reports of Committees*, Vol. 14: "Putumayo Atrocities" (London, 1913).

Chapter XI. The Chilean Experience

[1] The most useful sources for the history of British investments in Chile are *Stock Exchange Year-Book* for the years 1876–1950 and the *South American Journal* for the same period. The *Annual Reports* of the Council of the Corporation of Foreign Bondholders are not of much service, since these reports deal mainly with defaulting countries. Page references to works so well indexed as the *Year-Book* and the *Journal* seem superfluous; but see especially the following specific citations to the *Journal*: Vol. 76, p. 198; Vol. 110, pp. 148 and 270; Vol. 112, pp. 131–133; Vol. 131, p. 95; and Vol. 147, p. 67. Although a long and careful scrutiny of the *Year-Book* is required to ferret out

the British companies operating in Chile, since this manual's data are not classified by countries, the capitalization and dividend records of these companies are not difficult to trace through the years after the names of the companies are once discovered. The names of the most important of the some 50 or 60 British economic enterprises active in Chile at one period or another are mentioned in the text, particularly in the second part of this chapter.

The *Journal's* statistics for totals of investments and annual nominal returns give a somewhat distorted view for the years 1931 through 1940 because they include the nitrate investment without giving due consideration to the admixture of the American capital or large injections of water. The peak of the British investment, according to the *Journal* (Vol. 119, p. 312), was not reached until the end of 1935, when the nominal figure stood at more than £94.5 million. In my opinion, the investment was close to its maximum at the end of the year 1926, when the nominal aggregate of British capital in Chile was £78,866,640. The *Journal's* estimates for some of the years preceding 1926 and following 1940 are a little too low.

[2] Statistics for miscellaneous investments before 1910 are my own; beginning with 1910, they are taken from the *South American Journal*.

[3] Figures on average rates of return are my own for the years before 1910 and the *Journal's* thereafter. No allowance is made for loss of capital.

[4] There was a good deal of bickering between the company and the Chilean authorities over water rates. The company's side of the case is stated by the *South American Journal* (Vol. 76, p. 575, for illustration).

[5] Shareholders were paid £8 in cash for each £5 share (*Stock Exchange Year-Book*, 1930, p. 1457).

[6] Vol. 76, pp. 776–777.

Chapter XII. Profitable Ventures in Uruguay

[1] This chapter is based mainly upon the familiar three sources: Council of the Corporation of Foreign Bondholders, *Annual Report* for the years 1880–1949; *Stock Exchange Year-Book* for the years 1887–1951; and *South American Journal*, Vols. 76–148 (1914–1950). Uruguayan government securities are described in detail in the first two and listed in the third. British economic enterprises trading securities on the London Stock Exchange and operating in Uruguay are listed annually in the *Year-Book* and described from time to time in the *Journal*. Specific page references have been reduced to the minimum in the analysis here presented.

[2] Statistics in this and the two preceding paragraphs are in part my own compilations based on the three sources mentioned in note 1 and in part the estimates presented by the *South American Journal*. I have supplied the estimates for the years 1880, 1890, and 1900. Those for later years are taken from the *Journal*, especially Vol. 76, p. 226; Vol. 110, p. 179; Vol. 143, p. 174; and Vol. 147, p. 104. The *Journal* has published estimates for the year 1913 and for the years 1923 through 1949, based on the face value of securities quoted in London at the end of each year.

[3] Vol. 110, p. 179.

[4] Vol. 119, p. 97. Simon Hanson, in Chapter XI of his *Utopia in Uruguay* (New York, 1938), deals at some length with the difficulties and complaints of British investors. Important among these were the claims of a Franco-British organization, Rambla Company of Montevideo, Limited, set up in 1911 to build a sea wall and reclaim a large area of land on the outskirts of the capital. *Stock Exchange Year-Book* for 1914 and subsequent years gives a brief account of the tribulations and reclamations of this company. Apparently no mutually satisfactory settlement was ever reached. The Rambla Company was dissolved in 1933.

[5] Statistics on rates of return are my own for the years preceding 1910. For the years 1910 and following they are those published by the *South American Journal*, volumes and pages cited in note 2. For the price received by the British for their Uruguayan

Notes

railways and the losses, actual or theoretical, suffered by each company, see *Stock Exchange Official Year-Book* for 1951, Vol. 1, pp. 330 ff., under "Central Uruguay Railway," "Midland Uruguay Railway," "Midland Uruguay Extension Railway," "North Western of Uruguay," "Uruguay Northern," and "Quarahim International Bridge Company." No account of capital losses has been taken in computing rates of return.

[6] *South American Journal* for July 11, 1936 (Vol. 119, p. 41), quotes the chairman of the board of Atlas Electric and General Trust to the effect that over £6 million had been invested in the Montevideo tramway system. I suspect that this is an exaggeration.

Statistics on rates of return on the nominal capital of the various companies included in the second part of this chapter have been compiled from the *Stock Exchange Year-Book*, particularly from the volumes for the years 1887, 1892, 1896, 1902, 1914, 1926, 1931, 1939, 1950, and 1951.

Chapter XIII. Brazil: Large Recipient of Capital

[1] Like most of those preceding it, this chapter is based mainly upon three voluminous sources: Council of the Corporation of Foreign Bondholders, *Annual Report* for each of the years 1876–1949; *South American Journal* for the same period; and *Stock Exchange Year-Book* for the years 1877, 1881, 1891, 1896, 1901, and 1914–1951. For reasons already mentioned, specific citations have been reduced to the minimum. For statistics on British investments in Brazil and income therefrom for 1910 and subsequent years I have found the following references in *South American Journal* helpful: Vol. 76, p. 110; Vol. 110, p. 106; and Vol. 147, p. 55. I have depended upon the *Year-Book* for the years preceding 1910. I have accepted with some reservations the estimates of the *Journal*, which seem too high for the capital in economic enterprises, especially railways and public utilities, since the *Journal*, as already noted elsewhere, based its estimates upon the securities quoted on the London Stock Exchange, whether owned by Englishmen or not, assuming that the difference would be adjusted by English investments quoted on other exchanges or not quoted at all, an assumption which seems unwarranted in the case of Brazilian railways and utilities because large blocks of the securities of some of these were held by capitalists of Canada, the United States, and other countries.

[2] The majority of the Brazilian quoted railway securities owned by Englishmen in 1890 and earlier had a government guaranty of 7 per cent, and part of the rest had a guaranty of 5 and 6 per cent; and these guaranties were usually made good, particularly during the reign of Dom Pedro II, which did not terminate until late in 1889 (see *South American Journal*, Vol. 29, p. 315; and Vol. 31, p. 502). The rates of return on the railway capital for the years 1913 and following are those given by *South American Journal* and are somewhat too low — because some unprofitable non-English securities are included — even if capital losses were considered.

[3] *Stock Exchange Official Year-Book*, 1951, p. 366.

[4] For the early dividend record of this company I have had to depend on Michael G. Mulhall, *The English in South America* (London, 1878), p. 453.

Chapter XIV. Argentina: Late Major Field of Investment

[1] Estimates of total overseas investments by residents of the British Isles vary widely. Perhaps British foreign investments aggregated £1.6 billion in 1890, £2 billion in 1900, £3.5 in 1913, around £4 billion in 1929, and £3.3 billion in 1947. But see C. K. Hobson, *The Export of Capital* (London, 1914), pp. 37, 205, 207; J. A. Hobson, *Imperialism*, 3rd ed. (London, 1938), pp. 52, 62, 375; and Cleona Lewis, *The United States and the Foreign Investment Problem* (Washington, D.C.), p. 60.

My estimates of British investments in Argentina are based as usual mainly upon three sources: Council of the Corporation of Foreign Bondholders, *Annual Report* for the years 1880 through 1949; *Stock Exchange Year-Book* for the same period; and *South*

British Investments in Latin America

American Journal for the years 1914 and 1931–1950, especially Vol. 76, p. 168; Vol. 110, p. 82; Vol. 117, p. 326; and Vol. 147, p. 42. Such data as I have taken from the first two may be easily checked by consulting the indexes under "Argentina," or, in the case of the *Year-Book*, under "railways" or the names of the various companies mentioned in this chapter.

² I have arrived at these estimates of British investments in Argentine public utilities and real estate after a long and careful scrutiny of the *Stock Exchange Year-Book* for the years 1891 through 1950.

³ Statistics on income and average rates of return are based mainly on the *South American Journal*, especially Vol. 115 (June 23, 1934), p. 621 and Vol. 147 (Jan. 28, 1950), p. 42, and the rates are figured on the par value of capital paid up, without any allowance for losses of capital.

⁴ See, for example, Vol. 118, p. 561; Vol. 127, p. 88; Vol. 138, p. 301. The companies included in the *Journal*'s calculations were: (1) Argentine Land and Investment, (2) Argentine Northern, (3) Argentine Southern, (4) Córdoba, (5) Forestal, (6) Port Madryn (liquidated in 1935), (7) Río Negro, and (8) Tecka. Numbers 1, 3, 5, and 8 were the most profitable.

⁵ The capitalization and dividend record of this company and of the 7 others dealt with in this section have been determined by thumbing thousands of pages of the *Stock Exchange Year-Book* covering the years 1880 through 1950. The statistics may be tested by consulting the indexes under the various company names and examining the pages that recite their history.

Chapter XV. A Sample of British Overseas Companies

¹ *The Conditions of Peace* (New York, 1942), pp. 268–269.

² R. F. Harrod, *The Life of John Maynard Keynes* (London, 1951), pp. 346–356, 393, 446.

³ *The Latin-American Policy of the United States* (New York, 1943), Chaps. XIX–XX.

⁴ This discussion occurred at a session of the annual meeting of the American Historical Association in New York in the middle 1940's.

⁵ These companies have been selected after long and careful scrutiny of the *Stock Exchange Year-Book*. Since the indexes are very complete, it has seemed sensible to omit references to particular years and pages. Supplementary information has been obtained from the *South American Journal;* and for the same reason given in respect to the *Year-Book*, specific citations to the *Journal* are also omitted. The *Journal* not only publishes quotations of the securities of the 23 companies analyzed here; it also presents annual accounts of their dividends and occasional summaries of their history. But all these data may be easily found by consulting the index to each volume.

⁶ Statistical data on these 23 companies have been compiled from *Stock Exchange Year-Book*.

Chapter XVI. A Recent Decade of British Investment

¹ This large pamphlet not only classifies British overseas capital in considerable detail, according to both its nature and its geographical distribution; it also takes account of companies registered abroad as well as at home, separates the investment in government securities from the investment, usually more profitable, in business enterprises, and lists the latter under two headings: share capital and loan capital (bonds and debentures).

The book by A. R. Conan, mentioned in connection with Tables 35 and 36, is useful for its general summary of British overseas investments at the middle of the twentieth century, but Conan says little about profits and must surely exaggerate the total of capital involved.

Notes

Chapter XVII. British Views on Foreign Investments

[1] *The Progress of the Nation* (London, 1851), p. 628.
[2] *State Papers, British and Foreign* (London) XLII, 385.
[3] *Ibid.*
[4] *A Short Inquiry into the Profitable Nature of Our Investments* (London).
[5] *Economist* (London), August 20, 1892.
[6] *Imperialism: A Study* (London, 1948), pp. 85, 86–87. There are several editions of this work; the first was published in 1902 and the second in 1905.
[7] C. K. Hobson, *The Export of Capital* (London, 1914), p. ix.
[8] *Ibid.*, pp. ix–xxv.
[9] "Foreign Investment and National Advantage," in *Nation* (London), XXV (1924), 584–587.
[10] "Foreign Investments and British Public Opinion," in Quincy Wright, ed., *Foreign Investments* (Chicago, 1928), pp. 100–114.
[11] Vol. 115 (1934), pp. 249–250.
[12] *The Conditions of Peace* (New York, 1942), pp. 268–269. See also R. F. Harold, *The Life of John Maynard Keynes* (London, 1951), pp. 246–256 et passim, and Royal Institute of International Affairs, *The Problem of International Investment* (London, 1937), pp. 1–15, 102–109.

Chapter XVIII. Views of the Latin-American Recipients

[1] Carlos Calvo, *Derecho internacional teórico y práctico de Europa y América*, 2 vols. (Paris, 1868 and many subsequent enlarged editions); Rafael F. Seijas, *El derecho internacional Hispano-Americano*, 6 vols. (Caracas, 1884–1885). Consult also *The Calvo Clause*, an excellent monograph by Donald R. Shea published in 1955 by the University of Minnesota Press, Minneapolis.
[2] Scores of references could be given here. I mention only the following: Tancredo Pinochet, *La conquista de Chile en el Siglo XX* (Santiago, 1909); Pablo M. Minelli, *Las inversiones internacionales en América Latina* (Havana, 1938); Osario da Rocha Diniz, *O Brasil em face dos imperialismos modernos* (Rio de Janeiro, 1940); and the various standard collections of public addresses by Lázaro Cárdenas, Getulio Vargas, and Juan D. Perón.
[3] James Brown Scott, ed., *The Proceedings of the Hague Peace Conferences: The The Conference of 1907*, 3 vols., (New York, 1921–1922), I, 616; II, 137–143, 226–310, 555–560.
[4] Simon G. Hanson, *Utopia in Uruguay* (New York, 1938), deals fully with state economic enterprises in Uruguay.
[5] Ray Stannard Baker and William E. Dodd, eds., *The Public Papers of Woodrow Wilson: The New Democracy* (New York, 1926), I, 66–67.
[6] *Ibid.*, II, 342.
[7] Department of State, *The Lansing Papers*, I, 463, 467.
[8] Vol. 6, pp. 575–576.
[9] Samuel I. Rosenman, ed., *The Public Papers and Addresses of Franklin D. Roosevelt*, Vol. 12 (New York, 1950), p. 177.
[10] *Ibid.*, pp. 201–202.
[11] Senate Committee on Foreign Relations, 84 Congress, 1 sess., *Hearings*, "Mutual Security Act of 1955," pp. 300–301.
[12] During the first half of the year 1950 the Economic and Social Council of the United Nations published a series of mimeographed monographs on this subject under the following broad titles: *Survey of Policies Affecting Private Foreign Investment* and *Economic and Legal Status of Foreign Investment in Selected Countries of Latin America*. These studies deal with ten of the Latin-American republics: Argentina, Brazil, Chile, Colombia, Cuba, Guatemala, Mexico, Peru, Uruguay, and Venezuela.

Under the title of *Economic Controls and Commercial Policy*, the U.S. Tariff Commission published a similar series of monographs on all the countries during the years 1945–1947. The U.S. Department of Commerce published two surveys, one in 1952 and the other in 1954, under the title of *Factors Limiting U.S. Investments Abroad*.

[13] For the constitutional provisions on expropriation see Russell H. Fitzgibbon, *The Constitutions of the Americas* (Chicago, 1948), index under "property, right of and social functions of." Most of the Latin-American constitutions in force as of January 1, 1948 (the date of available data) provided for fair and prompt or prior indemnification. But procedures in such countries as Mexico, Bolivia, Brazil, and Argentina have not always conformed with the terms of the constitutions. Argentina's new constitution of 1949 contains this clause (see Article 40): "The price of expropriation of public service concessionary undertakings shall be the original cost of assets involved in operations, less the sums that may have been amortized during the period since the granting of the concession, and less sums in excess of a reasonable profit, which shall also be considered as repayment of the capital invested." The subject of expropriation was a hotly contested issue between the delegation of the United States and those of several of the Latin-American governments at both the Chapultepec Conference of 1945 and the Ninth International Conference of the American States which met in Bogotá in 1948. A summary of the proceedings of the first was published by the State Department in 1945 under the title of *Inter-American Conference on the Problems of War and Peace*. A similar summary of the second was published by the State Department in 1948, with the title of *Ninth International Conference of American States*. The U.S. Senate Committee on Banking and Currency, *Report* No. 1082, 83 Cong., 2 sess., dwelt at length on the subject of investment climate and indicated that it was rather unsatisfactory in most countries of the region (1953).

[14] As quoted by Galo Plaza, in *Problems of Democracy in Latin America* (Chapel Hill, 1955), pp. 48–50.

[15] Quoted in *ibid.*, pp. 63–64.

[16] *Ibid.*, pp. 82–83.

[17] Ángel del Río, ed., *Responsible Freedom in the Americas* (New York, 1955), pp. 205–223, for the addresses of Bowers and Santos.

[18] *Ibid.*, pp. 44, 45, and 54.

[19] *Congressional Record* (daily), Aug. 6, 1956, pp. 6270–6271. What will be the fate of private enterprise when government salaries, by and large, exceed those to be had in any other employment? When do government officials and employees expect to begin to practice the austerity that they recommend to the "dear" people?

APPENDIX A

BRITISH GAS COMPANIES IN LATIN AMERICA

Havana was probably the first city in Latin America to utilize artificial gas. In 1844, about thirty years after this new source of light and heat began to be used in the British Isles and a decade or so after it was introduced into the United States,[1] James Robb of New Orleans and Miguel de Silva of Havana obtained a concession from the Spanish government to operate a coal-gas plant in the Cuban capital. Organizing the Compañía Española de Alumbrado de Gas, they began to light Havana's streets by means of the new illuminant before 1850, probably in 1848. A second gas concession was granted in 1877, to Juan Domingo Stable, who transferred it to the Havana Gas Light Company, a New York corporation, which inaugurated its plant in 1882. The Spanish American Light and Power Company, also a United States corporation, leased both of these properties in 1883 and soon absorbed the two companies.[2] By 1890 — perhaps several years earlier — gasworks had been established in Cienfuegos and Santiago.[3]

During the 1850's, gaslights appeared for the first time on the streets of several of the Latin-American cities — Rio de Janeiro,[4] Buenos Aires,[5] Santiago, Copiapó,[6] Valparaíso,[7] and Guayaquil,[8] and probably Recife,[9] Lima,[10] Mexico City, and Veracruz.[11] During the subsequent decade the first plants were erected in Bahía, Ceará, Nictheroy,

---

[1] *Encyclopedia Britannica*, under "Gas."

[2] Cuba, Direccion general del Censo, *Informe general del censo de 1943*. (Havana, 1945), p. 539.

[3] *Special Consular Reports* (Washington, 1891), Vol. 6, reports from Cienfuegos and Santiago.

[4] *The Journal of Gas Lighting*, II (London, 1851–1852), 177, 378. *Water Supply* and *Sanitary Improvement* were phrases soon added to the title of this journal.

[5] *Ibid.*, V (1856), 259, 484–485, 661. The Buenos Aires plant was built by William Bragge, an English engineer.

[6] Mrs. C. B. Merwin, *Three Years in Chile* (Columbus, Ohio, 1860), p. 80; George A. Peabody, *South American Journals, 1858–1859* (Salem, Mass., 1937), p. 163. The Copiapó Gas Company, Limited, was organized in England in 1858.

[7] Merwin, *op. cit.*, p. 123. The city of Valparaíso was "lighted with gas for the first time" on September 18, 1856; gaslights appeared on the streets of Santiago sometime between September 1855 and May 1859.

[8] J. Fred Rippy, *Latin America and the Industrial Age* (New York, 1947), p. 72; *Commercial Relations of the United States* (Washington, 1859–1860), *passim* (Guayaquil).

[9] *The Journal of Gas Lighting*, VI (1857), 30.

[10] *Ibid.*, II (1851–1852), 405.

[11] *Ibid.*, V (August 19, 1856), 484: "The last West Indian Mail brings advices of the lighting of the city of Mexico with gas. Vera Cruz has been [thus] lighted for some time past."

British Investments in Latin America

Pará (Belém), São Paulo, and São Luiz de Maranhão,[12] and perhaps in some additional towns of Chile and Peru. During the next twenty years artificial gas began to be used in Montevideo, Pelotas, Porto Alegre, Rio Grande, Caracas, and a few more urban centers; by 1890, in short, gasworks were in operation in numerous cities and towns of Brazil, Argentina, Chile, Peru, and Cuba, although artificial gas was still not widely used, and perhaps would never be widely used, in other Latin-American countries.[13]

Many of the early gasworks in Latin America were financed by Englishmen who built even more plants than they ever owned.[14] The extent of British ownership is set forth in the following lists, which give the names of the British companies, the date when each was founded, and the capitalization of each.[15]

British Gas Companies in Latin America, End of 1876

Bahía Gas Co., Ltd. (1860); £150,000.
Buenos Ayres (New) Gas Co., Ltd. (1875); £303,750(?).
Ceará Gas Co., Ltd. (1866); £38,255(?).
Montevideo Gas Co., Ltd. (1872); £550,000.
Nictheroy (Brazil) Gas Co., Ltd. (1867); £85,220.
Pará Gas Co., Ltd. (1862); £166,870.
Rio de Janeiro Gas Co., Ltd. (1865); £720,000.
San Paulo Gas Co., Ltd. (1869); £80,000.
São Pedro (Brazil) Gas Co., Ltd. (1871); £110,000.

British Gas Companies in Latin America, End of 1890

Bahía Gas Co., Ltd. (1860); £150,000.
Belgrano (Buenos Ayres) Gas Co., Ltd. (1878); £300,000.
Buenos Ayres (New) Gas Co., Ltd. (1875); £700,000.
Ceará Gas Co., Ltd. (1866); £38,255.
City of Santos Improvements Co., Ltd. (1880); £135,000. Owned waterworks, sewage system, and gas plant.
Montevideo Gas Co., Ltd. (1872); £599,000.
Pará Gas Co., Ltd. (1862); £186,265.
San Paulo Gas Co., Ltd. (1869); £161,205.
South Barracas (Buenos Aires) Gas and Coke Co., Ltd. (1888); £40,400(?).

Although the number of British-owned companies remained the same for 1875 and

---

[12] Michael G. Mulhall, *The English in South America* (Buenos Aires, 1878), pp. 525, 531; *The Journal of Gas Lighting*, XIX–XXIII, index under the towns mentioned. This magazine usually gives the date of inauguration of each plant as well as some account of its construction.

[13] *Special Consular Reports* (Washington, 1891), Vol. 6, contains reports of consuls from the various Latin-American countries on the utilization of artificial gas. The coverage is not complete, but more than twenty plants are mentioned.

[14] This statement is based upon a careful examination of *Journal of Gas Lighting* for the years 1851 to 1890. The British investment was confined mainly to Argentina, Brazil, and Uruguay.

[15] These lists were compiled from *Stock Exchange Year-Book* for the years 1876, 1877, 1890, and 1891. This manual may have failed to include some of the smaller companies as well as some of the firms financed in part by British residents in Latin America. The date of a company's organization does not correspond to the date of the first use of gas, which usually occurs several months (sometimes even a year or two) later; but artificial gas was certainly utilized in Rio de Janeiro before the company listed for that city was organized — ten years before — and it was probably used in Santos before 1880, the date of the founding of the British company in that city.

Appendixes

1890, three of the old companies had passed from British control by 1890, three new firms had taken their place, and the nominal investment had increased. The properties at Rio and Nictheroy had been acquired in the late 1880's by French or Belgian capitalists; those at Pelotas, Porto Alegre, and Rio Grande — all owned by the São Pedro company — apparently had been taken over by the Brazilians.[16]

During the twenty years following 1890, further changes occurred and British holdings increased, as the following list for 1913 will disclose. Figures for capital invested are not given, however. Many of the gas companies had become subsidiaries of large utility corporations and the capitalization of the subordinate companies could not be accurately discovered from *Stock Exchange Year-Book* for 1913 and 1914, from which the list was compiled.[17]

British Gas Companies in Latin America, 1913

Bahía Blanca Gas Co., Ltd. (1907).
Ceará Gas Co., Ltd. (1866).
City of Santos Improvements Co., Ltd. (1880). Owned gas plant (?).
Maranhão Obras Públicas Co., Ltd. (1909).
Mexican Gas and Electric Light Co., Ltd. (1881?); absorbed (1902) by Mexican Light and Power Co., Ltd., a Canadian firm.
Montevideo Gas Co., Ltd. (1872).
Pará Gas Co., Ltd. (1898); reorganization of the old British company founded in 1862; controlled by Pará Electric Railways and Lighting Company, Ltd. (1905).
Primitiva Gas Company of Buenos Aires, Ltd. (1910); reorganization of Primitiva Gas and Electric Lighting Co., Ltd. (1901), which took over an Argentine company of similar name; the new British corporation controlled:
  Belgrano (Buenos Ayres) Gas Co., Ltd. (1878).
  Buenos Ayres (New) Gas Co., Ltd. (1875).
  La Compañía Gas Argentino (1869?).
  River Plate Gas Co., Ltd. (1897).
Rio de Janeiro Gas Co., Ltd. (1904?); reorganization of the old British firm founded in 1865; controlled by Rio de Janeiro Tramways, Light and Power Co., Ltd. (1904), a Canadian corporation.
San Paulo Gas Co., Ltd. (1869); controlled by São Paulo Tramways, Light and Power Co., Ltd. (1899), a Canadian corporation.
South Barracas (Buenos Ayres) Gas and Coke Co., Ltd. (1888).

---

[16] *Journal of Gas Lighting* traces briefly the history of these companies; see the index of each volume under "Rio de Janeiro," "Nictheroy," etc.

[17] Englishmen owned an interest in the Bahía Tramway, Light and Power Co. (1905), a Maine corporation which had taken over the old Bahía gas property, and in the Lima Light, Power and Tramways Co. (Empresas Eléctricas Asociadas, 1910), a Peruvian corporation which probably controlled the gasworks in Lima. Vera Cruz Electric Light, Power and Traction Co., Ltd. (1906) probably took over the Veracruz gas plant, if it was still in operation. The list therefore does not present a complete record of British investments in Latin-American gas enterprises; in fact, it merely lists the companies (perhaps not quite all of these) whose securities were traded on the London Stock Exchange during the years 1912 and 1913, as revealed by the *Stock Exchange Year-Book*.

APPENDIX B

BRITISH INVESTMENTS IN LATIN-AMERICAN ELECTRIC UTILITIES

Electric lights made their appearance in several of the leading cities of Latin America during the 1880's, within a decade after they began to be used in the United States and Europe, but electricity was not widely used in this part of the world until after 1900.[1] In introducing the new electrical inventions and devices, Englishmen, as usual, were prominent among the pioneers. They organized two or three electric companies for the purpose of operating in Latin America before 1890,[2] and they had investments in at least fourteen electric enterprises operating in the region by the end of 1900,[3] in some eighty organizations by the end of 1913,[4] and in approximately a hundred, including subsidiaries, by the close of 1926,[5] when their holdings seem to have reached the peak.[6] The following lists for the ends of the years 1900 and 1926, which include the names of enterprises in which British capital was either dominant or more or less significant and the date of organization and capitalization of each, are intended to indicate the location [7] and magnitude [8] of British influence.

British Investments in Electric Utilities in Latin America, End of 1900

Anglo-Argentine Tramways Co., Ltd. (1877); £1,530,035. Obtained in 1899 a concession to electrify its lines; electrification in progress.

---

[1] See J. Fred Rippy, *Latin America and the Industrial Age* (New York, 1947), pp. 80, 119, 132, 208–217. The telephone and the telegraph — also electric utilities, of course — are not included in these notes.

[2] The River Plate Telephone and Electric Light Co., Ltd., was organized in 1882 and the River Plate Electricity Co., Ltd., in 1889 (see *Stock Exchange Year-Book* for 1901, under "River Plate Electric Light and Traction Co., Ltd.," and "United River Plate Telephone Co., Ltd."). The date for the organization of the third firm, Mexican Gas and Electric Light Co., Ltd., has not been ascertained; perhaps it was organized in 1883 (see Ernesto Galarza, *La Industria Eléctrica de Mexico* (Mexico City, 1941) Chs. I and II, and *Mexican Year Book* for 1908 (Mexico City, 1909), pp. 512–523, for the beginnings of the Electric Age in Mexico).

[3] *Stock Exchange Year-Book* for 1900 and 1901.

[4] *Ibid.* for 1913 and 1914.

[5] *Ibid.* for 1926 and 1927, and *Moody's Manual: Public Utilities* (New York) for the same years.

[6] During the next decade controlling interest in several of the British companies was acquired by American and Foreign Power Co., of the United States.

[7] Largely in Argentina, Brazil, and Mexico; but also in Chile, Uruguay, Venezuela, Peru, Ecuador, Bolivia, Colombia, Costa Rica, and perhaps in Paraguay and Cuba.

[8] Exact aggregates of actual investments are unknown. The nominal investment at the end of 1900 was around £10,000,000, which increased to somewhat more than £100,000,000, including Canadian capital, by the end of 1926.

Appendixes

Buenos Ayres and Belgrano Electric Tramways Co., Ltd. (1898); £1,277,500.
Chilian Electric Tramway and Lighting Co., Ltd. (1898); £775,000. Property is in Santiago.
Costa Rica Electric Light and Traction Co., Ltd. (1898); £260,000.
Córdova Light and Power Co. (1896); $1,300,000. Maine corporation, organized by Theodore Newton Vail; property is in Argentina; controlled by La Capital Traction and Electric Company, Ltd. (see below).
La Capital (Extensions) Tramways Co., Ltd. (1898); £237,000. Vail is chairman of the board, but the capital is mainly English; electrification in progress.
La Capital Traction and Electric Co., Buenos Aires, Ltd. (1899); £1,196,010. Vail is chairman of the board; capital is largely English.
La Capital Tramways Co., Ltd. (1896); £370,000. Vail is chairman of the board; capital is mainly English; electrification is almost completed.
Mexican Electric Works, Ltd. (1897); £400,000. Siemens and Halske enterprise but considerable British investment; electric plant is in Mexico City.
Mexican Gas and Electric Light Co., Ltd. (1883); capital unknown. Controlled by Antony Gibbs and Sons, London; property in Mexico City.
Mexico Electric Tramways, Ltd. (1898); £1,027,753. Property is in Mexico City and the Federal District.
Primitiva Gas Company of Buenos Aires (1855?); capital unknown. Argentine company; Englishmen hold £300,000 in debentures of 1898; company owns an electric as well as a gas plant.
River Plate Electric Light and Traction Co., Ltd. (1896); £352,510. Acquired River Plate Electricity Co., Ltd. (1889).
São Paulo Tramways, Light and Power Co., Ltd. (1899); $14,026,636. Canadian corporation.

British Investments in Electric Utilities in Latin America, End of 1926

Anglo-Argentine Tramways Co., Ltd. (1877); £20,184,439. Controls:
  Buenos Ayres and Belgrano Electric Tramways Co., Ltd. (1898).
  Buenos Ayres Electric Tramways Co., Ltd. (1901).
  Buenos Ayres Grand National Tramways Co., Ltd. (1899).
  Buenos Ayres (New) Tramways Co., Ltd. (1888).
  City of Buenos Ayres Tramways Co., Ltd. (1888).
  La Capital (Extensions) Tramways Co., Ltd. (1898).
  La Capital Traction and Electric Co., Ltd. (1899).
  La Capital Tramways Co., Ltd. (1896).
Atlas Light and Power Co., Ltd. (1926); £6,282,235. Controls:
  Argentine Tramways and Power Co., Ltd. (1912), operating in Santa Fé, Argentina.
  Córdoba Electric Tramways Construction Co., Ltd. (1908?), operating in Córdoba, Argentina.
  Córdoba Light and Power Co. (1896).
  La Sociedad Commercial de Montevideo (1896?).
  La Transatlántica Compañía de Tranvías Eléctricos (1900?), operating in Montevideo.
Bahía Tramway, Light and Power Co. (1905); $10,886,300. Maine corporation; some British investment; property sold in 1913 to municipality of Bahía; bonds received in payment still outstanding.
Brazilian Traction, Light and Power Co., Ltd. (1912); $16,587,900. Canadian holding company controlling, in addition to telephones and gasworks:
  Brazilian Hydro Electro Co., Ltd. (1922).
  Rio de Janeiro Tramways, Light and Power Co., Ltd. (1904).
  São Paulo Electric Co., Ltd. (1910).

British Investments in Latin America

São Paulo Tramways, Light and Power Co., Ltd. (1899).
Jardím Botánico Tramways Co. (1882).
Buenos Aires Town and Docks Tramways, Ltd. (1920); £573,459. Reorganization of Buenos Aires Port and City Tramways, Ltd. (1905).
Buenos Ayres Lacroze Tramways Co., Ltd. (1905) capital unknown. Incorporated in Argentina; controls Buenos Ayres City and Suburban Tramways, Ltd. (1911); British investors hold £1,540,980 in debentures.
Cartagena (Colombia) Waterworks, Ltd. (1905); £750,199. Also owns an electric plant.
Ceará Tramways, Light and Power Co., Ltd. (1911); £348,508. Operating in Fortaleza and Ceará, Brazil.
City of Santos Improvements Co., Ltd. (1880). Owns electric plant and tramways as well as waterworks.
Compañía de Electricidad de la Provincia de Buenos Aires, Ltd. (1911); £1,818,444. Incorporated in Argentina; acquired an Argentine firm of the same name organized in 1905; Englishmen have minority investment.
Compañía Hispano-Americana de Electricidad (1920); 262,523,450 Spanish pesetas. Incorporated in Spain; owns properties in Europe as well as in Argentina; some British investment; controls:
    Compañía Argentina de Electricidad (1900?).
    Compañía Hidro-Electrica La Florida (date unknown).
    Empresa de Luz y Fuerza Buenos Aires–Mendoza (date unknown).
Costa Rica Electric Light and Traction Co., Ltd. (1898); £415,244.
Ecuadorian Corporation, Ltd. (1926); £598,411 (?). Canadian corporation; succeeded an English company of the same name organized in 1913; owns electric utilities and various other properties in Ecuador.
Electric Light and Power Company of Cochabamba (1908). Bolivian corporation; British investors own £111,140 in bonds of 1911.
Havana Electric Railway Co. (1926); $17,246,170(?). Maine corporation; properties are in Camagüey, Santiago, and Havana; Englishmen probably have some investment.
International Light and Power Co., Ltd. (1913); $4,985,000 plus £431,400. Canadian corporation; controls:
    Compañía de Electricidad de Mérida (date unknown), operating in Mexico.
    Compañía de Luz y Fuerza de Paraná (date unknown), operating in Argentina.
    Paraná Tramways Co., Ltd. (date unknown).
    South Brazilian Railways Co., Ltd. (1910).
    Venezuela Electric Light Co., Ltd. (1915?), operating in Caracas, Venezuela.
International Power Co., Ltd. (1926); $11,500,000. Canadian corporation; owns properties outside of Latin America and controls:
    Bolivia Power Co., Ltd. (1925), operating in La Paz and vicinity, and Oruro Power Company.
    Porto Rico Railways Co., Ltd. (1906).
    Venezuela Power Co., Ltd. (1925), operating in Maracaibo and Barquisimeto.
La Plata Electric Tramways Co., Ltd. (1909); £550,450. Acquired the property of La Plata and Ensenada Tramways Co., Ltd. (1890), in province of Buenos Aires.
Leopoldina Terminal Co., Ltd. (1911); £2,353,600. Owns warehouses in Rio de Janeiro and a fleet of ferry boats as well as electric tramways in Nictheroy, Brazil.
Lima Light, Power and Traction Co. (Empresas Eléctricas Asociadas, 1910); capital unknown. Incorporated in Peru; British capitalists own a large part of preferred stock, and debentures amounting to a total of £1,901,480.
Lima Railways Co., Ltd. (1865); £588,700. Electrified in 1904–1905; lines connect Lima with Callao and Chorillos.
Manáos Tramways and Light Co., Ltd. (1909); £550,800.
Mexican Light and Power Co., Ltd. (1902); $52,434,692. Canadian corporation; controls:
    Alameda River Hydro-Electric Co. (date unknown).

Appendixes

Mexican Electric Light Co., Ltd. (1905).
Mexican Southern Power Co. (date unknown).
Pachuca Light and Power Co. (1910).
Mexico Tramways Co., Ltd. (1906); $30,475,000, plus £1,461,500. Canadian corporation; most of the sterling securities are held in England; controls Mexico Electric Tramways Co., Ltd. (1898).
Minas Geraes Electric Light and Tramways Co. (1912); capital unknown. Brazilian firm operating in Bello Horizonte; Englishmen own £92,880 in bonds of 1913.
Monterey Railway, Light and Power Co., Ltd. (1905); $12,699,273. Canadian corporation; owns waterworks and sewers as well as Monterey Light and Power Co. (1903?); property is in Mexico; some British participation.
Motor-Columbus, A. G. (1923); 135,500,000 Swiss francs. Swiss corporation; probably some British investment; controls (besides properties located outside of Latin America):
   Compañía Americana de Luz y Tracción (1918), operating in Asunción, Paraguay.
   Compañía de Electricidad de Corrientes (date unknown), operating in Argentina.
   Compañía de Electricidad de Dolores (date unknown), operating in Argentina.
   Compañía Italo-Argentina de Electricidad (1911).
   Lima Light, Power and Tramways Co. (1910).
   Sociedad Anónima Luz Eléctrica y Fuerza Motriz de Pergamio (date unknown), operating in Argentina.
North Mexico Power and Development Co., Ltd. (1919); $13,500,000. Canadian corporation; reorganization of Mexican Northern Power and Development Co., Ltd. (1909); located in Chihuahua.
Pará Electric Railways and Lighting Company, Ltd. (1905); £715,000. Also controls a gas plant.
Pernambuco Tramways and Power Co., Ltd. (1913); £1,701,092. Operates in Recife, Brazil, and vicinity.
Rio de Janeiro Suburban Tramways, Ltd. (1910); £652,500.
River Plate Electricity Co., Ltd. (1902); £533,000. Property in Argentina.
Société Internationale d'Energie Hydro-Electrique ("Sidro") (1923); 162,500,000 Belgian francs. Belgian holding company; probably some British investment; besides investments outside of Latin America, the company owns securities of Mexican Light and Power Co., Ltd., and Mexico Tramways Co., Ltd.
South American Light and Power Co., Ltd. (1902); £303,200. Property in Bahía Blanca, Argentina.
Southern Brazil Electric Co., Ltd. (1913); £1,187,750. Controls subsidiaries in Amparo, Campinas, Paranagua, and Piracicaba.
Southern Electric Tramways Co., Ltd. (1905); capital unknown. Argentine corporation; British investors hold £130,000 in debentures issued in 1926.
Tucumán Tramways, Light and Power Co., Ltd. (1914); £1,208,545. Controls two subsidiaries; operates in Argentina.
United Electric Tramways Company of Caracas, Ltd. (1906); £287,900.
United Electric Tramways of Montevideo, Ltd. (1904); £350,000 (?).
Whitehall Electric Investments, Ltd. (1922); £10,928,072. Owned by the Weetman Pearson interests; controls:
   Compañía Chilena de Electricidad (1919?).
   Compañía de Electricidad de Valparaíso (1920?).
   Compañía de Luz y Fuerza Motriz de Orizaba (1908?), operating in Mexico.
   Compañía Eléctrica de Tampico (1911?).
   Compañía Hidro-Eléctrica (1923?), operating in Chile.
   Compañía Eléctrica de Córdoba (1910?), Mexico.
   Puebla Tramway, Light and Power Co. (1908), in Mexico.
   Vera Cruz Electric Light, Power and Traction Co., Ltd. (1906).

INDEX

Aiken, Senator George D., quoted, 213
Alberdi, Juan B., favors foreign investments, 208
Alessandri, President Arturo, takes control of Chilean nitrate deposits, 228
Alfaro, Flavio Eloy, favors foreign investments, 208
Argentina: British investments in, 12, 19, 20, 22, 23, 24, 25, 28, 30, 31, 33, 34, 35, 36, 37, 38, 39, 40, 41, 42, 43, 44, 45, 49, 50, 53, 54, 55, 56, 67, 69, 71, 73, 74, 76, 78, 79, 80, 81, 82, 85, 87, 90, 159–67; profits from British investments, 67, 72, 76, 79, 85, 161–67; defaults on government bonds, 28, 162

Balgooyen, Henry W., quoted on foreign investments, 5
Balmaceda, President José, threatens nationalization of nitrate deposits, 211
Balta, José, favors foreign investments, 208
Banks and other financial firms, British-owned in Latin America, 34, 35, 37, 41, 43, 45, 67, 71, 73, 74, 80, 85, 89. *See also* individual countries
Barrios, Justo Rufino, favors foreign investments, 208
Batista, Fulgencio, cordial toward foreign investments, 216
Batlle, President José, curtails foreign investments, 211
Bemis, Samuel Flagg, mentioned, 171
Bolivia: British investments in, 12, 19, 23, 24, 25, 31, 32, 37, 38, 40, 49, 50, 53, 54, 55, 56, 67, 68, 69n, 73, 74, 77, 80, 82, 85, 87, 88, 89, 124–25, 126–28; rates of return from British investments, 67, 85, 126–28; issue of sterling bonds, 31, 32
Bonds, Latin-American, British investments in, 17–22, 26–32, 37, 45, 68, 78, 85–86. *See also* specific countries
Bowers, Claude G., advocates "Marshall Plan" for Latin America, 218

Brazil: British investments in, 12, 19, 20, 22, 23, 24, 25, 26, 28, 29–30, 32, 33, 34, 35, 36, 37, 39, 40, 41, 42, 43, 44, 45, 48, 50, 51, 52, 54, 55, 56, 57, 66, 67, 68, 69, 70, 71, 72, 73, 74, 76, 77, 78, 79, 82, 84, 85, 87, 89, 90, 150–58; rates of return from British investments, 67, 72, 76, 79–80, 85, 152–58; defaults on government bonds, 26, 153, 158
Breweries, British-owned in Latin America, 41, 43, 71, 83. *See also* individual countries
British companies, most profitable: in Latin America, 34, 43, 44, 62, 73, 74, 81, 82, 89, 175; in Africa and the Orient, 179, 181–83
British investment boom: of the *1820*'s, 17–25; of the *1880*'s, 36–50; of *1902–1913*, 52–56, 57–60, 66–74
British investment experience in Latin America, summarized, 6–13
British investments in Latin America: early, 17–25; in *1880*, 25–35; in *1890*, 36–50; in *1900*, 45; in *1913*, 66–74; in *1928*, 75–83; *1939–1949*, 84–91
British investments in other regions, 7, 178–84
British investments overseas, *1939–1948*, 185–94
Bryan, William Jennings, and foreign investments in Latin America, 211, 212

Calvo, Carlos, and the Calvo Clause, 209, 210
Capital, flow of British to Latin America, 11, 17–21, 23, 24, 25–26, 36, 45–46, 66, 75
Cárdenas, Lázaro, and the foreign investor, 216
Carr, E. H., quoted on foreign investments, 171, 204–05
Chile: British investments in, 12, 19, 20, 21, 23, 24, 25, 27–28, 29, 32, 33, 34, 36, 37, 38, 39, 40, 41, 42, 43, 44, 45, 48, 50, 53, 54, 55, 56, 57–65, 67, 68, 69, 70, 71, 72, 73, 74, 76, 77, 78, 79, 80, 81, 82, 85, 87, 133–41; profits from British investments, 57–65, 67, 72,

246

Index

73, 74, 76, 78, 79, 85, 135–41; defaults on government bonds, 27, 135
Colombia: British investments in, 12, 19, 20, 21, 23, 24, 25, 27, 28, 32, 34, 37, 38, 39, 40, 43, 45, 47–48, 50, 52, 54, 55, 56, 67, 68, 69, 70, 72, 76, 78, 79, 81, 82, 85, 87, 89, 113–22; rates of return from British investments, 67, 72, 76, 79, 85, 115–22; defaults on government bonds, 27, 32, 38, 114–15
Costa Rica: British investments in, 19, 25, 26–27, 28, 32, 37, 39, 40, 49, 50, 51, 54, 55, 56, 67, 68, 77, 79, 85, 87, 88, 90, 105–09; small returns from British investments, 67, 85, 105–09
Cuba: British investments in, 12, 25, 33, 34, 36, 37, 38, 39, 41, 43, 50, 54, 55, 56, 67, 68, 69, 70, 71, 72, 76, 78, 79, 83, 87, 88, 89, 109–12; meager profits from British investments, 67, 85, 109–12

Davis, Norman, 111
Dawson, John, and Chilean nitrate of soda, 58, 59
Díaz, Porfirio, favors foreign investments, 208
Díez de Medina, Fernando, denounces foreign investors, 218–19
Defaults of Latin-American governments on sterling bonds, 18, 26, 32. *See also* specific countries
Doheny, Edward L., garners profits from Mexican oil, 102
Dominican Republic: British investments in, 23, 25, 31, 32, 36, 37, 38, 39, 40, 49, 50, 54, 55, 56, 67, 69, 73, 76, 77, 79, 84, 105, 109; meager returns from British investments, 105, 109; defaults on government bonds, 32, 38, 109
Drago, Luis, and claims of foreign investors, 210

Economist (London), quoted, 200, 204
Ecuador: British investments in, 12, 19, 25, 27, 28, 32, 37, 38, 40, 41, 49, 50, 54, 55, 56, 57, 67, 68, 70, 71, 72, 77, 79, 85, 90, 114–16, 120–21; meager returns from British investments, 79, 120–21; defaults on government bonds, 27, 32, 38, 114–15
El Salvador: British investments in, 19, 27, 37, 49, 50, 54, 55, 56, 57, 67, 68, 69, 70, 72, 77, 79, 85, 87, 90, 105–09; meager returns from British investments, 79, 85, 105–09; defaults on government bonds, 27, 106
Electric utilities, lists of British in Latin America, 242–45

Estancias. *See* Real estate

Financial firms. *See* Banks
Flour mills, British-owned in Brazil, Chile, and Peru, 41, 83, 89, 137
Foreign investments: presumed importance of, 3–4, 10, 13, 171, 195–96, 201–02; impact in Latin America and elsewhere, 8–10, 200–02; motivations of British, 17–18, 197–99; views on, 197–219
French investors, experience in Latin America, 12–13

García Moreno, Gabriel, approves foreign investments, 208
Gas companies, British, in Latin America, 43, 340–41
German investors' experience in Latin America, 13
Gómez, Juan Vicente, approves foreign investments, 208
Gregory, Theodore E., quoted on foreign investments, 203
Guano, British investment in Peruvian, 35
Guardia, Tomás, favors foreign investments, 208
Guatemala: British investments in, 19, 25, 27, 28, 37, 50, 54, 55, 56, 67, 68, 69, 71, 72, 77, 85, 87, 90, 105–09; meager profits from British investments, 106–07; defaults on government bonds, 27, 32, 72, 106
Guzmán Blanco, Antonio, approves foreign investments, 208

Haiti, British investments in, 19, 23, 56, 76, 77, 84, 105
Harvey, Robert, and Chilean nitrate of soda, 58, 59, 62, 63
Hegan, J. and Company, builders of Arica and Tacna Railway, 29
Heilperin, Michael, quoted on foreign investments, 5, 6
Hobson, C. K., quoted on foreign investments, 201–02
Hobson, John A., condemns foreign investments, 200–01
Honduras: British investments in, 19, 25, 27, 28, 32, 37, 38, 39, 40, 48, 50, 53, 54, 55, 56, 67, 68, 77, 85, 87, 105–09; meager gains from British investments, 67, 85, 87, 106
Humphrey, Senator Hubert, quoted on investments in Bolivia, 113–14

Imprudent investments, 17–32, 105–09, 113–14, 124–32, 151, 153

247

Inglis, G. M., and Chilean nitrate of soda, 58
Irigoyen, President Hipólito, approves foreign investments, 208
Isaacs, Harold, quoted on foreign investments, 6

Keynes, John Maynard, views on foreign investments, 171, 202–03, 204

La Gran Colombia, 19, 27, 114
Lansing, Robert, quoted on foreign investors in Latin America, 212–13
Leguía, Augusto B., approves foreign investments, 208
Lockett family, 58
Losses, British, in Latin America, 18–25, 86–87, 104, 109, 113, 121, 123, 125, 126–27, 158, 174

Machado, Gerardo, approves foreign investments, 208
McGregor, "King" Gregor, of Poyais, 21
Manufacturing plants, English-owned in Latin America, 35, 37, 41, 43, 45, 71, 82–83, 89. See also individual countries
Mexico: British investments in, 12, 19, 20, 22, 23, 24, 25, 26, 28, 32, 37, 38, 39, 40, 41, 42, 45, 47, 50, 52, 54, 55, 56, 66, 67, 68, 70, 71, 72, 76, 78, 82, 85, 87, 88, 89, 90, 95–104; meager average returns from British investments, 67, 72, 78–79, 85, 87, 97–104; defaults on government bonds, 26, 32, 79, 95, 98
Mining, 43; early British investment in Latin-American, 17, 18, 22–25, 32; summary of British investments in, 46–57. See also British companies, individual countries
Mining investments, profitable British in Africa and the Orient, 179–83
Mining Manual, 40, 46, 54, 55, 56
Mitre, Bartolomé, approves foreign investments, 208
Murray, Hon. Thomas, quoted on high salaries of U.S. bureaucrats, 220

Nash, Robert Lucas, praises foreign investments, 200
Nation (London), 203
New Granada. See Colombia
Nicaragua: British investments in, 19, 25, 27, 37, 40, 43, 49, 50, 53–54, 55, 56, 67, 68, 70, 77, 105–09; scanty profits from British investments, 85, 87; defaults on government bonds, 27, 106
Nitrate companies, lists of, 60, 62, 73
Nitrate of soda, British investment in Chilean, 37, 57–65, 138–39
North, John Thomas, "Nitrate King," operations of in Chile, 58–63

Palmerston, Lord, policy regarding foreign investments, 199–200
Panama, British investments in, 26, 33, 54, 56, 67n, 68n, 76, 77, 84, 105
Paraguay: British investments in, 12, 19, 23, 25, 31, 32, 37, 39, 40, 41, 50, 54, 55, 56, 67, 68, 69, 77, 85, 90, 124–26; meager profits from British investments, 67, 85, 87, 124–26; defaults on government bonds, 31, 32, 125
Peak: of British investments in Latin America, 75–83; of investments in Latin-American mines, 52–56
Pearson, Weetman Dickinson (Lord Cowdray), profits from activities in Mexico, 102–03
Perón, Juan Domingo, reduces and controls foreign investments, 211, 216
Peru: British investments in, 12, 19, 21, 23, 24, 25, 29, 32, 33, 35, 37, 38, 39, 40, 41, 43, 45, 49, 50, 51, 53, 54, 55, 56, 67, 68, 70, 71, 72, 74, 78, 79, 82, 83, 85, 87, 90, 128–32; meager returns from British investments, 67, 72, 74, 76, 79, 85, 87, 130–32; defaults on government bonds, 28, 32, 38, 129
Peruvian Corporation, large and unprofitable British enterprise, 38, 40, 44, 69, 71, 74, 129, 131, 132
Petroleum investments, British: in Latin America, 70, 82, 88, 90, 101–02, 122, 131, 132, 175, 177, 225; in other regions, 178, 179, 192, 193, 194
Porter Doctrine on protection of foreign investments, 210
Porter, G. R., quoted, 199
Poyais, Kingdom of, 19, 21
Prado, Manuel, approves foreign investments, 216
Problems in international investment: recent, 3–5, 12–13; of British investors in Latin America, 10–13, 18, 20–23, 26–28
Profit from foreign investments, 18, 21–22, 32, 173–74
Public utilities, British investments in Latin-American, 33, 34, 39, 45, 70, 73, 80–81, 239–45. See also Electric utilities, Gas companies, and individual countries

Index

Quebracho, 184; exploitation of by Forestal Land, Timber and Railways, 73, 175

Railways, British-owned in Latin America, 25, 32, 33, 34, 37, 39, 44, 68–69, 72–73, 78, 79–80, 86, 89–90. *See also* individual countries

Ranches, British-owned in Latin America. *See* Real estate

Rates of return on British overseas investments: general, from Latin America, 7, 10–12, 17, 21, 22–23, 32, 35, 42–45, 67, 72–73, 76–83, 85–88, 174; from other independent countries, 178–79, 189–92; from the Commonwealth and Empire, 178–83, 186–89. *See also* British companies and individual countries

Real estate, British investments in Latin-American, 18, 23, 25, 35, 37, 40–41, 43, 45, 70–71, 81, 89. *See also* Argentina, Brazil, Mexico, Paraguay, Uruguay

Reyes, Rafael, approves foreign investments, 208

Roosevelt, Franklin Delano, quoted on foreign investments in Latin America, 213

Rubber: failure of British investments in Latin America, 70, 158n; profits from investments in other regions, 178, 179, 180

Santos, Eduardo, urges "Marshall Plan" for Latin America, 218

Sarmiento, Domingo Faustino, approves foreign investments, 208

Seijas, Rafael, writes critically of foreign investors, 209

Shipping companies, British investments in Latin-American, 34, 35, 44, 67, 69, 71, 85

Socialist tendencies in Latin America, 214–18

South American Journal, 44, 58n, 67n, 68n, 70, 71n, 73, 74, 75, 76, 77n, 78, 79, 80, 83n, 84, 85, 90, 91, 96, 97n, 106, 109, 110, 127, 128, 134, 136, 138, 143, 144, 149, 151, 152, 160, 163, 204. *See also* notes, pp. 223 ff.

Stock Exchange Year-Book, 40, 42, 46, 56, 58n, 113, 126, 137n, 143, 180n. *See also* notes, pp. 223 ff.

Submarine cables, British investments in, 33, 39, 43, 70. *See also* individual countries

Tea plantations in India and Ceylon, British profits from investments in, 178, 179, 180, 181, 194, 195

Times (London), quoted, 203

Tin, Malayan and Siamese: British profits from, 178, 179, 180, 182

United Nations, highly-paid staff of, 220

United States citizens' investments in Latin America, 13, 56–57, 226

United States government, postwar aid to foreign countries, 205–07

Uruguay: British investments in, 12, 25, 30, 31, 33, 34, 35, 36, 37, 39, 40, 41, 42, 43, 45, 49, 50, 51, 53, 54, 55, 56, 67, 68, 69, 70, 71, 72, 74, 76, 77, 78, 79, 81, 83, 85, 89, 142–49; rates of return from British investments, 67, 72, 74, 76, 79, 81, 83, 85, 143–49; rare defaults on government bonds, 31, 144

Valentine, Alan, quoted on foreign investments, 5

Venezuela, British investments in, 12, 19, 24, 25, 28–29, 31, 37, 38, 39, 40, 44, 45, 47, 50, 51, 53, 54, 55, 56, 67, 68, 69, 70, 76, 78, 79, 81, 82, 85, 89, 114–23; average meager profits from, 67, 72, 76, 79, 85, 114–23

Views on foreign investments: British, 197–205; Latin-American, 208–11, 214–19; of some United States officials, 211–14; recent, of the United States government, 205–07

Wilson, President Woodrow, quoted on foreign investments in Latin America, 211, 212, 213

EUROPEAN BUSINESS
Four Centuries of Foreign Expansion
An Arno Press Collection

Anstey, Vera. *The Economic Development of India.* 1952

Baster, A. S. J. *The Imperial Banks.* 1929

Baster, A. S. J. *The International Banks.* 1935

Blount, Edward. *Memoirs of Sir Edward Blount.* 1902

Braake, Alex L. Ter. *Mining in the Netherlands East Indies.* 1944

British Electrical and Allied Manufacturers' Association. *Combines and Trusts in the Electrical Industry.* 1927

Brode, Heinrich. *British and German East Africa.* 1911

Burden, William A. M. *The Struggle for Airways in Latin America.* 1943

Calvert, Albert F. *Nigeria and Its Tin Fields.* 1910

Crouchley, Arthur Edwin. *Investment of Foreign Capital in Egyptian Companies and Public Debt.* 1936

Davies, A. Emil. *Investments Abroad.* 1927

Deterding, Henri. *An International Oilman.* 1934

Ferns, Henry S. *Britain and Argentina in the Nineteenth Century.* 1960

Fitzgerald, Patrick. *Industrial Combination in England.* 1927

Gregory, Theodore. *Ernest Oppenheimer and the Economic Development of Southern Africa.* 1962

Henry, James Dodds. *Baku.* 1906

Hussey, Roland Dennis. *The Caracas Company, 1728-1784.* 1934

Jucker-Fleetwood, Erin Elver. *Sweden's Capital Imports and Exports.* 1947

Korthals-Altes, J. *Sir Cornelius Vermuyden.* 1925

Laves, Walter Herman Carl. *German Governmental Influence on Foreign Investments, 1871-1914.* 1977

Levy, Herman. *Monopoly and Competition.* 1911

Liefmann, Robert. *Cartels, Concerns and Trusts.* 1932

Marcus, Edward and Mildred Rendl Marcus. *Investment and Development Possibilities in Tropical Africa.* 1960

Meakin, W. *The New Industrial Revolution.* 1928

Michell, Lewis. *The Life and Times of the Right Honourable Cecil John Rhodes, 1853-1902.* Two vols. in one. 1910

Miller, Benjamin L. and Joseph T. Singewald. *The Mineral Deposits of South America.* 1919

Mulhall, Michael G. *The English in South America.* 1878

Nordyke, Lewis. *Cattle Empire.* 1949

Nute, Grace Lee. *Caesers of the Wilderness.* 1943

Patterson, E. M., editor. *America's Changing Investment Market.* 1916

Pinner, Felix. *Emil Rathenau und das Elektrische Zeitalter.* 1918

Riesser, J. *The German Great Banks and Their Concentration in Connection with the Economic Development of Germany.* 1911

Rippy, J. Fred. *British Investment in Latin America, 1822-1949.* 1959

Rondot, Jean. *La Compagnie Française des Pétroles.* 1962

Roth, Cecil. *The Sassoon Dynasty.* 1941

Senior, Nassau W. *A Journal Kept in Turkey and Greece in the Autumn of 1857 and the Beginning of 1858.* 1859

Siemens, Georg. *History of the House of Siemens.* Two vols. 1957

Southworth, Constant. *The French Colonial Venture.* 1931

Spender, John A. *Weetman Pearson, First Viscount Cowdray, 1856-1927.* 1930

Thorner, Daniel. *Investment in Empire.* 1950

U. S. Department of Commerce, Bureau of Foreign and Domestic Commerce. *Investments in Latin America and the British West Indies.* 1918

U. S. Federal Trade Commission. *Report of the Federal Trade Commission on Foreign Ownership in the Petroleum Industry.* 1923

U. S. Office of the Alien Property Custodian. *Alien Property Custodian Report.* 1919

U. S. Office of the Alien Property Custodian. *Annual Reports.* Four vols. in one. 1943/45/46/47

Van Oss, S. F. *American Railroads as Investments.* 1893

van Winter, Pieter J. *American Finance and Dutch Investment, 1780-1805.* 1977

Vlekke, Bernard H. M. *Nusantara.* 1943

Wallace, Donald H. *Market Control in the Aluminum Industry.* 1937

Wellington, Dorothy Violet Wellesley. *Sir George Goldie, Founder of Nigeria.* 1934

Wheeler, John. *A Treatise of Commerce.* 1931

Wilkins, Mira, editor. *British Overseas Investments, 1907-1948.* 1977

Wilkins, Mira, editor. *European Foreign Investments, As Seen by the U. S. Department of Commerce.* 1977

Wilkins, Mira, editor. *Foreign Investments in the United States.* 1977

Wilkins, Mira, editor. *Issues and Insights on International Investment.* 1977

Williamson, John W. *In a Persian Oil Field.* 1930

Wilson, Arnold T. *The Suez Canal.* 1933

Wilson, Charles Henry. *Anglo-Dutch Commerce and Finance in the Eighteenth Century.* 1941

Wood, Gordon. *Borrowing and Business in Australia.* 1930

Wortley, B. A. *Expropriation in Public International Law.* 1959